PUNK PLAYTHINGS

Provocations for 21st Century Game Makers

PUNK PLAYTHINGS

Provocations for 21st Century Game Makers

Chris Lowthorpe
Sean Taylor

CRC Press
Taylor & Francis Group
Boca Raton London New York

CRC Press is an imprint of the
Taylor & Francis Group, an **informa** business

AN A K PETERS BOOK

CRC Press
Taylor & Francis Group
6000 Broken Sound Parkway NW, Suite 300
Boca Raton, FL 33487-2742

© 2018 by Taylor & Francis Group, LLC
CRC Press is an imprint of Taylor & Francis Group, an Informa business

No claim to original U.S. Government works

Printed on acid-free paper

International Standard Book Number-13: 978-1-4987-7022-4 (Paperback)
978-1-138-29580-3 (Hardback)

Visit the Taylor & Francis Web site at
http://www.taylorandfrancis.com

and the CRC Press Web site at
http://www.crcpress.com

Contents

Forewords

Being playful, like being thoughtful, acquiescent, or combative, is simply one of the many states of being we occupy day to day. As social creatures, we often use playfulness to interrogate our social and physical environment, to build relationships, and to establish boundaries. We may not describe this as gameplay but we engage in situations many times every day that require us to interpret rules of social and professional norms and make decisions about how we behave in order to achieve the outcomes we desire. As we get older, how we perceive and engage with play is re-contextualized and the grammar we use to describe it evolves, but essentially we negotiate the world by engaging similar strategies to those we used to test our parents' patience or the strength of a rope swing.

Right now video games are going through those difficult teenage years, where the desire to be a grownup is engaged in a constant battle with the desire to run and jump and shout out loud. Like a teenager, the route to maturity for games cannot be negotiated using the tools or experiences available to us, we learn as we go. Over time we start to hang out with different people in different places and, while we might still feel like teenagers inside, externally our maturity is judged by the company we keep, the places we go, and the things we do.

For video games that means you will now find them in the museum or art gallery, in the classroom or medical center, and in festivals and events being used by musicians and performers to reinterpret their performances; they are the subject of research conferences where academics discuss the way that games allow us to develop our understanding of ourselves and our interactions with ideas and actions. The maturity of a medium is not defined by the age of its audience but more by the way it enters culture. Culture, of course, is a two-way street. This book shows, for the first time, how our culture and traditions can influence our approach to designing and making games as well as being designers and makers.

I first came across Chris teaching a games course in a provincial art school. Having one eye open for people with a cultural studies background and an interest in video games, I immediately picked up on the influence Chris was having on the student artists and designers as it came through in the fluency and maturity of their understanding of their work. I pointed this out to a senior academic, recommending that they hold on to Chris jealously as academics with his knowledge and enthusiasm for games are hard to find. Imagine my delight to discover shortly afterward that he'd been moved to another department...Meanwhile in Dundee, a small games studio was building a reputation for excellence, reliability, and productivity, building small casual games for digital TV set-top boxes. Denki would develop over 150 games for that platform and develop a design process that was as close to anything I'd seen to a reliable and reproducible approach to designing a stream of high-quality products.

The "Denki Way," as it became known, was developed by the inspired and mercurial Gary Penn and the insightful and forensic Colin Anderson. The studio practices an all-encompassing approach to design and development that values craft and quality with a player-centered approach to all aspects of planning, design, and production. When the opportunity arose for a study of design practices in the games industry, funded by the Economic and Social Research Council here at Abertay University, Denki and Chris seemed like an irresistible match.

In the eye of the storm at Denki sat Sean Taylor, producer and the man tasked with implementing the "Denki Way" and ideally placed to guide Chris through the twist and turns of the process; how it had developed from principle to practice and what it meant for day-to-day life in the studio. Collaboration turned to friendship through a shared passion for pop culture, fashion, and music. What started as research soon became a crusade to improve design practice in the games industry, learning from previous experiences in other media, particularly in advertising and design agencies. Their approach borrows the ecosystem of the music industry and the emerging "authenticity culture" in catering and hospitality; the soft politics of the hipster movement influenced their thinking. Conceived over craft beer and artisan pretzels, this book is the joyful issue of their union.

Punk Playthings is overtly political. It challenges game makers to line up alongside rebellious visionaries from Malcolm McLaren to Quentin Tarantino; to recognize that they are part of a disruptive tradition that casts a skeptical eye to its past and a jealous eye to its future. In these pages, commercial success is neither motivation nor shameful desire but a consequence of authenticity. Here, game making is a response to the urge to engage with others and, in its authentic state, a means by which to critique contemporary society, its values and its institutions. Engagement, for Chris and Sean, is not a transaction—not downloads or in app purchases—but an ethos that begins in the studio (or even at the bar), expressed in shared cultural values. They emphasize the need for an agreed vision (manifesto) and a commitment to your craft that is matched by a commitment to your players, a cultural appetite that informs every aspect of production and an openness to the influence of the past on the potential of the future.

This book brings to mind Flannery O'Connor's answer to a question about why she writes. In her response, "I write to discover what I know," the author captures the fundamental condition of creative production. She points out that grand visions quickly turn to philosophy but that the creative impetus begins in the individual experience; it is the personal made public and the intimate made explicit. In speaking of what we know, we preserve authenticity and offer up an invitation to players to enter into the confidence of the game.

As the introduction says, this book is not for everyone. Game makers, designers and developers are an increasingly diverse group. Over my 15 years of practicing teaching and researching in games, I have worked with at least three games industries and visited enormous games factories, micro-studios, and sole traders. I have witnessed a technology industry become a creative industry, become a cultural industry and be all of these at once. The one thing I find everywhere I go is a spirit of adventure, a desire to look over the horizon to bring back what they find. This book is written in that spirit and if you're a fellow traveler, this book might just be for you.

Gregor White
Professor of Applied Creativity
Head of School of Design and Informatics and the
UK Centre for Excellence in Computer Games
Education at Abertay University

I was pleasantly surprised when Sean told me that he and Chris would be writing a book inspired by Chris' time studying Denki's development methods. I've always intended to share more about the lessons Denki has learned as independent game developers, but never quite got around to it for various reasons. The idea of having someone else start the ball rolling was more than welcome. However, I was a little concerned when Sean asked me to write a foreword for the fruits of their labor: *Punk Playthings*. That's because it's hard to imagine anyone less "punk" than me—a balding, middle-aged geek who grew up doing what I was told, keeping away from those unruly characters who might lead me astray and finding solace in that quintessential antithesis of punk rock music—prog rock.

That said, I've always had a healthy respect for mavericks—those people I saw doing their own thing because they inherently knew it was right, even when everyone around them was telling them otherwise. Fortunately, upon joining DMA Design in 1993, I had the opportunity to work with an entire company of mavericks early in my career and that experience lit in me a desire to carry the torch forward after DMA abandoned its pioneering roots and jumped aboard the *Grand Theft Auto* gravy train at the end of 1999. I never really considered it this way at the time—but with this benefit of hindsight and the perspective I've gained from this book you're about to read—I guess you could say that leaving the safe harbor of DMA to start Denki was ... a little bit punk?

Having now read *Punk Playthings*, I certainly recognize a few hallmarks I wouldn't have beforehand. Denki was born of the kind of frustration and rebellion this book champions—frustration at the dysfunctional development methods our industry considers "normal"—and rebellion at the widely held belief that the creative process of making games is somehow sacred: a dark art, full of superstition and ritual, complete with its high-priests who claim a deeper understanding and insight. As far as I've been able to tell from my own experiences, all those approaches ever do are create convenient shadows that charlatans can hide in after making poor decisions so as never to be held to account for their outcomes, or used to frighten developers into compliance. I wanted Denki to kick the doors open, to throw back the curtains, let in some light and show everyone that game development wasn't anything to be worshiped or revered without question but rather a wonderful new art-form to be explored, studied, and challenged by a digital generation of artisans in just the sorts of ways *Punk Playthings* encourages. So I guess you might say that was a little bit punk too?

When I launched Denki with my co-conspirators in 2000, we rejected commercialism as our prime motivator, unlike the majority of our games industry peers at the time. Not in the sort of naive, idealistic way that *Punk Playthings* wisely warns young game creators away from, but by placing money in its rightful place as a key resource to be respected rather than a principal guiding aim to be chased at any cost. Of course, everyone says they're not motivated by the money, but we only really find out whether we are or not when it's on the table right in front of us. That's why one of my proudest moments remains Friday March 10, 2000, when I and my fellow Denki founders looked a £1.6 Million offer to buy the company outright straight in the eye and said, "no thanks—our independence matters more to us." I guess that was pretty punk.

The independence we bought ourselves that day enabled us to build Denki entirely without compromise and grow it into a sort of creative laboratory for game development, crystallizing our culture slowly around our core principles without any impurities. We were able to find people along the way who shared our goal of making game development more transparent and effective and who wanted to build games with a focus on the substance rather than the surface. Every time we did make money, we didn't spend it on flashier offices—as anyone who has ever visited Denki HQ will attest—or fast cars or any of the other vanity traps young game developers often fall into. Instead, each time we amassed the kind of money that might have bought us bigger houses or faster cars, we spent it on funding more research in the Denki games laboratory, exploring original concepts that inspired us or refining the techniques that would help us master the craft of game making. I guess that was pretty punk.

The development method we arrived at—which we rather unimaginatively refer to as "The Denki Way"—certainly helps us make games more effectively, but it was never intended to be prescriptive; it was intended to be provocative. Sure, no one blinks at the mention of video games and digital toys in the same sentence today, but back in 2000 when Denki shunned the "games company" descriptor and announced itself as "A Digital Toy Company," the suggestion of computer games as digital toys was more likely to start a fight than inspire thoughtful discussion. In some ways, we were wearing the *I Hate Pink Floyd* t-shirts of our day. So, you know, maybe that was properly punk too.

Oh yeah—and now I come to think of it—Denki never really had a commercial hit either. What could possibly be more punk than that, right?

I've been lucky enough to meet and work with some truly inspirational mavericks over the years and the authors of this book certainly fall into that category. Sean is a kindred spirit who embodies the ideals Denki was founded on better than I do. He's held us all accountable to those ideals in practice and he continually challenges their underlying assumptions without deference in order to make them better. Chris is his perfect counterpart—every bit as curious, insightful and fearlessly questioning as Sean, but forged in the academy rather than tempered in the furnaces of creative factories. Between them, they have a formidable insight and perspective on the most pressing issues today's game makers will need to overcome if they want to work in play for the long term. And I'm really pleased to see so many of those insights successfully captured and shared within the pages that follow.

It's been something of a bittersweet experience reading through the wisdom Sean and Chris have carefully distilled into *Punk Playthings*. Part of me is deeply jealous that I didn't have this book when I was starting my career in game development 25 years ago. There are lessons on almost every page that are worth their weight in gold— lessons that took me months—sometimes years—to learn. There are innovative approaches to game development in here that I literally bankrolled and wasted tens, or maybe hundreds, of thousands of pounds on before discovering their limitations—all expertly deconstructed and exposed for the misguided thinking they always were, so that no one else has to waste their time or money going down those dead ends again. I seriously wish I could go back and hand my younger self a copy of this book when I was starting Denki.

Then again, maybe it's just as well this stuff wasn't in circulation back then because after reading this book I've realized I'm so punk I'd probably have rebelled against it all anyway. Now I'm just left wondering what pisses off today's new generation of game makers the most? What aspects of "the games industry" are they going to rebel against? By the time they've finished reading *Punk Playthings*, they'll have the perspective and manifesto to marshall themselves to change it.

I sincerely hope that *Punk Playthings* hands them the match they need to light their anger into a healthy, two-fingered salute to conventional wisdom.

Kick out the jams motherfuckers.

Colin Anderson
CEO
Denki
Dundee, Scotland

Acknowledgments

Chris says

Thanks to Professor Gregor White for glimpsing a glimmer of potential many years ago then consistently helping me realize it. To Colin Anderson and Gary Penn for their friendship, openness, and generosity. And to my dad for putting *Pong* in his seaside amusement arcade 40 or so years ago—this is your fault.

Respect to my fellow gunslinger, Sean, for much the same things he's kindly written about me. Plus his razor-sharp insight into making games and careful nurturing of my now deep appreciation of nocturnal Scottish culture. *¡Larga vida la conspiración!*

Thanks to friends at the University of Abertay, Dundee—Dr Iain Donald and Dr Dayna Galloway in particular—and some of the wonderful students I've taught over the years (hello, Rosie!).

Most importantly, I *really* could not have written this book without the love and support of my wife and best friend, Marie-Claire. This book is for you.

Sean says

I'd like to thank Gary Penn for helping me to think differently about the design of game design and Colin Anderson for giving me the impetus to articulate it. I'd also like to thank my co-conspirator, Chris, for his endless enthusiasm, inspiring provocations and ever-insightful criticisms.

Finally, this book is dedicated to my wife, Zoe. This book would not have been possible without her love and support. Thank you.

We both say

Chris and Sean would like to thank Louie Isaaman-Jones for his sterling work making this book look unique. When he's not selecting music, crafting cocktails, or tending to urban woodland, Louie does distinctive design for some of London's most maverick nights, record labels, agencies, and companies. If you want him to make something of yours look better, say hello:

Email: info@louieij com

Web: http://www louieij com/

Instagram: https://www instagram com/louieij

Authors

Dr Chris Lowthorpe is an award-winning game educator and playful provocateur. He earned his doctorate from the University of Abertay, Dundee—currently Europe's top game school—where he also won the 2014 Innovation in Teaching Award. Chris has taught and mentored some of the brightest talents in UK games and provided game education, development, and entrepreneurship consultancy to academic, cultural, and commercial organizations.

An unreconstructed East Anglian, Chris is a lifelong *Pong* fanatic, trained chef, amateur cocktail crafter, ex-London tour guide, socialist-turned-pragmatist, retired DJ and Acid House veteran. Somehow, all this is connected. He lives in the middle of a Suffolk field with his wife, Marie-Claire, extensive record collection, trusty Jeep, and the occasional pheasant.

Web: https://www.playhaus.online
Twitter: https://twitter.com/chrislowthorpe
Instagram: https://www.instagram.com/chrislowthorpe/

Sean Taylor is an award-winning game producer and playful provocateur. In 1996, Sean dropped out of college to join the organized chaos of DMA Design—midway through the production of the original *Grand Theft Auto*—and has been making games ever since. For 10 years, Sean was the producer at Denki—Dundee's digital toy factory—where he helped design, develop, and produce hundreds of games across web, mobile, television, console, and social—most notably, the BAFTA-winning *Quarrel*. He has worked on some of the world's largest and smallest game projects—creating a lot of value and a lot more mistakes along the way.

Made in Scotland and currently residing in Dubai, Sean helps game makers around the world do the things that they do better so they can do better things.

Web: https://www.playhaus.online
Twitter: https://twitter.com/kwangchow
Instagram: https://www.instagram.com/kwangchow/

Introduction

1,2,3,4...

"Hello Peter, Hello Paul,
Saints and sinners, welcome all,
Tommy Cannon and Bobby Ball,
Hello, Hello, Hello, Hello!"

The Beloved
Hello (1990)

Is It Me You're Looking For?

Before we get started, we would like to thank you for buying this book (*muchas gracias*), borrowing it (cheers), or possibly stealing it (bloody cheapskate). We also want to discuss expectations. If you're reading this in the hope of discovering a silver bullet for entrepreneurial game making success—forget it. That's the next book. If you wanted a prescriptive how-to handbook for the step-by-step creation of compelling playful experiences—sorry, no dice. Don't worry. There are plenty of people out there who will gladly nickel and dime you with snake oil promises for both the above. But if you're looking for a book to provoke, challenge, and sometimes frustrate you—while maybe forcing the odd nod of recognition or occasional outburst of emphatic agreement—you could be in luck.

This book is a compass, not a map. It is both probe and provocation, not a comfortable confirmation of game making biases and orthodoxies. You might love it and hate it at the same time. That's fine. All we ask is you keep an open mind. Do that and who knows what might happen? This book is not for everyone. But it might just be for you.

Who's Better, Who's Best?

"We tried and we failed
And we tried and we failed
Oh, we tried and we failed
We tried and we failed
And we tried ...
Cash on the nail ... it's just a fairytale!"

The Smiths with Sandie Shaw
Jeane (1984)

This is a book born out of failure. Primarily, the failure to settle an argument. In January 2012, Denki—the independent game studio in Dundee, Scotland, where Sean worked—launched *Quarrel* for the Xbox. A strategy word game best described as *Scrabble* × *Risk* × *Countdown*, *Quarrel* was initially published on the App Store in August the previous year. The game quickly received critical acclaim, culminating in the BAFTA Scotland Best Game Award for 2011. But the development story of *Quarrel* was not a happy one.

Denki first envisaged *Quarrel* in 2008, finishing a version for Xbox Live Arcade (XBLA) two years later. And this is where the trouble began. Following prevailing industry orthodoxy, the studio started shopping *Quarrel* around to publishers. The game acquisition teams loved it but once they passed the game up the decision tree, problems started. The executives in finance and marketing departments—what Denki CEO Colin Anderson terms "the bit more commonly known as The Industry"—were not interested (2012). The publishers gave many reasons for rejecting *Quarrel* but one signal persisted through the noise: gamers don't buy word games. Anderson didn't agree. He believed "gamers know a good game when they see one and will happily invest in it" (Anderson 2012). Denki pressed on. When it published the iOS version a year later, critical reaction and the winning of a BAFTA supplied signals Anderson could be right. So on the day of *Quarrel*'s XBLA launch, in his usual engaging and candid style Anderson penned an article for Gamasutra describing what had occurred and provocatively asking: who was right, the game industry or *Quarrel*?

The answer was neither. *Quarrel* was not the commercial success Denki hoped for. The certification process and legal wrangling necessary for publishing on XBLA had become "excruciating" for independent developers (Carmel 2011). Denki proved no exception. Worse, the company had chosen the wrong publisher for the game. But *Quarrel* had to be released if it was going to recoup its development costs. Finally, the game emerged, but only at great commercial, cultural, and personal cost to the company. Despite all its best intentions, it transpired that Denki had sold *Quarrel* out to the wrong people.

But Denki's failures do not mean the industry was right. What the story of *Quarrel* exposed were the limits of industry orthodoxy. The old ways of thinking, making, and selling were no longer working in a newly disrupted landscape. A game that had been a notable critical success, that connected and resonated with players during open playtesting and following its App Store launch, had somehow managed to sink without trace. For Denki, *Quarrel* was proof, traditional industry methods were now useless at selling quirky games or esoteric experiences. The orthodoxy was based on notions of the mass, of bloc demographics, and of push advertising. Instead of attracting patronage directly from the like-minded, dogma demanded identikit games that conformed to established genres. These simply cannibalized concepts and mechanics from other successful games in an effort to appeal to the same audience, conveniently identified by proxies such as focus groups and personas. The resulting products were then neatly packaged and put on the "supermarket shelf." Games were beginning to eat themselves.

Turning Disruption into Money

Releasing *Quarrel* was futile yet valuable. The game failed commercially but it confirmed what Denki had suspected: the industry playbook hadn't changed but the playing field and rules of the game had. Radically. After learning this, Denki decided it needed to experiment with new approaches for making and selling games. It would need to adapt better and faster if it was going to negotiate the uncertainties of a disrupted marketplace and survive. This need was the provocation that led to a new project: Denki Skunk Works.

Skunk Works was a highly autonomous team working on experimental projects relatively unhindered by bureaucracy. Sean was instigator and leader of the project, Chris observed it for his doctoral research. The team sought to explore new thinking and perspectives by developing experimental products that provided heuristic learning. Skunk Works would learn quickly and fail fast by conducting insurgencies into the new and supposedly democratized marketplace generated by digital distribution. It was hoped this learning would eventually help Denki circumvent outmoded industry bullshit and achieve commercial success making its own games.

Denki already knew self-publishing presented as many challenges as opportunities. It brought increased uncertainty, a saturated marketplace, and the need for a new mindset and set of competencies. It was difficult to get a game discovered by customers or to persuade those that discovered it to make a purchase. In its impetuous idealism, the valorization of self-publishing by the indie sector tended to gloss over these challenges—it still does—but Denki had been playing the game too long to get fooled. The company had begun exploring approaches designed to help overcome these new challenges, starting with Steve Blank's Customer Development approach then progressing to Lean Startup principles advocated by Eric Ries and Ash Maurya. But Anderson soon realized adopting Lean Startup throughout Denki would be too radical, risky, and slow. Instead, the proposed Skunk Works would do it. So this team began a series of experiments to implement Lean Startup, build adaptive and entrepreneurial capacity, recognize and overcome the challenges of self-publishing, and most of all, to learn. One of the first things Skunk Works learned was that while Lean Startup had some useful ideas and approaches for game development, it was too clinical for creating compelling playful experiences. Worse, the team discovered that building adaptive capacity, encouraging entrepreneurship, and developing a heuristic mindset take time and therefore money. Unfortunately, both were running out for Denki.

Skunk Works came to an end due to lack of resources. By usual business metrics, it had been a failure. The project had not delivered commercial success from its experimental game, *Par Tribus*, and the only meaningful revenue now coming into Denki was from work for hire. The company had a proven repertoire for efficient high-quality making, so it seemed obvious its best chance for short-term sustainability lay in that direction. Denki gave up trying to create and sell original games for the foreseeable future. Instead, it went back to making games for other organizations. End of story.

Well, not quite. Because in many ways, Skunk Works was a success. It delivered what it was supposed to: valuable heuristic learning. Denki learned through failure that Lean Startup was not a silver bullet for game making. It also learned that the company was not—at that time—well equipped to sell its own games on the open market. And it learned all this fast enough to change direction and return to client work. As a result, Denki not only saved itself but has quietly prospered in the past few years. More personally, it made us realize that a heuristic mindset, nimble adaptability, entrepreneurship, and intrapreneurship are now crucial competencies for game makers. These are no longer luxuries; they are necessities. But this learning—complimented by secondhand learning from the failure of others—also led us to think there had to be other ways to skin the game making cat. There had to be different approaches beyond the well-trodden but increasingly deteriorating AAA or indie pathways. Some new roads less traveled. We started discussing and exploring hundreds of examples that imparted more learning and it is a curated collection of these that appear in this book. Many come from the world of games but many do not. All helped us develop a set of first principles that form the foundation for our approach to making games in the early 21st century.

Career Opportunities

"Anger is an energy!"

Public Image Limited
Rise (1986)

Another catalyst for this book was the serial tendency of game startups in our local ecosystem to fail after a year or so. Many had been "incubated" by much-vaunted programs funded by public money, others by a national broadcaster. Most featured students we had previously taught or mentored, who we knew were extremely talented and had been educated on perhaps the best university game program in Europe. It was obvious something was seriously wrong when so much creative talent was being wasted. We investigated further and began to identify why this was happening: the funding of snowflake ideas instead of sustainable teams, pressure to incorporate not speculate, monocultural and orthodoxical mentorship, exhortations to endlessly make that treated selling as an afterthought or dirty word, self-limiting "indie" cultures and identities, and those holding the purse strings often being more interested in "conserving the institution" than the future of talented young people. It made us sad and angry to see all this entrepreneurial spirit wasted and enthusiasm crushed. And it is this anger that detonated this book and underpins its provocative approach. We *really* care about this shit.

Walls Come Tumbling Down

"Creativity is just connecting things ... [Creative people] connect experiences they've had and synthesize new things ... the broader one's understanding of the human experience, the better design we will have."

Steve Jobs
interviewed by Gary Wolf in Wired (1996)

This book is a mosaic. It adopts a contextual and inductive approach where exemplars act as tesserae assembled to make up a unified whole. Or at least, that's the plan. We display little respect for boundaries between mediums, industries, sectors, specialisms, or disciplines. We want this book to function as a trading space for ideas and learning sourced from across domains and cultures. We agree with Steve Jobs—the broader your cultural inputs, the better your creative outputs. Monocultures are simply systems devoted to reducing the variation that helps ecosystems evolve (Turner 2008, p.45). A monocultural mindset has no place in creative or artistic ecosystems, serving only to increase homogeneity and diminish originality. Creativity scholar Keith Sawyer argues "you can't create in a vacuum" (2006, loc.3414). We agree. For Sawyer, creativity is a sociocultural, interactional, collaborative phenomenon—contextually dependent on wider culture and society. And creating games is no different. Even though it sometimes seems like its own island, as a creative endeavor game making is really part of a vast, connected archipelago. A tessera in the cultural mosaic, to extend the metaphor. And when everything is connected, you can learn from *anywhere*. All you have to do is embrace knowledge-gathering, expand your cultural capital, think laterally, and make interesting new connections. Poach, plunder, and pilfer good ideas. Appropriate everything worth taking and reimagine it as something fresh.

You will find each essay here functions as a stand-alone piece but is, of course, connected to everything else. This means you don't have to read this book in sequential order if you don't want. You will also notice essays and examples raise points and themes that repeat and resonate throughout this book. Sometimes we make these explicit, sometimes they remain implicit. There are also shifts in authority, tone, and perspective. We make no apologies for this. We're exploring a complicated, fluid, and uncertain landscape where there are no easy answers. This book constitutes the process of our thinking rather than a completed product of discovery. We employ examples and case studies as probes and provocations, as means of insight to enable pattern recognition, rather than to deliver the fleeting chimera of objective truth. Like Marshall McLuhan, we see ourselves as safe-crackers who don't know what's inside. We just sit down and start to work. We listen, test, accept, and discard. We try out different sequences until the tumblers fall and (hopefully) the doors spring open (*Playboy* 1969). We have no fixed perspective. And we are happy to revise anything we say that later proves to be nonsense or doesn't provide deeper understanding. The nearest we come to advocating anything is our manifesto, a set of first principles that both informed and emerged from the iterative process of writing this book. Outside of those, we pretty much leave you to make your own connections and draw your own conclusions. We've got total confidence in your level of intelligence. After all, you're reading this book. Plus, it gives you something to do. Who said games have the monopoly on interactivity?

Rip It Up and Start Again

Although this book begins with failure, it is not about failure. It is about taking failure and learning from it, then using that learning to develop alternative approaches. This book is about learning from other people, from other cultures, domains, and sectors, from the distant or recent past. But it is definitely not about following prescriptive rules and dogma or getting stuck in nostalgic quicksand. The past is for building on, not living in. This book is about encouraging a truly independent mindset and approach for creating expressive playful experiences that resonate through culture. It is about embracing chaos, flipping the bird to orthodoxy, making new and unusual connections and, of course, doing it yourself. For this is the true essence of punk—not mohawk haircuts or ripped t-shirts—and the reason this book is called *Punk Playthings*.

Thick as Thieves

Finally, the thinking that appears on these pages is the product of two minds. It is the result of a conspiracy. And that conspiracy grew from serendipity, as so many creative things do. A few weeks after Chris began research at Denki, he was dispatched to a conference in Glasgow. So was Sean. Neither of us knew the other was attending, as we had only exchanged pleasantries at this point. By chance, we found ourselves attending the same talk and sat together. Afterward, we discussed the content and discovered we had reached roughly the same conclusions. So, in the absence of anything more interesting on the agenda, we withdrew to one of Glasgow's fine hostelries to discuss things further. And so the journey began.

In the five years since, we have continued these conspiratorial conversations. Incessantly. During visits to Dundee's best bars and pubs, our respective homes, London restaurants, workspaces, and most recently—due to geographical distance—on Slack. During this time we kept working our day jobs, adapted our thinking, and iterated our principles. The book you're reading is a different proposition to the book we began. And that's as it should be. Writing is thinking—as is any creative act. But at some point, you just have to stop. At some point, you have to expose your conspiracy and invite others in—if only to make it real. And so, dear reader, here is your invitation.

Chapter 1

The Road Less Traveled

Abstract

There are exceptional games but there is nothing exceptional about games. As a medium, it is no better or worse than any other.

This chapter explores creative mavericks who rejected the conventional wisdom and subverted the orthodoxical practices of their chosen mediums and domains. It argues that game makers themselves must move beyond the ghetto of the gamer—and the nostalgic clichés of traditional game development—to become genuinely independent in their thoughts, intentions and actions. To invent the future, games must take the road less traveled.

No Gods, No Masters

"A man with no enemies is a man with no character."

Paul Newman
(quoted in Verlhac and Dherbier 2006)

"Imagination is its own form of courage."

Francis J Underwood
House of Cards (2015)

Eclectic Skeptics

We worry too much about what people think of us. And we accept too much of what we're told. Now, this might sound rich coming from a book constantly telling you stuff. But that's not what this book is about. What we're doing is sharing provocations that will hopefully make you stop and think. What you do then, that's totally up to you. Nobody is infallible; no one has a monopoly on truth, despite what snake oil sellers would have you believe. And that's always worth remembering. Be an eclectic skeptic. Form your own character. Accept no gods, no masters. Look around, process and evaluate your context, assimilate information, then find new perspectives and imagine new realities. Leave the Kool-Aid on the shelf and resist restrictive silos. We don't follow prescriptive rule books—why should you?

More than a Woman

"Men liked to put me down as the best woman painter. I think I'm one of the best painters."

Georgia O'Keeffe
(quoted in Chadwick 1990)

Consider Georgia O'Keeffe. Today regarded as one of the great artists of the last century, O'Keefe spent much of her life resisting categorization. She lived uncompromisingly on her own terms and her work was equally resolute. In the 1920s she started to paint plants and flowers—nothing new you might think—but O'Keeffe had a different perspective. Instead of a traditional still-life viewpoint, she decided to paint flora as if viewed through a magnifying glass—up close and extremely personal. Works such as *Black Iris* garnered critical and public attention, helping establish O'Keeffe as one of America's most innovative modernists (Messinger 2004). These paintings also led to critics making myriad associations with the female body, due mainly to the popularity of Sigmund Freud's ideas at the time. Throughout the 1920s, her work was continually described in Freudian terms, labelled as "feminine" concerning perspective and method of expression. O'Keefe hated this. She viewed these interpretations as lazy ideological constructions that reinforced ideas of sexual difference, leading to more social and cultural segregation between genders (Chadwick 1990). In this construction, women painters were "feminine," "emotional," and "elementary," subconsciously obsessed with their bodies and close to the earth, whereas men were "masculine," "rational," and "intellectual." O'Keeffe never apologized for her gender—often exploring and celebrating her womanhood—but she believed such thinking only continued to marginalize female artists and reinforce patriarchy. It kept her firmly in the category of "great woman artist" but excluded her from being a "great artist."

In 1929, O'Keeffe started to visit New Mexico and became enchanted by the landscape and iconography of the desert there. Again, she adopted a new perspective, juxtaposing skeletal objects with desert landscape imagery, playing with size and scale. These works were provocative and unsettling, surreal and often masculine in form, far from the perceived femininity of her earlier work. For the rest of her life she would continue to shift perspectives in her paintings, moving close-up and abstracting her favorite landscapes, reimagining clouds from above through an airplane window. O'Keeffe would live in the brutal, beautiful desert lampooning men who talked about the "Great American Adventure" but had "never crossed the Hudson" (Imagine 2016). She was an outsider prickly as a local cactus who ploughed her own idiosyncratic furrow. Fellow outsider Joan Didion argued O'Keeffe was "equipped early with an immutable sense of who she was and a fairly clear understanding she would be required to prove it" (1979, p.129). And this she did by remaining fluid, shifting perspectives by zooming in and out, resisting categorization and in the process, disrupting the patriarchal art world.

Today there are major retrospectives of O'Keeffe's work in the most prestigious museums and galleries in the world. Her resolutely maverick life is the subject of biographies and documentaries. Georgia O'Keeffe is now described simply as "a pioneer of 20th-century art" (Tate 2016) or "American Painter" (*Encyclopedia Britannica* 2016); the words "female" or "woman" conspicuous by their increasing absence. Her continued resistance to being sidelined and categorized, her insistence on being judged solely on her work rather than her gender, finally paid off. Today Georgia O'Keeffe is simply one of the best painters.

An Englishman in New York

"We Sell—or else!"

David Ogilvy
Confessions of an Advertising Man (2013)

With David Ogilvy it's often hard to separate the myth from the man; he was equally at home selling himself as he was selling his clients' products. But that's part of what makes him so fascinating. Born in England of Scots and Irish extraction, Ogilvy won a scholarship to Oxford to read history. By his own admission he "screwed up" his university education, leaving in 1931 to work as an apprentice chef in Paris (Tungate 2007). A year or so later, he took a job peddling Aga cooking stoves to French chefs in London restaurants. During this time as a door-to-door salesman, Ogilvy discovered and refined his talent for selling and closing a deal, becoming so successful his boss asked him to write a manual for the other salesmen. Decades later, this book was still being praised by *Fortune* magazine as an exemplar for sales manuals, at the time it led Ogilvy to his first job in advertising (Tungate 2007). But the lessons he learned on the streets of London never left him, granting Ogilvy a unique perspective that led him to become perhaps the most quoted and revered "ad man" ever. The tough streets were a world away from the glamour of advertising but closer to the customer. And it was here Ogilvy heuristically and memorably, realized that "the customer isn't a moron, she is your wife" (2013, p.124). Long before advertisers started to think of people as individuals or even personas—these were the days of the masses "understood" by distant proxy—Ogilvy beat them to the punch by actually getting out and meeting people. Fancy that. He learned and never forgot that customers were more than abstractions or catch-all demographics—they were people too.

Ogilvy always maintained advertising was simply a sophisticated form of selling. No more, no less. Immersing himself in the industry during his early career, he spent time learning from New York's most successful ad men. But Ogilvy was a natural skeptic. He evaluated learning and information, abandoning what didn't resonate with him and adopting and synthesizing what did—before adding his unique twist. He rarely followed trends, preferring to formulate his own opinion and forge his own path.

At his height during the 1960s—advertising's creative revolution—Ogilvy was skeptical of "creativity" as a silver bullet solution or an end in itself. He even banned the unthinking use of the word within his agency, describing it as "hideous" (Ogilvy 2013). Ogilvy valued creative people, but their value resided in an ability to sell products. He believed advertising needed to be entertaining but always in the service of being persuasive, famously quipping, "We make advertisements that people want to read. You can't save souls in an empty church" (2013, p.125). But this razor-sharp focus on selling ran counter to the prevailing industry zeitgeist. At the time most agencies were focusing on making "clever" or "arty" ads. Ogilvy insisted a good advertisement didn't need to be clever; it needed to sell a product without drawing too much attention to itself (2013, p.108). The salesman in him meant Ogilvy could never forget agencies existed, first and foremost, to sell products for their clients. For him, the best advertising was well researched, based on a "big idea" and able to sell a product by communicating its benefits in an engaging way. Simple as that.

David Ogilvy changed advertising in many ways—usually by running counter to prevailing orthodoxies or trends. He even believed the best way to win new clients was not to spend precious resources on speculative "creative" pitches but to do great work for existing clients. Imagine that. The company he founded still bears his name, adheres to many of his ideals and is one of the world's most successful agencies. His desire to champion nonconformity, to pay well, to promote a positive corporate culture, to inspire people—plus his constant playful provocations in print—had a massive effect on the way advertisers thought about their work. Ogilvy reminded advertising of what it did and encouraged the industry to value itself for doing it. Advertisers weren't artists; they were salesmen who put on an entertaining and engaging show. This unique perspective and healthy skepticism reminded the industry of its essence at a time many were losing sight of it: "We Sell—or else!"

Insert Coin

> *"The things I had learned about getting you to spend a quarter in one of my midway games, I put those sales pitches in my automated box."*

> **Nolan Bushnell**
> *(quoted in Kent 2000)*

Meet someone else who divides opinion. Meet Nolan Bushnell. Celebrated and criticized in almost equal measure, there's one thing most people agree on: Nolan Bushnell pretty much invented the modern game industries. You're reading this book, so you already know about Atari, the iconic company Bushnell formed in 1972. Atari developed the seminal *Pong*—the first commercially successful arcade video game—and quickly followed it with other canonical titles. Then the company released the hugely successful cartridge-based Atari 2600 console in 1977. This machine took video games into both the home and the mainstream. It also unintentionally kick-started independent development when disgruntled Atari employees left to found Activision—the first independent game development company. So far, so familiar. But what we want to discuss is how Atari came to happen in the first place. And yes, you guessed it. It's about gaining a different perspective and imagining a new reality.

Nolan Bushnell loves ideas. At high school he loved philosophy, debating and playing imaginative pranks on friends. Nolan was a smart kid. And like many smart kids he enrolled to get a college education, joining the University of Utah in 1962 to major in engineering. Utah was one of the top schools in computer science—then a relatively new discipline—and Bushnell became fascinated by the subject. By befriending teaching assistants he gained regular access to the computer lab, where he played early computer games such as *Spacewar!*, taught himself to code and eventually made games of his own. His college education enabled Bushnell to understand computers and computer games. But he also attended another place of learning during this time.

The story goes that after losing his tuition money in a poker game, Bushnell was forced to take a job to earn money. He did this running arcade games at the Lagoon amusement park, just outside Salt Lake City. He started on the midway, working a stall where punters knocked down stacked milk bottles with a baseball at a quarter a shot. Bushnell soon realized the key to his job wasn't to stack the bottles; it was to attract players and get them to part with their coins. So he became a "midway barker"— drumming up patronage from the passing public. After a while, he was moved to the pinball and electro-mechanical game arcade. Here he used his engineering knowledge to maintain the machinery, but all the time he was observing and learning how the games worked, honing his understanding of the business (Kent 2001, p.29). Bushnell immediately realized each coin-operated machine was fundamentally a stand-alone business.

And he also discovered just how successful these mechanical businesses were, making as much as $200* a week per machine (NPR 2017). Bushnell saw opportunity and decided to get an intimate understanding of the tactics and tricks pinball and other games used to attract patronage then keep patrons parting with their money. He observed how the machines put on a show through an "attract mode" designed to entice passersby, in just the way he'd been drumming up business by barking on the midway. This understanding would serve him well in the future. The amusement park would be Bushnell's second education.

With his new perspective, Bushnell realized the future lay in combining the computer games he loved with the coin-operated analog arcade games he'd learned so much from at Lagoon. His first attempt was a false start. *Computer Space* had an eye-catching cabinet that attracted players—a trick learned from the arcades—but the gameplay was so complicated it required pages of instructions nobody wanted to read. The game was a failure, but Bushnell quickly learned from this. He started Atari and gave his new employee, Al Acorn, a brief to create a computer game as an exercise. Depending on who you believe, this was influenced either by the rudimentary computer tennis games Bushnell had played in college, or directly by the tennis game on the Magnavox Odyssey. Whatever the truth, Acorn came up with a prototype, surpassing what Bushnell had imagined with innovations such as ball acceleration and ricochets. Bushnell named the prototype *Pong*. The team added a few tweaks—including a coin-operation mechanism and the beautifully simple instruction to "Avoid missing ball for high score"—then installed a prototype cabinet at Andy Capp's Tavern in Sunnydale, California. Bushnell knew Atari had something special but he also knew it didn't have the money or manufacturing muscle to mass-produce it. So he flew to Chicago in a bid to sell *Pong* to one of the biggest coin-op companies, Bally Manufacturing. In a myopic business decision on par with Dick Rowe turning down The Beatles, Bally rejected the game outright. Bushnell says it did so because *Pong* was a two-player game and the orthodoxy of coin-operated machines "didn't allow for a two-player game if there's not a one-player game" (quoted in NPR 2017). Bushnell was bitterly dejected and decided to return to California. But before he left, he decided to call Al Acorn. It was a call that would change both Bushnell's life and the history of entertainment.

---

* Approximately $1600 per week when adjusted for 2017.

When Nolan got through to Al, his employee recounted how the team had received a request from Andy Capp's to service *Pong* because the game had malfunctioned. When Acorn arrived at the bar, he had opened up the coin box to play a free game and test the machine. To his astonishment, hundreds and hundreds of quarters gushed out all over the floor. The game had stopped working simply because it could not take any more money! After some quick calculations, Bushnell realized Bally rejecting the game was the best thing that could have happened. He decided Atari would build and license *Pong* itself. It had just enough money to build 12 cabinets and as Bushnell recalls, "the minute I got off the plane I submitted the order for the parts ... and we were off to the races" (NPR 2017). The era of the commercial game industries had begun.

Imagine

O'Keeffe, Ogilvy and Bushnell had impact because they looked at the world around them and imagined it both different and better. They glimpsed another reality, then worked to bring that vision into being. Georgia O'Keeffe saw a world where women artists would be in the artistic canon on their own terms and merit. David Ogilvy envisaged an advertising industry that delivered value to its clients by selling its products to real people in a nonpatronizing, entertaining and persuasive way, rather than thinking of people as a malleable mass to be manipulated through self-indulgent creative cleverness. And Nolan Bushnell imagined arcades full of beautiful, bright, bleeping video game machines bringing joy to millions—and hopefully, millions to him. Of course, these are not the only examples. History is full of people who dared not only to dream but to make those dreams reality—people like Ada Lovelace, the Wright Brothers, Marie Curie or Steve Jobs. None of them adhered to orthodoxy or gave much credence to trends. All had maverick tendencies and were often difficult. But running against orthodoxy is only for the headstrong. To be truly independent of mind, you need a healthy suspicion of accepted wisdom, conventions and opinions. You have to be skeptical but not cynical. You must question the status quo while continually learning from a wide range of influences, experiences and failures to imagine and realize new alternatives, new directions, new realities. You need the courage to imagine something new and the character to make it happen. If you can do that—who knows? You might make the world a better place.

FIGURE 1.1 Atari *Pong* arcade cabinet. (Courtesy of Rob Boudon, http://creativecommons.org/licenses/by/2.0.)

FIGURE 1.2   Portrait of Georgia O'Keefe by Alfred Stieglitz. (Courtesy of Wikimedia Commons, https://commons.wikimedia.org/wiki/File%3AO' Keeffe-(hands).jpg)

I Wanna Be Adored

"When I discover who I am, I will be free."

Ralph Ellison
The Invisible Man (1965)

"If I was you, I'd be a bit careful about this idea of independence. We're all connected."

Gil Scott-Heron
(quoted in PIAS 2016)

Me, Myself and I

The landscape is changing: AAA is a niche business, "gamer" a subcultural ghetto, "indie" increasingly a genre and identity. All are becoming meaningless, mostly empty clichés. Don't get cornered. Don't believe the hype. Putting #indiedev or #indielife on a tweet doesn't make you independent. It only shows your desire for acceptance. Never mind the virtue signaling. Be independent of mind. Be independent of action. Be yourself.

Out of One, Many

Gaming culture and industry were disrupted by the "casual revolution" during the mid- to late 2000s. First proposed by ludologist Jesper Juul, this concept describes a process of video games ceasing to be a subcultural activity—limited mostly to young males who self-identify as "gamers"—and becoming increasingly mainstream by connecting with "casual players" through "casual games." These games were accessible, demanding less time or knowledge of gaming subcultures and conventions to enjoy. Juul (2010) argues the phenomenon was mainly the result of two trends: the rise of "mimetic interfaces," where a player performs a physical activity mimicked on-screen—e.g. Nintendo's Wii console or games like *Guitar Hero*—and the rise of downloadable casual games.

While mimetic interfaces contributed to the casual revolution, in hindsight they were—as shiny tech often is—a fad. More important was the emergence of downloadable games, or to be more accurate, digital distribution. This frictionless method of distributing games—enabled by the faster internet connections available from the mid-2000s—heralded a massive shift for game makers. Now their intangible game products and services could be delivered directly to the consumer, apparently eliminating the need for the publishers who had traditionally dominated the relationship. Self-publishing was viewed as the silver bullet that would democratize making and selling games. And in their rush to self-publish, game makers left physical retailers reeling and traditional publishers sidelined. Out of this chaos Apple, Google and Valve elevated themselves to dominance. A similar phenomenon—exacerbated by rampant piracy—had massively disrupted the music industry only a few years earlier. Even so, many established game makers initially dismissed digital distribution, ignoring or underestimating the disruption it might cause. They were more interested in exploiting existing customers by engineering demand for their shiny plastic guitars.

But if these game makers had heeded lessons from the music industry, they might not have been so dismissive. The music business had made more money than ever during the late 1990s, but by the mid-2000s those profits—and the industry itself—were in freefall (Goldman 2010; Witt 2015). By ignoring digital distribution, the industry subjected itself to closures, mergers, rationalization, layoffs and a desperate search for new business models to survive (Witt 2015). If game makers had paid attention and joined up the dots, they might have realized that what happens to one creative industry can happen to another. But few were watching. And it was this failure to observe the wider context, to look and learn—coupled with the financial meltdown of 2008—that led inevitably to closures of medium and large developers around the world, plus mergers, rationalization, layoffs and a search for new business models to survive.

Digital distribution also changed gaming culture by making games ridiculously accessible to anyone with a smartphone or tablet, not just those with proprietary consoles. Such accessibility resulted in a "mainstreaming" of games throughout wider culture and society. We're all gamers now—to the point where that epithet is anachronistic and meaningless. The "traditional" pre-casual revolution gamer is now a niche audience, served by a niche console industry overly reliant on flashy technology—such as virtual reality—or the formatting of intellectual property (IP). Formatting involves the endless extension and exploitation of successful franchises—death by sequel where explorative innovation gets crushed by the logic of risk aversion and mitigation—or games eating themselves through the constant recycling of popular mechanics and tropes. Or sometimes both.

But as the audience for games has changed, so has the industry that makes them. It's no longer tenable to talk about a singular game industry—if it ever was; there are only game industries with vastly diverging realities. Workers made redundant from the big studio closures started their own small studios, realizing the digital distribution that once put them out of work might also represent an opportunity. They were joined by waves of young game makers—many fresh from college and university—who also saw the App Store, Google Play, Steam and others as an easy way to get their games directly to players. By 2014, research in the UK found 95% of game developers were small or micro-studios (Mateos-Garcia et al. 2014). Further investigation confirmed that over 65% of all studios employ fewer than four people and that nearly 70% of UK developers were founded post-2010, after the casual revolution (TIGA 2016; Ukie 2016). This rapid proliferation and diversification denote the much discussed and touted "rise of the indies" (Parker 2011; Gamasutra Staff 2013).

Independence Day?

But what does being indie—or more accurately, an independent game maker—mean? Nearly a decade on from the financial meltdown and disruption of the casual revolution, the answer is increasingly little. Indie game development has mostly become a badge of identity and aesthetic genre. *The Guardian* writer Keith Stuart has suggested indie game development now represents an extension of the 1960s "counterculture" (2012). But this presupposes the existence of a singular dominant culture to run counter to—an idea absurd in the fractured and atomized cultural milieu of the late 2010s. Or that repeating the self-indulgent navel gazing of the hippy counterculture is even desirable; as the punks always said, "Never trust a hippie." Worse, such a perspective treats indie as a singular homogenous culture itself. It ignores the diversity among so-called independent developers, from celebrated superstars like Jenova Chen—the central character in Stuart's article—to the thousands of unknown and unseen people making a variety of games in a variety of contexts. There's a world of difference between the cultural impact Chen achieved with his powerfully resonant experiences and the myriad of indie vanity projects and "lifestyle businesses" churning out conformist mediocrity. Instead of providing a viable alternative to the mainstream—based on radically different ethics and values, modes of production or ownership—the majority of these projects have zero meaningful impact, culturally or economically. The lucky ones quickly cease to exist. Others make just enough to perpetuate a shambling "indie lifestyle" for yet another go-round. But that's not real independence—it's entrapment.

Again it's worth looking at the music industry for historical parallels. In the wake of the 1970s punk revolution, the music industry in the UK and US witnessed an explosion of indies. Record labels like Rough Trade, Factory, Beggars Banquet, Fast Product, Postcard, Beserkely, Sub Pop, Matador and hundreds of others popped up everywhere. These labels were mostly set up by mavericks inspired by the do-it-yourself ethos of punk. They wanted to bypass the major labels that dominated the industry and do things on their own terms. These labels took risks by putting out content wildly different from the mainstream on a shoestring budget, often through the collaborative distribution of records and tapes (there were no digital downloads in 1982). Indies often controlled their supply chain and took products directly to the consumer. As a result, they were seen as "sticking it to the man" in an explosion of authenticity. And in the beginning, they probably were.

But as the 1980s progressed, indies became increasingly commonplace. Concurrently, the music they released became less known for its eclecticism, radical values, DIY ethos or alternative modes and means of production, more recognized simply as a genre. Most people buying "indie music" cared less and less about who owned the record label, how it distributed its products or treated its artists. Instead indie came to symbolize a band of usually white, usually middle-class musicians with jangly guitars and precious lyrics that appealed to college students. The apogee of this indie genericism was the so-called C86 movement—named after a compilation cassette distributed free with *New Musical Express* in 1986—described by Creation Records boss Alan McGee (quoted in Music for Misfits 2015) as "wet shite" and criticized by John Peel for its "shambling" self-conscious primitivism. C86 advanced the proliferation of twee indie bands peddling bubblegum indie tunes. It also gave birth to the Indie Kid™. These were children of the bourgeoisie who wanted everyone to know just how fiercely independent they were, so they adopted a uniform. Soon the streets were packed with teenagers clad exclusively in black jeans and plimsolls, cardigans and floral shirts. Indie was now everywhere. The major labels were finished. The future was bright. The future was indie.

Only it wasn't. By the end of the 1980s, an indiepocalypse was starting. Many of the best-known independents were going out of business. And there waiting in the wings were the major labels, ready for a spot of cherry picking. Majors are sluggish beasts; their size and bureaucracy make them slow to recognize and adapt to market disruption. They often get out-innovated by hip young gunslingers like the indie labels of the 1980s. But these big companies have things the gunslingers don't: stability, infrastructure, business acumen and money. And so these lumbering giants have learned to inno-vate in a different way, through mergers and acquisitions. As indie music became popular, the majors started to poach the most suc-cessful artists by offering huge advances the independents could never match. Or, if the indie label had a great roster and identity, the majors quietly acquired it. After all, by the late 1980s, it was becoming clear that most indie labels didn't have much in the way of business or selling smarts. Started as hobbies to initially put a record out, many couldn't adapt to scale and sustain themselves in a cut-throat industry. Even Factory Records—perhaps the seminal indie label of the era—had gone to the wall by 1992, its successful acts snapped up by London Records. Factory had done the hard, risky, explorative work of finding and developing artists, but it was a major that would fully exploit the rewards.

This strategy is still popular. Large media and entertainment com-panies learned the lessons of the 1980s. Instead of trying to out-innovate young gunslingers, they scour domains they operate in for the best talent and ideas. In games, big companies connect with universities to discover nascent talent or monitor innovative startups and studios as they experiment with their own energy, time, capital and risk in the marketplace. Once the market has fil-tered out the wheat from the chaff, the big players swoop in and acquire the successful entity and its intellectual property. It's a smart approach. And many game startups are now following examples from the tech sector, banking on getting acquired by a large studio or funded by venture capital (VC). Indeed, the delight-ful experiences made by Jenova Chen's supposedly "indie" thatg-amecompany would not have happened if the studio had not been bankrolled by Sony straight out of university. But all this complex-ity muddies the waters. Recognizing who is indie and who isn't is increasingly difficult. As a consequence, the term is ever more asi-nine and irrelevant.

From Safety to Where?

There's also an existential problem for indie game development: an extinction event. As with the indie record labels of the 1980s, there are now way too many independent game makers operating in a saturated marketplace who are just not that good at selling things. Consequently, these studios are either failing to scale or simply fail-ing. We've both seen this happen first-hand. It's upsetting to watch talented and enthusiastic young game makers have their dreams shattered. But one of the culprits is the term "indie" itself and the attitudes it often encourages and legitimizes.

To be indie in the creative industries has become a badge of identity, a form of self-valorization. It has increasingly little to do with how you go about your business, more that you adopt and display an outsider posture and lifestyle. This lifestyle celebrates being apart from—and somehow above—the dirty business of making money. And the indies that subscribe to such posturing see themselves as inherently "authentic" and "radical," heroically fighting the evil forces of capitalism one Steam or App Store release at a time. But this results in a proliferation of the worst kind of lifestyle businesses: ones that cannot afford to sustain the lifestyle they celebrate.

There is an acute problem with sustainability in independent game development. Few people like to talk about it, fewer seem to care. Most high-profile industry veterans tell young people simply to make stuff and do what they did, even though the environment for today's game makers is radically different from two or three decades ago. This "advice" is irresponsible but these stars have made their money. Perhaps worse, however, is the constant posturing and virtue signaling of the indie scene itself, which obfuscates and ignores the sustainability problem. Get past the valorization and the harsh truth is, if you're operating in the entertainment business—as game makers are—then whatever you identify as, you're in business. Simple. And if you want to survive in business, you have to take it seriously and make money. Whatever you make, you need to make and sell it effectively. Then you can pay yourself, your collaborators and of course, fund the continued production of more, perhaps better, experiences. If you want to be a radical outsider, great. We love radicals and outsiders. But then be truly radical and operate entirely outside the business of making games. Be a hobbyist or dillettante, make games for fun in your spare time, funded by your day job. Or adopt the artistic approach and attract patronage. These strategies remove the pressures of having to make money from your games just to survive, so you can be as radical as you dare, defiantly flipping the bird to big business and late capitalism. But if you want to be more than a hobbyist, to be a prosperous and sustainable independent game development business, then you might take some tips from XL Recordings.

Contra

Founded in 1989, XL was a side project of Groove Records, a record store in London's Soho (Teather 2007). Richard Russell, a young hip-hop enthusiast from suburban Edgware, was a regular customer who began working at the label. XL's early releases were niche, consisting of house and techno tracks from mostly unknown British and European artists. But by the early 1990s—as the UK dance and rave scene grew exponentially—these releases started to cross over to the mainstream. Most famous were *On a Ragga Tip* by SL2, *Charly* by The Prodigy and *The Bouncer* by Russell's own Kicks like a Mule. Somewhat amazingly, given their frenetic and challenging sound, these records reached numbers two, three and seven, respectively, in the UK singles chart. Simon Reynolds— music industry and rave culture historian—believes that had XL closed at the end of this period, it would still be remembered as a "legendary label" (cited in Jonze 2011a). But it had no intention of closing.

As the 1990s progressed, Russell took full control of XL. He widened its appeal beyond dance music, nurturing the roster and carefully adding new artists. And by mid-decade, early signing The Prodigy was achieving sustained success. The band's second studio album, *Music for a Jilted Generation*, reached number one in the UK; its third, 1997's *Fat of the Land*, achieved the same feat in 26 countries including the US. This success marked a turning point for the company, providing revenue and key learning for Russell as he expanded the label. The Prodigy had been allowed to develop its own sound, free from record label interference. When the band went mainstream around the globe, Russell realized the key had been affording it this creative control. He decided XL would move forward always guided by the principle of "letting musicians develop their vision instead of trying to dilute the work and make it more digestible" (Teather 2007).

Alongside creative control for artists, another XL first principle is quality control. The label only signs artists it likes, both musically and personally. In a 2011 interview, Russell stated that a cornerstone of XL's success was to only "put good records out." This might sound simplistic but to achieve such quality control the label signs only one or two artists per year, despite receiving over 200,000 unsolicited demos. Instead of the scattergun approach so often used in the music industry, XL is highly selective. This makes its success even more astounding, particularly when you consider the quality and cultural impact of its signings. Names such as The Prodigy, Dizzee Rascal, Vampire Weekend, The White Stripes, MIA, The xx and Adele read like a who's who of the last 20 years in alternative popular music.

A further XL principle is people over ideas. Russell (cited in Jonze 2011a) argues this is key to developing sustainable and scalable success for both artist and label: "the music [the artist] has done when you sign them is barely relevant. It's not even the start. It's much more about the person and their ideas and strength of character and the direction they want to go in." XL Recordings is not interested in developing a house sound or style; it is more about nurturing diverse artists with strong personalities and strong tastes to achieve their best works (Jonze 2011a). And it is this diverse roster—enabled by its adaptable artist-centric approach—that has been the secret to XL's success and sustainability.

Someone Like You

XL Recordings signed Adele Laurie Blue Adkins in 2006, on the strength of a Myspace demo she recorded as an 18-year-old student. Two years later, the label released her first album, *19*, which was an instant critical and commercial success. Further success followed when Adele's second album, *21*, was released in 2011 and went 16 times platinum within a year. Another four years later, *25*, her third studio album, was certified ten times platinum within six months and became the best-selling album worldwide in 2015 (Adejobi 2016; BPI 2016). Adele has continually broken music industry records and become the richest British singer ever (Ellis-Petersen 2016). And she has done it by crafting and performing music that resonates across cultures while signed to an independent record label. XL gave her "the freedom to become a blockbuster artist on her own terms ... [and] recognized and nurtured her talent" (Ellis-Petersen 2016). At the same time, it demonstrated that the major labels aren't the only ones who can scale an artist at a global level (Sullivan 2012).

XL's guiding principles meant it refused to pressure Adele to do things she didn't want to, such as perform at festivals or deliver to the kind of structured release timetable demanded by a major (Jonze 2011b). Rather it gave the singer a plentiful period of artistic development—alongside a sensible financial burden—in her early years (Ingham 2015). And it let her choose where and when she wanted to perform or appear, important for a star wary of the limelight (Ellis-Petersen 2016). In return, Adele's phenomenal success has given XL an invaluable financial cushion. Sales of *21* alone earned the label some $67 million in profit during 2011 (Rolling Stone 2012). These earnings allow XL to engage and invest in new artist development for the foreseeable future. The label is independently free to take more risks and sign increasingly experimental acts like Ibeyi—a French-Cuban duo that sings mostly in Yoruba—or Haitian hip-hop artist Kaytranada. For XL Recordings, Adele has been not only the mother of invention but the guarantor of its independence.

Crystalized

Adele left XL when her three album deal expired in summer 2016. Many in the industry were shocked but others were encouraged. Three album deals were label policy and XL had stayed true to this principle by extending the same freedom to its biggest earner (Adejobi 2016). A couple of months later, Richard Russell was awarded the Pioneer Award at the AIM Music Awards. Introducing him, Damon Albarn called XL Recordings "the greatest modern independent label in the world" and Russell "a genius" (PIAS 2016). Hyperbole aside, Albarn has a point. But much of the genius lies in those few simple principles Russell formulated to guide XL. It is these that have allowed it to adapt and scale. Signing artists with powerful artistic visions and distinct personalities, rather than one good song, means they are more likely to develop into sustainable commercial entities. Strong characters might cause tension, but by extending them full creative control this is minimized, allowing them to get on with what they're best at—making great music. And by signing only a few artists each year, the label has the resources to nurture and scale talent on the roster. This gives artists the best chance of achieving both cultural resonance and commercial success. XL's extraordinary hit rate is a testament to this approach. The success of artists such as The Prodigy, Vampire Weekend, The xx and Adele helps the bottom line, long-term sustainability and enables the company to take more risks with new artists.

Make It Last Forever

Independent game developers can learn much from Russell and XL. The label has learned how to make money and compete with the majors while staying faithful to its guiding principles. Russell doesn't spend his time flaunting his outsider, antiestablishment identity at every turn, moaning about how hard life is fighting "the man." Instead, Russell has beaten the man at his own game. He has ensured the label remains truly independent by realizing everything is connected. XL's successful insurgencies into the commercial mainstream free it from the shackles of VC investment, public sector funding or constantly trying to survive. This means the label can make its own decisions to sign who it wants when it wants, offering artists a fair deal and the creative control to help them develop. XL has learned to be sustainably independent through commercial success because Russell realized early on that being indie doesn't entitle you to a living.

Real independents can't afford to ignore making money because it doesn't fit an indie identity. Do that and you won't be independent for long. If you want to be in the business of making games, you need to act like it. There is nothing wrong with making money so you can make better, more creative, more radical games. But there is everything wrong with a self-limiting identity that either ignores or devalues the realities of business in an attempt to celebrate itself. As Jim Reid, indie hero and legendary lead singer of The Jesus and Mary Chain argues, "There is a lot of aiming too low [in indie] ... but we always wanted to be on Top of the Pops" (Music for Misfits 2015). The lesson is: if you want to be truly independent, forget transient regard from the uniformed worthies; sustained popular adoration is far more liberating.

FIGURE 1.3 Author Chris Lowthorpe's 12" vinyl of *Charly* by The Prodigy. (Reprinted with permission from Chris Lowthorpe.)

Weapons of Mass Destruction

"There are, in fact, no masses; there are only ways of seeing people as masses."

Raymond Williams
Culture and Society (1963)

*"Cause I'm not like everybody else,
I'm not like everybody else."*

The Kinks
I'm Not Like Everybody Else (1966)

Massing

Raymond Williams argued the concept of the "masses" was a product of industrialization. People left the countryside to "mass" in the new industrial towns, where they then massed together in the new factories. As a result of this physical massing, a further social, political and cultural massing occurred as the newly urbanized workers came to view themselves—and be viewed—as the "working class." From this massing a variety of ideas emerged, including mass production, mass action, mass democracy, mass communication, mass entertainment and the mass market. And for most of the 20th century, we thought about things through the lens of the mass and the masses.

Mass Effect

Growing up in 1980s Britain, mass entertainment and mass audiences still dominated. Television was king, even though there were only four channels until satellite and cable television services launched at the end of the decade. Radio, monopolized by the BBC, was also popular. News came primarily from these sources or the newspapers. This was a broadcast landscape. A place where one voice called to the masses and had a good chance of being heard and even believed. Shared viewing experiences were common, as evidenced when more than 30 million people (53% of the UK population) watched the 1986 Christmas Special of BBC soap opera *EastEnders* (BARB 2017). This remains the most watched TV show of all time in the UK, excluding special events. Out of the next 24, only one aired after 2000. And even that was the return of 1980s favorite *Only Fools and Horses* (BARB 2017). The most watched program of 2015—an episode of *The Great British Bake Off*—was seen by less than 25% of the population; and that figure included the two channels it broadcast on (SD and HD) plus the on-demand viewing figures from BBC iPlayer (BARB 2017). So, what changed?

In entertainment: a lot. The media landscape has shifted from broadcasting to narrowcasting to microcasting. First, cable and satellite providers disrupted mass entertainment by offering more choice tailored to increasingly targeted audiences. Today, Netflix gives us what we want, when we want it. Streaming platforms such as YouTube or Twitch go even further, catering for super-niche audiences by enabling individuals to create, stream and watch hyper-tailored and targeted content on individual channels. The days of shared viewing experiences on a nationwide scale are a thing of the past. The masses appear to be no more.

Trumped

But the mass is a powerful and persistent concept; we've used it for so long it's hard to change. Even smart people still get blindsided by myths of the mass, as the US presidential election of 2016 revealed. The Democratic party relied on a strategic playbook predicated primarily on demography, the statistical study of populations. Studies have consistently shown the US experiencing considerable demographic change, becoming more ethnically and racially diverse as over 59 million people immigrated to the nation during the last 50 years (Cohn and Caumont 2016). Most of these immigrants have come from Latin America and Asia. Indeed, in the four years between the 2012 and 2016 elections, the Latino electorate alone had grown by 17% (Krogstad 2016). This change was thought the key to electoral success by the Democrats, as the foundation of their playbook was the "bloc vote." This is a concept predicated on the belief that people vote en masse according to an aspect of their identity. Because of the bloc vote theory, Democrats believed Latinos were the reason Hillary Clinton would beat Republican candidate Donald Trump. Traditionally Latinos vote Democrat. Consequently, as there were more Latinos voters than ever—and Trump had publicly antagonized the Latino population—the thinking was they would vote for Clinton in record numbers and swing the election. But this didn't happen.

The problem is the bloc vote is rooted in ideas of the mass. It selects people by an aspect of their identity—most often ethnicity, race or gender—then groups them together accordingly. Once people are conceptualized as a homogenous mass, it's easy to ascribe certain traits or behaviors to them, or in extreme cases, discount or dehumanize them. The Democrats weren't attempting anything nefarious, but they were making the mistake of predicting people's thinking and behavior on a single aspect of their identity. Consequently, a thesis emerged that proposed virtually all Latinos would vote Clinton. Another one suggested that most women would too, particularly as Clinton would be the first female president and Trump seemed an unapologetic misogynist. The majority of African-Americans were also assumed to be Clinton voters. But this thinking was fallacious because it ignored individual difference and the multivalent complexity of identity.

Raymond Williams knew the concept of the masses was problematic. Individuals don't conceive of themselves as part of a mass: "the masses are always other people, ones we don't know or can't know ... to other people we also are the masses. The masses are other people" (1963, p.289). In other words, we don't think of ourselves as part of a homogenous mass but as an individual with a unique identity. This identity is complex, often fluid and multilayered, with particular aspects dominant at different times. But, however we self-identify at certain moments, one thing that remains constant is our belief that we are individual and unique. The trouble is when we think of other people as a mass—Latino voters, for example—we simplify their identity, conceiving of them purely through the frame we have used to lump them together. Such reductionism loses sight of the individual, attributing conformity to diversity. We forget people are emotional individuals who experience different life events; these inform the way they think and act, which can often be selfish and irrational. This forgetting is what sabotaged the Democratic playbook.

Of course, the majority of Latino voters did cast their ballot for Hillary Clinton. But not as many as the bloc vote strategy predicted or relied on. Exit polls suggested only 65% of Latinos voted for the Democratic candidate, with 29% actually voting for Trump. This represented a smaller percentage than those who voted for Obama in 2012 (Krogstad and Lopez 2016; Luhby and Agiesta 2016). In the key swing state of Florida, things were even worse. Here 35% of Latino voters went for Trump, with that figure soaring to 54% among Cuban Latinos (Krogstad and Flores 2016). Women also supported Clinton less than expected, with the percentage down on the previous two elections where the candidate had been male. Surprisingly, 42% had supported Trump despite accusations of sexual abuse and misogyny against him (Tyson and Maniam 2016). Fundamentally, the bloc vote had failed to materialize as predicted because the playbook treated people as a one-dimensional mass governed by a single aspect of their identity. The truth was far more complex, located in individual life experiences and hidden heterogeneity within demographic groups. The split between Cuban and non-Cuban Latino voters evidences such complexity. And a day after the election, Mexican-American journalist John Paul Brammer further highlighted this by arguing the Latino vote is made up of men, women, immigrants, natural-born citizens, the college-educated, farmers, conservatives and progressives who all get lumped together as a homogeneous mass in a way white people tend not to be (2016). The same goes for the "female vote" or the "African-American vote." It is no longer viable, nor desirable, to think about people in such a reductionist and simplistic way. Mass voting blocs can no longer be relied on to elect presidents, if they ever truly could be. And treating people as homogeneous lemmings is not only insulting but liable to result in a nasty surprise come Election Day.

The mass is pretty much dead. It was a phenomenon of industrialized societies where people, production and communication were increasingly concentrated. But as society in so-called developed nations becomes more postindustrial and atomized, the idea of a mass anything is becoming untenable, categorizing individuals by a homogenizing demographic or assumptive persona more unreliable. It's difficult to change the way we think, but today everyone is an individual. Or at the least, they believe they are. Things for everybody are now really for nobody. Everything is niche. So the trick is to be selfish, to make and do things for yourself. Create something intoxicating you want to experience. The chances are others will too.

The Haçienda Must Be Built!

"The idea was to start the club for yourself, cos there was nowhere in Manchester that gave you what you wanted. There was nowhere you could get in, dressed normally."

Peter Hook
(quoted in Savage 1992)

Manchester's legendary Haçienda nightclub is a great example of selfish creation resonating with a niche group and becoming successful. There are many legends and tall tales about the club but perhaps the most insightful recounts a moment just before it opened when Tony Wilson, head of Factory Records, was showing friends around. One of them, looking at the Haçienda's cutting edge architecture and costly interior design, asked who Factory was building the club for. Wilson responded the Haçienda was built for "the kids." The friend pointed out "the kids" were currently interested in watching bands in the corner of a grotty room while wearing long drab clothes and old raincoats, so why was Factory building a glossy New York discotheque for them? Wilson recalls being "rather stumped. I couldn't answer that question" (Wilson 1992). By identifying "the kids," Wilson was thinking in conventional terms of the mass. But he was dead wrong—the Haçienda wasn't for the masses at all.

The Haçienda was primarily for Rob Gretton, New Order's manager. At the time there was nowhere in Manchester Gretton wanted to go—especially to meet members of the opposite sex—so he dreamed up a new nightclub (Gretton 1992). He proposed his grand vision to members of New Order—his charges and Factory's most successful band—who liked it and were persuaded to put up a substantial amount of funding. Peter Hook, the band's bass player, argues there was no sense of doing it for "the kids" or giving back to the people of Manchester. Hook (1992) says: "the main priority for it was the fact that people like you, yourself and your friends mainly, didn't have anywhere to go." This sentiment is echoed by others such as Stephen Morris (1992), who remembers: "I don't think we were thinking about the people of Manchester at the time. We were doing it for selfish reasons." In another place or time, this might be unremarkable. But what made the Haçienda different was its context. It was the antithesis of everything people in early 1980s Manchester thought a nightclub could or should be (Morris 1992).

Manchester was the world's first industrialized city. As such, it had been a hotbed of massing: physical, social, political and cultural. The size and population of the city exploded throughout the 19th century as it became an epicenter of mass production—known as "Cottonopolis"—and radical mass politics, driven by the newly massed and urbanized working class. But by the early 1980s, Manchester was well on its way to becoming one of the world's first postindustrial cities, due to extensive factory closures and job losses. Much of the city center was desolate. Once-bustling Victorian railway stations were parking lots, proud factories stood idle and derelict. And it was into this postindustrial decline that Factory decided to insert a colorfully modernist, late-night fun palace. It would be filled with designer furniture and located in a disused yacht showroom on Whitworth Street West. The arrival of the club was nothing short of an alien invasion. Mike Pickering, one of the Haçienda's most famous DJs, remembers it causing widespread confusion because: "there was nothing like it ... I don't think it's too outrageous to say that then it was completely beyond people" (1992). So, how did this enigma become one of the most influential and loved nightclubs ever?

It took time. The club struggled to make ends meet in its first few years, mostly as the result of overspends on construction and poor management. Luckily, Gretton and New Order hadn't quit their day jobs so could continue to subsidize it. The Haçienda opened seven nights a week—often with few customers—but weekends and live gigs were relatively busy. Gradually, the club attracted a following. It became known as a place where people who felt outside mass culture, mass entertainment and the mass market could feel at home. Unlike other clubs at the time, the Haçienda had no prescriptive dress code predicated on mainstream ideas of what constituted suitable nocturnal attire. At "the Haç" you could wear what you and your friends wanted and all tribes were welcome. The club also had an unapologetically out and proud gay night at a time when homosexuals were often ghettoized and ridiculed (or worse) in British culture and society. The music policy became ever more niche and experimental, with more and more nights playing cutting edge music. Within five years, the Haçienda—always a warehouse party waiting to happen—found itself at the epicenter of the late 1980s Acid House explosion, adopting new sounds from Chicago and Detroit before virtually anywhere else. It became ground zero for Manchester's urban regeneration, bringing hundreds of young creative people into the forgotten south side of the city center. Epiphanies happened every weekend on the dancefloor, bands formed at the bar and friendships were cemented for life. The Haçienda went from zero to iconic legend in under a decade, as its unique spirit percolated first through Mancunian culture then wider British and global culture too.

Today, the Haçienda itself is gone—an inevitable victim of the regeneration it spawned. But in 2016, thousands packed out London's Royal Albert Hall to hear a classical orchestra reinterpret electronic "hits" from the club's dancefloor. Books are written about the club and its design and influence are regularly celebrated. In 2013, two urinals from the club toilets even went on sale for £15,000 (Dex 2013). Taking the piss aside, it's clear the Haç still resonates through culture nearly two decades after it closed its doors. Not bad for club built so a few mates had somewhere to go of an evening.

It's the Context, Stupid

"Despite the continuing role of mass production in many societies, the task is to design for the individual placed in his or her immediate context ... Products should be personal pathways in the otherwise confusing ecology of culture."

Richard Buchanan
Branzi's Dilemma: Design in Contemporary Culture (1998)

Whatever you do, it's essential to think about individuals and their contexts. It's no good trying to make and sell to nonexistent masses. Instead, think about specific contexts filled with individuals, contexts like yours. Often individuals in similar social and cultural environments want similar things, regardless of more essentialist identities. The young people who built the Haçienda wanted somewhere to go away from the commercial mainstream, where they could dance to niche music, wear what they wanted to wear, be who they wanted to be. In the context of a newly postindustrial Manchester, enough people like them wanted the same thing. Unlike a Clinton campaign that imagined voters as mass blocs organized along racial or gender lines, Donald Trump's campaign also focused on individuals in their contexts. The campaign acknowledged that many people, regardless of gender or race, felt fed up and angry in their immediate environment. Common among these was a belief that things were changing for the worse, that they were being abandoned by globalization and looked down upon by a metropolitan liberal elite. Whatever the realities, instead of relying on mass demographics, Trump told compelling stories of "Making America Great Again" that resonated with those dissatisfied with their lot.

Making and selling playful experiences is not running a nightclub, nor is it running for office. But it is equally dependent on context and abandoning ideas of viewing people as a mass. Unlike the 19th and 20th centuries, there are fewer and fewer mass movements, more and more agile insurrections. Our postindustrial societies have atomized: cultures become subcultures, subcultures become tribes, tribes become cadres. And cadres are now becoming loose, fluid groups of individuals in specific contexts. The hipster—that cultural phenomenon of the early 21st century—may be easy to laugh at but is also extremely hard to define. Few individuals self-identify as hipsters, but they can often be recognized contextually by where they hang out, either physically or online (Peter York's Hipster Handbook 2016). Increasingly, those who can create experiences that resonate in these specific contexts and provide a "personal pathway" through an increasingly complex culture will be successful. These experiences may be niche and ephemeral—more one-hit wonders than extensive bodies of work—but for a moment they will feel vitally authentic. And authenticity, however manufactured and constructed, only occurs when an experience emotionally resonates with someone—voter, dancer, player or customer—in their immediate and specific environment. Mass is finally over.

FIGURE 1.4 Author Chris Lowthorpe's flyer for the Haçienda. (Reprinted with permission from Chris Lowthorpe.)

FIGURE 1.5   The efficient assembly line at the Volkswagen plant in Wolfsburg, Germany. (Courtesy of Roger Wollstadt, *Flickr: Wolfsburg—Inside the Volkswagen Plant*, http://creativecommons.org/licenses/by-sa/2.0.)

Yesterday

"Plunder and destroy, refuse to worship the past and remember that anyone can do it."

Sheryl Garrett
Cut and Thrust (1988)

"Yesterday, all my troubles seemed so far away..."

Lennon and McCartney
Yesterday (1966)

The Nostalgia Machine

Nostalgia ain't what it used to be. Just because the future is uncertain does not mean you should spend your time pining for a past that never existed. Reject romanticized traditions and false idylls—you don't know where they've been. Tradition can be a straightjacket, nostalgia a myth. Plunder the past, learn from history, then create your own myths. Remember, the past is for building on, not living in.

A Turn to Craft?

The past decade has seen an explosion of craft and artisanship. Beer, gin, denim, bicycles, bread, cheese, leather goods, even video games—all these and more are now being crafted rather than produced. Out goes the mass-made, processed and homogenized. In comes the handcrafted, authentic and unique. And this is a good thing. Mostly. Who but a masochist prefers insipid mass-produced lager over a flavorful "small batch" beer, crafted by enthusiasts in your local microbrewery? Why would anyone eat a nutrition-free slice of processed white bread when there's a delicious hunk of artisan sourdough waiting to be savored?

Cost is one answer. Anything crafted by a skilled artisan is likely to be more expensive than its mass-produced counterpart, due to the extra risk, care and time in making it. That's understandable. If a product uses the best raw materials, is carefully and painstakingly crafted by specialists in small batches, then you expect to pay more for it. It's "reassuringly expensive"—to quote an advertising campaign that for over two decades successfully sold mass-produced beer by channeling myths of rural idylls filled with happy artisans. And here lies the problem. There are two sides to the craft revolution: "craft" as a verb and "craft" as a noun.

Oh, I Believe in Yesterday

"In recent years the words 'crafted' and 'hand-built' have become absorbed into the language of advertising and packaging and into popular culture in general."

Christopher Frayling
On Craftsmanship (2011)

"Craft" as a noun draws on nostalgic myths of the happy artisan, a mythology that positions craft as both precursor and resistor to industrialized capitalism. This view supposes everything was better before industrialization, that the world was full of artisans leading charmed lives filled with carefree crafting of simple but unique objects. As Frayling (2011) argues, this is nostalgia masquerading as history. While industrialization had many downsides, preindustrial society was definitely no walk in the park. So, where does all this craft nostalgia come from? Frayling (after Wiener 1992) believes it is possible for nations to industrialize economically while not entirely industrializing culturally. Raymond Williams concurs, arguing that as industrialization progressed in Britain, artists, writers and poets were paradoxically hard at work mythologizing a simple, natural and unadulterated countryside, creating a dichotomy between the capitalist exploitation of the industrialized city and the disappearing rural idylls populated by happy artisans (1973). This Romanticism positioned the myth of a lost preindustrial golden age at the heart of British culture, creating a sense of retrospective regret and persistent nostalgia. For Williams, such nostalgia is "myth functioning as memory" (1973, p.43). And this myth persists in contemporary Britain, with versions existing in other so-called developed nations. It would seem one thing our atomized postindustrial societies still have in common is a deep nostalgia for their preindustrial salad days.

Nostalgic notions of craft highlight our enduring fascination with both the mythology of craftsmanship and a paradise lost (Frayling 2011). And when "craft" is used as a noun, it functions as a symbolic shorthand for this mythology. In the dense fog of nostalgia, the preindustrial era appears simpler, better, happier—a time free from the uncertainty that defines our modern realities. Of course, this is nonsense. The "maelstrom of modern life" has been with us for nearly five centuries (Berman 2010). But such nostalgic symbolism is seductive and reassuring, deceiving us with simplicity and reassuring us with cost. When put in the hands of accomplished marketers, it can be highly effective at persuading us to purchase "craft" at inflated prices—especially when it promises a slice of that simple, better, happier life. We're regaining our lost paradise, and we can feel good about it too—simply by looking at the price tag. "Craft" as a noun seduces consumers by piggybacking on these nostalgic myths and of course, on the reemergence of genuine small-scale, small-batch, artisanal makers that practice "craft" as a verb, as a process, as a careful but risky act, rather than as a product differentiation strategy. Not surprisingly given its power, more and more mass-producers and marketers are using craft as a noun to gain access to our wallets.

Crafty

In September 2016, some "low volume" beers produced by Heineken Ireland (a subsidiary of Heineken International) were accused of being mis-sold as craft beers throughout the Republic of Ireland. Allegedly, these beers were rebadged at the tap to look like local craft brews to deceive the consumer. No one seems to know who was responsible, but Heineken Ireland apologized and appointed an external body to investigate. The incident prompted the Food Safety Authority of Ireland to announce an investigation into the craft beer market and led to the Independent Craft Brewers of Ireland (ICBI) launching a quality mark to guarantee real craft beers (Hospitality Ireland 2016). The ICBI complained: "some companies are ... releasing products into the market which they're misrepresenting as craft beer and being vague about origin to suggest a provenance of craft beer from an independent Irish brewery" (Murphy 2016). Provenance is deemed crucial in craft brewing, both to ensure quality and highlight regionality. Industrial producers have been criticized by genuine craft brewers and beer enthusiasts for selling "craft" beers with no information regarding where the product is made or by whom, leading many to suspect surreptitious mass production by large-scale operations. By 2015, things had got so bad that Barrett Garese and friend Rudy Jahchan launched *Craft Checker*, an app that can tell you whether your pint is "from an authentic craft brewery or just a mass-market imitation craft beer" (Craft Check 2016). Now we like a craft brew, but we are not beer snobs. As Anthony Bourdain says, sometimes you just want any cold beer "to get a little bit buzzed and pleasantly derange the senses and have a good time and interact with other people" (quoted in Sellers 2016). But industrial brewers using "craft" as a noun—masquerading ordinary mass-produced beer as craft to charge more and gain access to the lucrative market eroding their core brands—is somewhat underhand, if not particularly surprising.

Levi's, the world's most famous jean manufacturer, also employs "craft" as a noun. The company launched its Made & Crafted line in 2009, but although the name focuses consumer attention on the act of making—deploying "craft" as a verb to emphasize nostalgic mythology and notions of quality—the reality seems somewhat different. In a 2013 interview, the design lead for the line said it was impossible to say "Levi's *Made & Crafted* quality is so much more superior than anything else that we do, because that's not necessarily the case" (Williams 2013). He then revealed that the Crafted element of the name was simply the result of the word being regularly used around the design studio at the time of naming—no doubt influenced by the rise of genuinely crafted denim and other products (Williams 2013). This sleight of hand—implying "craft" as a verb when it is more likely a noun—does not make Made & Crafted clothes poor products. But trading on nostalgic craft mythology to justify a reassuringly high price does perhaps make them a little disingenuous. Just calling something crafted does not make it so. But, in Levi's defense, a degree of redemption comes from Made & Crafted's attempt to reinterpret company heritage by adding a contemporary twist to the back catalog. Perhaps it is less a product that is being crafted here and more a curated concept.

Crafted

"Roy subscribes to the ideal that in order for something to be great, it has to be given time, work and patience."

Young Lee
A Conversation with Roy Slaper (2013)

The best exponents of the craft explosion adopt a DIY ethic and take skills, materials and approaches from the past, then marry them with a modern twist to create delightful new products and experiences. They employ "craft" as a verb: a skillful and careful act. Many learn almost forgotten skills or arcane knowledge. Care, quality and uniqueness trump nostalgia. That does not mean nostalgia is not present here. But this is a nostalgia for taking pride in your work and its outcomes, for knowledge that deserves saving from extinction. It is yesterday placed in service of tomorrow, enhanced by the attitudes, tools and opportunities of today. Most of these new craft makers are as expert with digital tools and services as they are with the traditional tools of their trade; some even craft digital artefacts. Virtually all use digital means to communicate their story and sell their goods. These artisans are plundering the past and remixing it with the present to create the future.

Take Roy Slaper in Oakland, California. Roy was a skilled metalworker who decided he wanted to make himself a pair of jeans, then set out to learn how. Sometime around 2010, he bought a couple of vintage sewing machines, put them in his apartment, sourced some denim and made his first pair. They were almost unwearable. But pleased he managed to make anything at all, Roy decided to carry on. He learned his craft through painstaking research, attending sewing groups and immense amounts of practice. There were plenty of failures, but after a few months, Roy was making wearable jeans. He also found a mentor who taught him more about the mysteries of denim. She introduced him to "a string of really smart people who seemed to be the gatekeepers of a lost art. It's funny to say that making jeans is a lost art but it sort of is" (Roy Denim 2016). The jeans continued to improve and Roy became further immersed in learning his craft, to the point where his apartment was so full of material and vintage sewing machines there was hardly enough room to sleep (Lee 2013). Unsurprisingly, news of this maverick maker started to spread through the Bay Area, leading to a handful of orders for his experimental products. Roy realized he couldn't go on making jeans in his apartment—the neighbors didn't like the noise for a start—so he rented space to use as a studio. As an experiment, he put up a basic website with pictures of what he was doing and a way to buy the single style he made. The localized word-of-mouth buzz quickly spread online to niche denim forums then resonated across social media. The orders started to roll in. His experiment had been a success, suggesting Roy could make a sustainable life and business as a one-man artisan jean maker. He started to professionalize, collaborating with stockist Self-Edge to produce videos of his making process that rapidly helped spread the word online. Half a decade later, Roy is considered "one of the best craftsmen in the world when it comes to hand-making jeans from start to finish" (Articles of Style 2015). He has bespoke denim woven for him by the prestigious Cone White Oak Mill in North Carolina. His small-batch collections are eagerly awaited by denim enthusiasts around the world and sell out almost immediately. And he still does everything himself, from the first chain stitch to the final Instagram post.

Games of Craft

"We like to handcraft, not mass produce."

Ken Wong
Behind the Scenes: Monument Valley (2014a)

The best thing about "craft" as a verb is that anyone with dedication can do it. From a metalworker with dreams of crafted jeans to a game designer with a vision for a crafted playful experience.

We talk about *Monument Valley* in more depth later, but for now, let's focus on Ken Wong's statement about wanting to "handcraft" a digital game. On first reading, such a statement seems counterintuitive. How can something intangible be crafted by hand? But Wong is alluding to the importance of heuristic learning and care. Frayling (2013) argues that what distinguishes craft is the care with which things are made, the fact they have been made by human beings for other human beings. He agrees with scholar David Pye (1968) that craft is an activity where quality is not predetermined but depends on the judgment, dexterity and care the maker exercises as they work. Both thinkers emphasize the importance of makers continually learning while doing. This primacy of care and heuristic learning is implicit in Wong's statement; he deliberately contrasts the idea of handcrafting something individual—carefully and lovingly made by a human being for a human being—with the impersonal homogeneity of something mass-produced by machines for the masses. This focus on collaborative craft has been echoed by the rest of the *Monument Valley* team, affirming how important the craft making of each level was to the success of the game (Wong et al. 2014b).

The craft of *Monument Valley* is not "craft" as a noun. The aesthetics of the game are resolutely digital and game-like—despite being influenced by artist M.C. Escher—and completely devoid of nostalgic notions of craft. Here craft is not superficial; it is put into the making of every level and espoused in the narrative of the development team. *Monument Valley* wants to be different to the soulless mass-produced. And such a process of crafting a digital game represents a coming to terms with (post) modernity, postindustrialism and the possibilities of digital technologies. This is craft articulated through the language of technology and entering the realm of production with its own networks, expertise and knowledge sharing (Frayling 2011; Carpenter 2011). And rather than being nostalgic resistance to modernity, this kind of crafting can be a boon to entrepreneurial makers in postindustrial contexts. Craft is a business model too. Just take a stroll around the so-called hipster area of your local city and look at the plethora of artisan coffee joints and bakers, craft brew pubs and jean makers. This is not a counterculture; it is rampant and unapologetic entrepreneurship. There is much to be learned here. And the most critical lesson is that by exercising care in making an experience the best it can be, by always remembering that you're humans making something for other humans, "craft" as a verb can set you and what you make apart. Craft doesn't have to be about a longing for yesterday; it can be a vision and strategy for tomorrow.

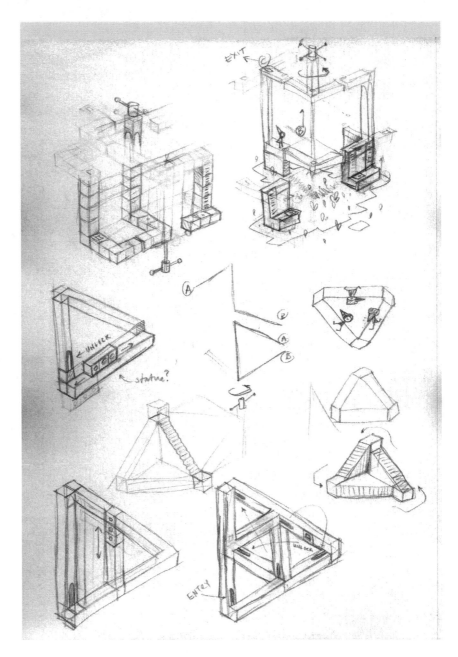

FIGURE 1.6 Early sketches of *Monument Valley*. (Reprinted with permission from ustwo games, ©ustwo Games 2014. All rights reserved.)

FIGURE 1.7   A screenshot from *Monument Valley*. (Reprinted with permission from ustwo games, ©ustwo Games 2014. All rights reserved.)

Canon Fodder

"Most of my heroes don't appear on no stamps..."

Public Enemy
Fight the Power (1989)

Checklist Culture

We are obsessed and surrounded by cultural lists: the 50 best movies, albums, books, games and restaurants. Ever. Each December we
pour over the end-of-year lists from columnists, critics and anyone
else with an opinion—just in case we missed something. Recently
we have become hooked on bucket lists: things to be experienced
before we shuffle off our mortal coil. Or more accurately, cultural
checklists for the terminally unimaginative. It sometimes feels like
our whole culture has been reduced to a series of lists to be checked
off rather than experiences to be discovered. Or even experienced.
But where does this obsession with grouping and categorization
come from? Who compiles these lists? And why should we care?

Imperfect List

*"[Beethoven, Mozart, Bach and Brahms] They're all heroes of
ours, ain't they? They're wonderful people. Oh yes, they really turn
us on!"*

Johnny Rotten
on Today with Bill Grundy (1976)

Compiling lists of culture is not new. For hundreds of years,
culture—mainly literature but also visual art and music—has been
compiled into a supposedly definitive list: the Western canon. This
identified works considered the most valuable in shaping and preserving Western culture, in particular so-called high culture, that is,
poetry, literature, classical music or fine art. The canon essentially
listed the works that laid the foundations for everything the West
is and stands for. Sounds interesting, right?

Well, yes and no. While great work was listed in the canon, it had
serious failings. It was exclusive and elitist. During the postmodern "culture wars" of the 1970s and 1980s, the canon was criticized for what it failed to contain, namely women or people from
nonwhite or non-Western backgrounds (think Georgia O'Keefe). It
became regarded as the exclusive preserve of "Dead White Men,"

a cornerstone of a patriarchal, white, Western culture that failed to recognize or value the work of women, nonwhites or minorities— or indeed anything from outside the West itself. Also, the canon excluded everything but rarified high culture. There was no room for the popular culture most of the Western population enjoyed in their everyday lives. No movies, no popular music, no TV, no comics and certainly no video games. The canon was fundamentally the preserve of a cultural elite who judged not only what work had cultural or artistic merit but as a result decided what might be worthy of preservation or funding. And these judgments reflected the elite's cultural tastes and snobbery. The postmodernists decided it was time to challenge all of this, believing such an imperfect list could benefit from that most postmodern of processes: a remix.

Sacred Cows Slaughtered Daily

Postmodernism was great at challenging and deconstructing the cultural status quo. It playfully subverted the orthodoxies of art, culture and society to reveal new narratives and points of view. Postmodernism argued that the "grand narratives"—religion, progress, capitalism— were either dead or dying. Modernism had failed to make the world a better place, artistic originality was impossible and the best we could all hope for were ironic and playful remixes of everything that had gone before. To postmodernists there was no singular historical truth, just competing historical narratives. Many of these—based on gender, ethnicity, sexuality, etc.—had been obscured or overlooked for decades. Similarly, there was no fixed meaning in a work of art or culture. It was irrelevant what the maker intended because the moment a work was complete, it was open to deconstruction and interpretation. The author might as well be dead. In short, postmodern thought was fundamentally against a singular view of anything. It was heterogeneous, inclusive, pluralist. It encompassed elements of Marxism, feminism, queer theory, postcolonialism, poststructuralism and any other "ism" that wanted in. Even capitalism. So the existence of a singular Western canon that exclusively defined what culture had value—and equally important, what culture was deemed valueless—provided a bright red rag to the postmodernist bulls of the late capitalist 1980s.

Postmodernism encouraged artists and creators to play. To deconstruct and reassemble, to perform cultural remixes by putting myriad influences through a creative blender. Sacred cows were slaughtered daily. Ex-arch modernist Philip Johnson remixed the quintessential modernist office block with a playful Chipperfield pediment; Malcolm McLaren remixed Puccini with hip-hop beats; Barbara Kruger remixed commercial advertising with a dose of feminist and anti-consumerist messages. The voices and narratives of the unheard became heard. Consequently, postmodernists subverted and remixed the existing Western canon, playing with its contents and producing new canons of alternative culture they valued instead. The exclusion of women and minorities was over. The barrier constructed between so-called high and low culture melted into air. The fight back against cultural and political elites was on. The people were sick and tired of being told what to think and do. Capitalism was starting to crumble and the cultural revolution was most definitely being televised.

All right, so that last bit is an overreach. The Anglophone West mostly voted for radical right governments that were both socially and culturally conservative throughout the 1980s. It continues to do so. And most people going about their daily lives at the time weren't particularly aware of the culture wars raging on university campuses, in academic publications and throughout the art world. Why should they have been? The people were less concerned with learning from Las Vegas than going there and taking it for every dime they could. But consciously or not, people were increasingly interacting with postmodern culture and postmodern ideas on a regular basis.

Your New/Old Arsenal

"Tell the truth, James Brown was old,
'til Eric and Ra came out with 'I Got Soul'!"

Stetsasonic
Talkin' All That Jazz (1988)

The technique of sampling in popular music—enabled by digital technology—was an inherently postmodern act. Samplers had been around in basic yet expensive form since the late 1960s, but by the early 1980s machines such as the E-mu SP1200 had become smaller and cheaper, consequently making sampling accessible. Young artists creating new musical genres such as electro, hip-hop, house or techno could now have a sampler in their bedroom. These creators used them to plunder content—vocal snippets, drum loops, guitar riffs, sound effects—from their influences. These usually took the form of extant recorded music but could also be more esoteric, including documentary narrations, speeches, civil defense broadcasts, porn soundtracks, Disney cartoons and so on. Manipulated by the sampler, these snippets were reconstructed into a sonic collage—or more accurately bricolage (see Levi-Strauss 1966)—to create something new from the culture that surrounded the creators. Well, newish. Records that achieved mainstream success—*Pump Up the Volume* by M/A/R/R/S or the Double Trouble remix of Eric B and Rakim's *I Know You Got Soul*—contained dozens of relatively obscure samples, exposing listeners to new pieces of culture many had not encountered previously. Often these were the product of another time, place or cultural group and they encouraged further exploration among the culturally curious. For example, many white middle-class kids in 1980s Britain developed an obsessive interest in Black American music of the previous decade, due to the funk, soul or disco samples used in new hip-hop and house records. This obsession would lead to a popular subculture known as Rare Groove in the mid- to late 1980s (Thornton 1995). Exploring these new/old cultures created more and more subcultures based around them, each sporting its unique canon constructed from the bottom up.

Although postmodernism is usually considered anticanonical, sampling is an example of how it could be extremely effective at exposing previously overlooked work and enabling the construction of new canons from it. Postmodern creators sampled, "quoted" and remixed culture continually, making ironic references, hybridizing genres, subverting meanings—all the time drawing attention to the obscure, the unknown and the undervalued. Never mind cultural appropriation, this approach shone a light on the forgotten and the marginalized, exposing and celebrating their culture. In the process, it created something new that both subverted and enhanced mainstream Western culture. True, postmodernism could be a cul-de-sac—its lack of belief in anything too often resulting in negative conservatism and a relativistic shrug of the shoulders—good at pulling things apart but less good at constructing or proposing alternatives. But this was more the case with politics, economics and science, rather than art and culture. Here postmodernism empowered creators to discover and curate canons constructed from an arsenal of diverse influences and passions. And the extreme extension of this empowerment is all those cultural lists and checklists of experiences to "do" before we die. The lists might have got out of control but the good thing is that canons are no longer for the elite. We've all got a provisional license to curate now. That's why we describe everything as curated, from DJ sets to booklists to menus (Rosenbaum 2014). You no longer need to know the Western canon to be culturally astute or creatively successful. Instead, you might know a lot about hard-boiled fiction, trashy novels, ambient music, JRPGs, or have an encyclopedic knowledge of movies from arthouse to grindhouse. Or all of these at the same time. And using that knowledge you might constantly mine, sample and expose your influences, creating an evolving canon of your own for fans to explore with every new thing you create. Or you might if your name is Quentin Tarantino.

Turning Shit into Gold

"Tarantino's influence ... is derived from his own pop-cultural cherry-picking: Every film he's directed or written has been loaded with countless homages, lifts and references to books, movies, TV shows and music that coalesce into a pop-cultural galaxy of their own."

Larry Fitzmaurice
Quentin Tarantino: The Complete Syllabus (2015)

Quentin Tarantino needs no introduction. He has been recycling, reusing and remixing supposedly disposable mainstream culture into critically acclaimed movies for a quarter of a century or so. Often considered the ultimate postmodern filmmaker, he is also one of the most gifted and controversial. But this is not an in-depth discussion of his work, nor a list of his best films to be argued over ad infinitum. What is interesting about Tarantino for our purposes is the way he constructs his own canon of "great" movies by sampling them, challenging and reshaping orthodoxy as he goes.

Film historian Foster Hirsch calls Tarantino's seminal *Pulp Fiction* a "terminally hip postmodern collage ... a succulent guilty pleasure, beautifully made junk food for cinéastes" (Clarens and Hirsch 1997). Strangely, this was partly meant as a put-down. But not only does Hirsch inadvertently write a great advertisement for the film, he also makes a fundamental mistake: neither Tarantino nor the influences he remixed in *Pulp Fiction* could have been described as "hip" at the time of the film's production.

Instead of referencing obscure arthouse or canonical movies such as *Citizen Kane* or *Battleship Potemkin*, Tarantino makes homage to the ephemeral and often failed popular culture of his childhood or teens. He kick-started the 1970s revival of the 1990s with *Reservoir Dogs*, then helped sustain it with *Pulp Fiction* and *Jackie Brown*. Although the first two are primarily tributes to hard-boiled fiction and film noir, they are liberally sprinkled with homages to late 1960s and 1970s culture—from *The Taking of Pelham 123* and *Mean Streets* to *Happy Days* and *The Brady Bunch*. And it's not just films being referenced; Tarantino's early movies were soundtracked with often forgotten songs from the same era, including *Reservoir Dog's* infamous "ear scene" accompanied by 1974 hit *Stuck in the Middle with You*. With *Jackie Brown*, Tarantino went even further, paying homage to the ultimate—and at the time, ultimately forgotten—1970s film genre blaxploitation.

Neither Tarantino nor his influences and homages were especially hip when he emerged in the early 1990s. He was seen as a hyperactive film geek—at a time when "geek" was still a pejorative term—and the 1970s regarded as "the decade that taste forgot," a terrifying land of flared trousers, trashy medallions and avocado bathroom suites. Instead, both the director and his influences became hip—and indeed important—because of each other. Tarantino is an incredibly skilled filmmaker who draws on and remixes eclectic personal influences—in the process taking advantage of our cultural amnesia—to create highly acclaimed work. He does this so well that his influences then become fashionable and valuable—hip because he uses them, not the other way around. Sometimes these influences are obscure. Sometimes they are from overlooked mainstream culture. The ten movies Tarantino chose for the British Film Institute's Director's Poll are revealing: over half appear solely on his list, including mainstream blockbuster *The Great Escape*. Tarantino, more than most directors, values mainstream movies and culture as much as the obscure. And just like his sampling, his valuing of the mainstream is not deployed with detached irony but lovingly, as genuine homage. Tarantino is a superfan of film and popular culture, not a detached observer. This fanaticism resonates with the culturally curious who watch his movies. People seek out the influences, finding new culture and helping compile the Tarantino canon. Willis (1997) described Tarantino as "turning shit into gold"—alluding to his fascination with toilet scenes—but equally, this describes perfectly his ability to create critically acclaimed and canonical work by recycling forgotten and disparaged influences.

Quentin Tarantino reinvigorated and changed film and wider popular culture by not adhering to the traditional "good taste" canon of the critical and cultural elite. His years as a video store clerk gave him a unique, bottom-up, idiosyncratic knowledge that he utilized superbly to create works both popular and critically acclaimed. Tarantino never completely abandoned the canon but he has helped reshaped it, while also creating his own alternative and personal version. And that's what an ex-record store assistant from Minneapolis did with alternative music too.

8.2

"Distinguish yourself ... just be unique and have an independent voice."

Ryan Schreiber
(quoted in Williams 2015)

Ryan Schreiber founded *Pitchfork* in 1995. Today it is the go-to place for serious—if at times rather earnest and pretentious—discussion and reviews on alternative music. A kind of *Rolling Stone* for hipsters. As a result, it divides audiences. Some love it. Some hate it. But that was always part of the plan.

Schreiber was inspired to start *Pitchfork* by the DIY ethos of fanzines and college radio. Working in a record store helped him gain an encyclopedic bottom-up knowledge of his medium while also being aware of its traditional canon, just like Tarantino. But Schreiber was irritated by the lack of criticality and insight delivered by the music press at the time, believing reviews lacked strong opinions, were too reverent and ultimately dishonest. He had a point. Due to dwindling circulation, the established music press relied heavily on advertising and access, leaving it vulnerable to pressure from record companies. The scathing reviews of Lester Bangs and Nick Kent were a thing of the past. If an artist got a bad review, that artist's label might threaten to pull adverts or access to promotional releases, or to other artists from across its roster. This imbalance of power had led to an almost comical collapse of criticality and depressing descent into irrelevance. The magazines had simultaneously become more conventional too. Schreiber knew something had to be done—and he thought the internet might be the answer.

The first iteration of *Pitchfork* launched online with the name *Turntable*. The content was sporadic and of variable quality— Schreiber had no writing experience—but it was at least critical, feeling more honest as a result. It changed its named in 1996, but few noticed. Schreiber continued working in the record store to pay the bills, plugging away with *Pitchfork* on the side, happy to be expressing himself and receiving some free promos of new music. It wasn't until 1997 when he recruited more writers to produce regular and more consistent content that *Pitchfork* started to gain traction. The next year he moved the operation from its origins in Minneapolis to Chicago and recruited even more writers. The site honed its distinctive voice and never looked back.

Today, *Pitchfork* is a barometer for alternative music. Its perceived frankness and criticality—aided by an authoritative yet tongue-in-cheek scoring system that rates everything from 10.0 down to 0.0—has gathered a loyal following. And yes, a few works have received the double zero. As *Pitchfork's* influence has grown, so has that of the culture it favors. It has helped break hundreds of esoteric artists—Sufjan Stevens, Animal Collective, Arcade Fire, Bon Iver and more—plus created its own canon of albums and songs. Every year *Pitchfork* compiles end-of-year lists that thousands immediately stream or download. It has challenged and revised existing canons for past work, compiling alternative lists of the best albums of the last four decades that repeatedly challenge the received wisdom found in more conventional publications.

Of course, anything as critical and opinionated as *Pitchfork* is bound to be criticized. Some dismiss its favored artists as "*Pitchfork* darlings," or its alternative canons as "hipster lists." But that's the point. By challenging mainstream and alternative music orthodoxies, sharing its influences, championing new talents and creating distinct canons, *Pitchfork* has become trusted, influential and wildly successful. It has progressed and changed the shape of alternative music, rebuilding it in its own image. In late 2015, the site was acquired by Condé Nast—publisher of *Vogue*, *The New Yorker*, *Wired*, *GQ*, etc.—for an undisclosed sum. Impressive for a site founded to air the opinions of a frustrated record store clerk.

Northern Soul: A Warning from History

> *"Open up your eyes and see it baby, Give yourself a better chance, Because time will pass you, Right on by ..."*

Tobi Legend
Time Will Pass You By (1968)

As you've no doubt realized by now, this is a celebration of discovering, curating and remixing your own influences. We believe drawing on and channeling things you genuinely love or value—rather than those you're told to value—results in creating more meaningful and expressive experiences. That doesn't mean traditional canons are valueless—throwing the baby out with the bathwater is never a smart move—just that these are no longer the only lists in town. If postmodernism has given us anything, it's permission to discover our own influences, sample and curate these in an informed way, accruing our own unique cultural capital to spend creatively. But sometimes it can lead us up a blind alley.

The roots of Northern Soul lie in the "rare soul" clubs of the English Midlands and North West in the 1960s. These were initially influenced by London clubs playing imported soul music on labels such a Tamla Motown, Stax and Atlantic. But by the early 1970s, this sound had lost popularity in London, replaced by the new heavier funk of James Brown or Parliament/Funkadelic. But in the North, crowds still preferred the driving beats of earlier soul to fuel their all-nighters at clubs like Wigan Casino or Manchester's Twisted Wheel. As a result, this music—and the subculture around it—became known as "Northern Soul." For a time it was incredibly vibrant, with thousands crowding dancehalls across the Midlands and the North to dance the night away. The problem was that the music fueling these nights was already out of date. By the mid-1970s, most songs were over a decade old and there were no more in production. Some records became Northern classics and these formed a canon of sorts. But DJs couldn't play these songs repeatedly all night, week in, week out—unless they wanted to bore everyone to death. So the search started for rarer and more obscure 45s to keep things alive. At first, these were songs that had not become hits on known labels such as Motown, or less successful efforts by known artists, but as these were discovered, played and eventually overplayed, the search moved to ever more obscure songs and artists. Most of these obscurities had not been released in the UK and finding them involved an army of record dealers and the odd DJ crate-digging their way across the United States. And as anyone with an intimate knowledge of crate-digging knows, there's always more chaff than wheat.

Northern Soul eventually became a creative cul-de-sac. Sure, the diggers found a few gems, but increasingly the scene became predicated on the scarcity of a record rather than its quality and appeal. This suited the record dealers but not the DJs, now asked to pay £40 or £50 pounds for a copy of The Triumph's *Walkin' the Duck*—a generic and mediocre sub-Motown instrumental—at a time when the average weekly wage was around £30. Nor in the long run did it suit much of the crowd, who were increasingly drifting away to other scenes that embraced new and evolving music rather than listening to poor imitations of the original Northern sound. By the early 1980s, the remaining Northern clubs demanded a strict diet of "clip-clop popular oldies," blacklisting DJs who tried to play new releases. This hardcore scene found itself isolated and in terminal decline as a result of its puritanical adherence to obscure and inane "stomping" records. Northern Soul was increasingly dancing on the spot. Even its famous motto, "Keep the Faith," began to feel more like a desperate plea than a rousing call to arms.

Northern Soul was an archival culture, where records expedite a cultural revival and allow "dancing to music recorded and forgotten in another world and another time" (Thornton 1995, p.69). These cultures are vibrant and fun for a time—even useful in preserving the obscure or forgotten—but ultimately cannot move forward if they don't create anything new. Many don't and some actively demonize it. Also, these cultures are usually monocultural, focusing on one cultural form and drawing exclusively from it. They are concerned with purity, not sustainability. As a result they have a limited shelf life. Northern Soul today is kept on life support by a small hardcore fan base, fueled by nostalgia and happy to stomp to a continual loop of mediocre old records. This stands in stark contrast to the dance music derived from the electro, techno or house movements of the 1980s. This has continually morphed and developed from its obscure subcultural roots to global domination. Meanwhile, Northern Soul has remained rigid and stuck in time. Time has passed it right on by.

Games without Frontiers

So how is this connected to making games? Sadly, game makers and game culture can also be dangerously monocultural. One reason is that game design orthodoxy has traditionally foregrounded gameplay mechanics over artistic or creative content. You choose your "core mechanic" first, then you mold everything else around and in service to it. That's how we ended up with hundreds of identikit first-person shooters (FPS) with interchangeable narratives tacked on. Like Northern Soul, these might be vibrant and entertaining for a time, but generic FPSs are the gaming equivalent to the "stompers" that made Northern Soul irrelevant. Of course, some designers try to be more creative with mechanics, hybridizing one game's mechanic with that of another. But these again draw solely on one source: games. And so do most of their concepts and content. Too much of this and games will eat themselves.

Ultimately, game makers need to challenge orthodoxy and cast a wider cultural net. We need to question whether the mechanic should always take precedence in the conceptual process. Surely there are alternatives, more inspiring starting points than simply what a player does? For example, what a player might *feel*. And we need to work harder at exploring new, unknown, alternative or forgotten culture, mining and sampling influences taken from beyond games to remix into something more vital and sustainable. With the internet, we don't even have to work that hard to do it. Gathering influences is simple but it is only valuable if you do something creative with it. The point is not to compile new lists; it is to create new and provocative content to be curated into future lists. Of course, some game makers are already doing this. But nowhere near enough. We need to explore other cultures, domains, art forms. We should pay homage to the past to influence and shape the future. But don't just regurgitate: recycle, reuse, remix. Push things forward. Otherwise, time might pass us by too.

Postmodern Playlist

Steinski—*Lesson 3* (1985)

M/A/R/R/S—*Pump Up the Volume* (1987)

Eric B and Rakim—*I Know You Got Soul (Double Trouble's Six Minutes of Soul Mix)* (1988)

Malcolm McLaren—*Madam Butterfly* (1984)

Sufjan Stevens—*Illinois* (2005)

Quentin Tarantino—*Pulp Fiction* (1994)

DMA Design/Rockstar — *Grand Theft Auto Series* (1997 - present)

Devolver Digital—*Hotline Miami* (2012)

Tobi Legend—*Time Will Pass You By* (1968)

FIGURE 1.8 The sampler that helped start it all: the E-mu SP-1200. (Courtesy of 2xUeL, https://commons.wikimedia.org/wiki/ File%3AE-mu_SP-1200_front_of_machine.jpg)

thatgamecompany: A Case Study in Aesthetics

In *The Substance of Style: How the Rise of Aesthetic Value Is Remaking Commerce, Culture and Consciousness*, Virginia Postrel (2003) argues that we live in an age of aesthetics where everyday decisions are informed by our sensory experiences, rather than clinical, rational information or functionality. In Postrel's view, aesthetics extend well beyond mere decoration to permeate the look, feel and emotion of all types of people, places and things.

thatgamecompany embodies Postrel's concept of aesthetic value. It is a studio deliberately designed to create compelling emotional experiences and challenge the perception of what games can be. Players expect—and receive—a greater depth from thatgamecompany: more emotion, more catharsis, more multisensory stimulus and a greater diversity of place, performance and feeling. A perfect harmony of substance, style and emotion.

Cloud

Kellee Santiago and Jenova Chen met as master's students at the University of Southern California (USC) where they were both enrolled in the Interactive Media Program at the School of Cinematic Arts. Neither Santiago—with a background in experimental New York theater—or Chen—a computer science student from Shanghai—were prototypical game makers. But both recognized the potential of video games as a means of communication and expression (Chaplin 2009).

An avid gamer as a child, Chen (2015) felt games had failed to grow up alongside him, lacking the emotional maturity to engage him as an adult:

> Film is very established; you have a genre for every single thing you want to feel. No matter your age, genre, nationality and mood there's something for you. But for games... You have a thriller, horror, action film, and sports victory film. But there is no romance, no drama, no documentary, and no thoughtful examination on life. These are basic feelings humans want to have in life, but they are just not available in games. That's why lots of people stop playing games as they grow older; they want to feel these things but games don't offer it.

Inspired by their studies at USC—particularly the classes of game designer Tracy Fullerton and her playcentric design methodology—both Santiago and Chen began to speculate on what games could be and their potential as an immersive and emotional means of expression. Over the next three years, the pair would collaborate on projects, exploring their notion of games as meaningful emotional experiences and eventually arriving at two provocative questions: could they make a game that expressed something different to gaming monoculture? If they could, would people be interested in playing such a game?

The answer to both questions was "yes." *Cloud*—funded by a $20,000 grant from USC—attracted over 400,000 downloads in four months (McCartney 2012). What set the game apart was the way it deliberately attempted to capture a feeling: what it was like to "be a kid, staring at the clouds and daydreaming" (Santiago 2010a). Rather than dictate an idea or present a game mechanic, the makers posed and probed a question: what if a game could trigger an immersive, emotional experience within a player?

> *"I actually, literally cried at the sheer beauty of it. I just wanted to let you know that your work engendered such motion. Cloud is just utterly impressive."*
>
> **Email from a *Cloud* fan**
> *Fullerton et al.* (2006)

Flow in Game

Fundamental to the success of *Cloud* and its emotional resonance was capturing flow: the sweet spot between ability and challenge for a player. Flow was the subject of Chen's MFA thesis, *Flow in Game* (2006), an exploration of how Mihaly Csikszentmihalyi (1990) flow theory could be used to deliver optimal, contextual experiences for different players within the same game.

Csikszentmihalyi defined "flow" as the feeling of complete and energized focus in an activity, with a high level of enjoyment and fulfillment (Chen 2006). During a flow experience, "we lose track of time and worries" as attention focuses on the performance of an activity and the pleasure derived from it (Chen 2007). This optimal experience is commonly referred to in a gaming context as being "in the zone."

Motivated by the observation that despite evolving into a "mature medium," video games were still perceived as shallow, aggressive and immature by the non-game-playing majority, Chen (2006) argued that the most effective way to challenge this perception was to create games nongamers could play and enjoy. He posited that descriptions of flow were "identical to what players experience when immersed in games" but he was also aware that "different players have different skills and expect different challenges" (Chen 2007). To confront perceptions and broaden their audience, games needed to transport different types of players to "personal flow zones" (Chen 2007). For a game to appeal to a broader audience—with these variable desires and abilities—Chen believed an experience could not be the same for all players (2007). This type design challenge is typically resolved through the introduction of binary choices such as "novice" or "hardcore" difficulty settings, or their in-game equivalent, passive dynamic difficulty adjustment. Chen disagreed with this approach, believing that too much noncontextual choice overwhelmed and distracted players, undermining the fundamental component of flow: "a sense of control and concentration of the task at hand" (2007). It was Chen's view that the best way to create games that challenged and entertained a broad, diverse audience was to offer implicit and adaptive choices embedded within the game's core activities. This method allowed for different users to enjoy the experience without their flow being interrupted or undermined. To illustrate and test this game design assumption, Chen created *fl0w*, a minimal browser game about exploring and evolving within a surreal biosphere as a simple organism. *fl0w* enabled players to intuitively curate their optimal experience. Personal gameplay choices and performance dynamically adjusted the difficulty level and pacing of the game, allowing gamers—and nongamers—of all abilities to enjoy the experience in their own way, at their own pace. Hailed as "beautiful, relaxing and confusing" (Parsons 2006), *fl0w* drew more than 5 million unique visitors in its first year of release and was named Internet Game of the Month by *Edge* (Chen 2006; Kong 2017).

fl0w the Game

As a breakthrough in emotional game design and validation that players desired resonant emotional experiences, the success of *Cloud* inspired Santiago and Chen to formalize their collaboration. But neither was "out to make a games company"; thatgamecompany would be a means to make their kinds of games—immersive, emotional experiences that challenged perceptions of what games are and who they might be for—on their own terms (Santiago 2010a). Idealist but definitely not a niche arts project, thatgamecompany was on a mission to "make commercially successful games ... as a communicative medium" (Santiago 2010b). There was no desire to operate at the fringes; Santiago and Chen wanted to infiltrate the mainstream industry, delight the broadest possible audience and inspire other game makers to abandon the gamer monoculture and push the medium forward.

For such a fantasy to become a reality, thatgamecompany required a very particular kind of partner: a publisher or investor who not only bought into its creative vision but could also help cultivate an environment where thatgamecompany could flourish. *Cloud* demonstrated potential to prospective partners but any deal came with significant risk. thatgamecompany required a partner prepared to invest time, energy and money while devolving complete creative control to a young team fresh out of university and full of idealist game design notions. Described by Santiago (2010b) as "part publisher and part mentor," Sony Santa Monica signed thatgamecompany on a three-game deal in spring 2006 to produce games exclusively for PlayStation Network (PSN). The deal benefitted both parties: it gave Sony exclusive "indie" games to differentiate the upcoming PSN service from the rival Xbox Live Arcade service and it gave thatgamecompany the reach and exposure to establish a brand in the mainstream (Santiago 2010b).

Sony Santa Monica incubated thatgamecompany within its Los Angeles studio, helping the young company learn about the "shipping process of making games and working with the publisher" while affording the critical distance to "discover a creative focus process" for itself (Santiago 2010b). The initial plan was to remake *Cloud* for its PSN debut but conscious of the risk of starting a project, a company and a publishing relationship simultaneously, Santiago (2010b) took the pragmatic decision to shift production focus to remaking *flOw*, as it was a more fleshed-out design and easier project to realize within constraints. Even so, remaking *flOw* represented a steep learning curve for the rookie team, who initially planned to make the game twice as large in a development schedule half as long. But with Sony Santa Monica's support—equipment, contractors and experienced production oversight—thatgamecompany released *flOw* on PSN in February 2007.

The most downloaded game on PSN in 2007, *flOw* received a host of award nominations including Best Innovation at the 2007 BAFTAs and Best Downloadable Game of the Year from the Academy of Interactive Arts & Sciences DICE Awards (Wikipedia 2016a). It also exhibited at the Smithsonian American Art Museum and the Museum of Modern Art, the latter describing it as a "wondrous experience of inhabiting a different kind of being, one endowed with surprising motility, behavior and mind" (2014). Most importantly for Santiago, *fl0w* "validated our process, our mission, all of the blood, sweat and tears we put into it" (2010b).

Flower

The success of *fl0w* demonstrated games could be more than macho thrills and instant gratification. Chen (2009) had no quarrel with video game machismo but believed it limited the potential of the medium by lacking a "complexity of feeling" or the daring to "evoke the other types of feelings." And complexity of feeling was what thatgamecompany decided to pursue next, using the next two years to create *Flower*: an "interactive poem" exploring the tension between urban bustle and natural serenity (Boyer 2009; Govan 2009).

Flower started out as a series of feelings thatgamecompany wanted to articulate in interactive form. From this starting point, the team embarked upon a protracted 14-month period of exploring how such feelings might be expressed and captured in a compelling emotional experience (Kong 2017). Throughout prototyping—and the 10-month production period that followed it—the game's design focused on keeping the player in a peaceful emotional state (Kong 2017). This meant continuously stripping away rogue elements of frustration or excitement that threatened to turn *Flower* into just another game. *Flower* was an "escape from stress and loneliness" according to Santiago, an "emotional shelter" that projected positivity onto its players (quoted by Carless 2009).

> "Three quarters of the development time involved was just prototyping—just getting the feeling right and the last fraction involved producing the actual game."
>
> **Santiago and Hunicke (2010)**

Released on PSN in February 2009, *Flower* delighted and conflicted critics. IGN's Ryan Clements (2009) hailed it as one of the "most beautiful games I've ever played." Eurogamer's Tom Bramwell (2009) also praised *Flower*'s beauty but criticized the $9.99 price tag placed on a "brief, film-length" experience. Perhaps Alice Liang (2009) best captured *Flower*'s intentions, rejecting the opportunity to offer any "analytical take on thatgamecompany's auteurist endeavor" and, instead, simply reveling in the joy of a beautiful, tactile, immersive experience.

With *Flower*, thatgamecompany again demonstrated a mainstream game did not have to be thematically conservative or emotionally repressed to connect with an audience. It was one of the most downloaded games on PSN in 2009 but possibly the only one that regularly, according to Jenova Chen (2009), moved players to tears:

> We have already had a few fans mail us about *Flower* to tell us they had tears in their eyes, or they cried after they played the first level because it reminds them of their dead mother, or it reminds them of the town they used to live in forty years ago. So why are we even asking if [games] can make people cry? Games have already accomplished that.

Santiago (2009) compared the making of *Flower* to "walking in the mist," a purposeful but "hard and painful" journey punctuated by blind trial and error. *Flower*'s development stretched thatgamecompany's creative capabilities and provoked it into evolving its creative process to realize ambitions. But could the process keep pace with Chen wanted to do next?

Journey

Inspired by a conversation with a former astronaut about how one's spiritual self is forever changed after seeing Earth from space, Chen identified the next positive emotion he would seek to capture and communicate inside an interactive experience: awe. After coming face to face with the sublimity of infinity, astronauts returned to Earth poignantly aware of their relative insignificance within the universe. Chen (2015) asserted that a typical game does the opposite; instead, it places the player at the "center of power." Chen believed that to feel genuine awe within a game, you had to feel small and be stripped of empowerment.

In an interview with Simon Parkin, Chen (2015) mapped what he believed to be the only three ways to create valuable games for adults:

1. Intellectual experiences, such as *Portal*, allowed players to see the world from a fresh perspective.
2. Emotional experiences, such as *Flower*, provoked genuine emotion, reflection and catharsis within a player.
3. Social environments where "intellectual or emotional stimulation could happen from other people."

Journey would explore the third way of mature game making: constructing an online multiplayer emotional exchange within an interactive space, cultivating social emotion and shared feelings among players. Chen (2015) wanted to create genuine connections between people, challenging the assumption that online multiplayer experiences meant sharing spaces and emotions with random "assholes":

> There's an assumption in video games that if you run into a random player over the Internet, it's going to be a bad experience. You think that they will be an asshole, right? But listen: none of us was born to be an asshole. It's the game designer that made them an asshole. If you spend every day killing one another how are you going to be a nice guy? All console games are about killing each other or killing one another together ... Our games make us assholes.

Chen believed the vast majority of multiplayer experiences were about task solving and when a player was in task-solving mode they could not possibly be in the right frame of mind to exchange emotion. To create the context for meaningful emotional and social connections between random players, *Journey* had to strip the player of empowerment: no names, no chatting, no quests, no words, no meta progression, no extrinsic rewards and, above all, no competitive play.

Ironically, exchanges in initial prototypes were characterized by players going out of their way to kill each other. In spite of the fact that everyone involved in making the game knew its intention was to communicate "positive things about humanity," their natural impulse was to seek out and perform actions that provided the strongest visceral feedback (Chen 2015). Inspired by discussions with a child psychologist friend, Chen took the radical step of stripping out gaming prerequisites—such as collision detection—that introduced the opportunity to engineer spectacular moments of gratifying negativity. Without personalized usernames, chat or the ability to harm each other, all that remained were moments of innocent, serendipitous, silent collaboration. Chen (2012a) likened this process of subtraction to a Japanese Zen Garden, "where the design is perfect when you cannot remove anything else." Stripped of clutter and convention, *Journey* possessed a raw, emotional resonance that surpassed even *Flower*.

Hours after release, players streamed unprompted onto thatgamecompany's forums and started discussing the anonymous players they had encountered on their personal journey:

> *"To my companion who appeared when things were darkest, who encouraged me on with song when thing's [sic] got tough and danger loomed overhead, who ran to my aid when I was down*

and who meditated with me near the end; thank you for an inde-scribably beautiful experience. It will stay with me for the rest of my days."

Monk (2012)

"Am I the only person who gets so full of grief when they lose a companion, they can't bear to complete that Journey and instead start a new one?

While Journeying, I generally (always) stick with the same companion from the bridge until we walk into the light together. I've never had to leave early, but occasionally will lose a companion about halfway through. I get really sad and turn off my console when that happens."

B_Squared (2012)

"I do sometimes get sad when people leave, especially when they leave mid-level. But I understand that people sometimes have other things to do. I also guess I have lost so many real people in my life that—as a metaphor—I know you have to just keep going."

Jo Pierce (2012)

The emotion, reflection and catharsis of *Journey's* meaningful shared experience was never more pronounced than in a letter Chen received from a 15-year-old girl named Sophia (quoted by Takahashi 2013), who shared a *Journey* with her father before he died from an illness:

"I want to thank you for the game that changed my life, the game whose beauty brings tears to my eyes. Journey is quite possibly the best game I have ever played. I continue to play it, always remembering what joy it brought and the joy it continues to bring."

—I am Sophia, I am 15 and your game changed my life for the better

The letter was one of many received from people who had lost family members and for whom *Journey* had provided a lasting and cherished memory. Fittingly, thatgamecompany (2017a) describe *Journey* as an "interactive parable" where:

> You wake alone and surrounded by miles of burning, sprawling desert and soon discover the looming mountaintop which is your goal.
>
> Faced with rolling sand dunes, age-old ruins, caves and howling winds, your passage will not be an easy one. The goal is to get to the mountaintop, but the experience is discovering who you're, what this place is and what is your purpose.

These are words that not only capture the "Hero's Journey" of the game but also serve as an allegory for the game's development, a challenging and protracted "trial of perseverance," according to Chen (2012b). *Journey* may have become the fastest selling game ever on PSN when released in March 2012 but it bankrupted thatgamecompany in the process (Chen 2013; Wikipedia 2016b). The making of *Journey* began in January 2009 but, constrained by a strict Sony development budget, it had only a one-year development schedule. Chen, a self-confessed perfectionist, was faced with a stark choice: ship on time and deliver an average experience, or stay true to the vision and hold off shipping until the game had "achieved its intended emotional impact" (Chen quoted by Parker 2013). Chen chose the latter and *Journey* ended up taking three years to design and develop. The team had to survive on half pay for the final six months and the studio temporarily shut down between project completion and release (Chen 2013). Producer Robin Hunicke described the experience as an "emotionally destructive development cycle" bound by two competing tensions: "passionately believing that something is possible and deeply fearing there's not enough time, not enough money and not enough faith to make it happen" (quoted by Dyer 2012).

> *"The fact of the matter is we signed an unrealistic schedule believing, in our heart of hearts, it would probably be extended later and we paid for that stress in the entire project. We were poor at extracting realistic individual estimations and people failed to confront the true costs of 'just in time' changes to the game."*
>
> **Robin Hunicke**
> *(quoted by Khaw 2012)*

The experimental creative process pioneered by Chen and Santiago was pushed to its very limits by *Journey*. Its production perfectly encapsulates —and amplifies —the natural contradiction that exists between probing new aesthetic frontiers and being beholden to the rational requirements of a major label benefactor.

Dandelions

Journey marked the conclusion of thatgamecompany's three-game deal with Sony and the end of an era for the studio. Shortly after release, Kellee Santiago left the company on amicable terms to seek fresh challenges, as did Hunicke and half the team (Alexander 2012). With Santiago's departure, Chen remained as sole leader, visionary and public face of the studio. Backed by a $5.5 million investment from Benchmark Capital in 2012, Chen (2015) left behind the relative security of being "under the wing of the giant mother Sony" to fully embrace entrepreneurship and independence. In early 2017, five years after the release of *Journey*, thatgamecompany teased their next title: a "game about giving" that seeks to "positively touch more players than ever before" (thatgamecompany 2017b). Chen (2015) is under no illusion as to how critical its success will be for investor confidence and the ongoing viability of thatgamecompany: "It does [being independent of Sony's distribution, marketing and editorial muscle] bring a lot of risks and extra pressure that the game has to be good. Otherwise, we're done. The company's gone." But Chen believes that by continuing to curate emotionally resonant experiences with enduring aesthetic value, the risk will be rewarded: "Our advantage is that we want to create positive things for people, unlike most people that make games. By sticking to that, we will have commercial success" (Chen 2015).

Punk Provocations

- What if you designed an experience around making the player feel an emotion?
- What if you observed nature then articulated it as an interactive experience?
- What if you defined the aesthetic value—the substance, style and emotion—of your game before you started making it?

FIGURE 1.9 A screenshot from *Cloud*. (Reprinted with permission from thatgamecompany, ©thatgamecompany 2005. All rights reserved.)

FIGURE 1.10 thatgamecompany tease their forthcoming game in early 2017. (Reprinted with permission from thatgamecompany, ©thatgamecompany 2017. All rights reserved.)

Chapter 2

Ideals Over Ideas

Abstract

Meaningful ideals and creative innovation have been replaced by cheap ideas and mediocre invention. Making is important—but only within the wider context of a clear purpose and magical vision. Understanding what you're trying to do and why it matters is not something to be explored as an afterthought. It is the essence of any designed experience.

This chapter probes the approximation of authenticity through provocative manifestos and playful cultural appropriation, arguing that critical thinking, polycultural synthesis and serendipity make a greater contribution to meaningful and resonant playful experiences than slavish authenticity, virtuous craft, or technical mastery.

What Side Are You On?

"I'm talking about drawing a line in the sand, Dude!"

Walter Sobchak
The Big Lebowski (1997)

A "just make it" mantra is prevalent in game making. Never mind context or vision the orthodoxy goes—just make something and everything will be fine. But this is the equivalent of building a bridge without measuring the gap. You end up with something nobody wants. Sure, making is essential but stop just making *stuff*. Before you start, ask questions like: What are we making? Why are we making it? Who are we making it for? And what does it all mean? Otherwise, you're only making noise.

Why We Create

"But he don't know what it means,
Don't know what it means,
And I say, yeah!"

Nirvana
In Bloom (1991)

Creative people act to express what they think or feel—even to find out what they think or feel. They create to explore and understand the human condition, their personal condition, to react against what exists, to express their anger, frustration, puzzlement, despair, or joy. Whatever the impulse, creativity is always part of an ongoing search for meaning. And that is something we are all engaged in. It is what makes us human. We seek meaning in the senseless, to find "the sermon in the suicide ... the moral lesson in the murder of five" (Didion 1979, p.11). Or we search for meaning in something new, something wonderful, something transformative. And it is here that great art delivers. Art alters our perceptions; it connects with us, it provides new meanings while challenging the old. As Simon Schama says, "Great art has dreadful manners ... the greatest paintings grab you in a headlock, rough up your composure and then proceed in short order to rearrange your sense of reality" (2006, p.6). But that is what we want. Or at least, it is what we should want. To be shaken out of the quotidian by the protean. To shatter the dumb complacency of the mediocre. To have the banality of routine disrupted by delight—if only for a few minutes. It is this meaning that reminds us we're alive. We constantly search for it. Some of us even search for the same things. That's why meaning is key to creating experiences people truly want. Humans cluster around meanings, ideals and narratives, not single snowflake ideas.

Really Saying Something

"I don't know what I think until I write it down."

Joan Didion
The White Album (1979)

Consider what has meaning to you. What makes you emotional, inquisitive, or angry? If you reflect, then articulate a creative and provocative response; it can resonate across cultures. Learn to probe prod and make a dent in the world. Like Marshall McLuhan. In the 1960s, this Canadian media theorist articulated prescient provocations about the coming of the "electronic information revolution." He identified the transformative effects it would have on culture and society, three decades before computers and the internet went mainstream. At a time when the orthodoxy dealt in the masses and delineated specialisms, McLuhan argued that new electronic media would soon return us to tribalism. That increasingly we would reside in a connected "global village" where specialism was irrelevant. Sound familiar?

Not surprisingly, McLuhan's thinking upset people. It disturbed their complacent refusal to imagine a future radically different from their present. But some—especially in academia—were more disturbed by the way he articulated his thinking. McLuhan eschewed long-winded logical argument and definitive answers in favor of rapid-fire aphorisms and punchy provocations. For example: "We look at the present through a rearview mirror. We march backward into the future" (McLuhan and Fiore 1967, p.74). McLuhan called these *probes*. He viewed himself as an explorer, a pioneer penetrating new media landscapes to kickstart debate and enhance understanding (McLuhan and Zingrone 1997). Many of his probes—most famously "the medium is the message"—passed into everyday usage. McLuhan became an intellectual and cultural icon. He was interviewed in *Playboy* magazine and featured in the Woody Allen masterpiece *Annie Hall*, where he performed a cameo settling an argument about his theories. Later, he would be cleverly referenced in an episode of *The Sopranos* and become "patron saint" of the influential technology magazine *Wired*. Today, he is viewed as perhaps the most influential—if controversial—media theorist of the 20th century. No wonder the other academics didn't like him.

McLuhan was a provocative thinker. But he knew thinking has to be articulated to have real value or impact. It's no use saying the same old thing, in the same old way, to the same old people. To draw a line in the sand and stand out from the crowd, you must expose and communicate your ideas and ideals. Challenging the status quo requires crafted articulation of provocative content. McLuhan was a master at this. He knew that turning complex ideas into resonant probes connected with real people. He understood that to resonate, you must articulate.

Manifest Destiny

The manifesto has long been the articulation of choice for radicals of all kinds. It was first democratized by English dissenters in the 17th century and soon became almost obligatory among revolutionary groups. Famous early examples include the US Declaration of Independence (1776) and the *Communist Manifesto* (1848). But at the beginning of the 20th century, the manifesto became the property of artists and creators. From the Futurists onward, every art and design movement worth its salt had a manifesto declaring what was wrong with the world and what it was going to do about it. These manifestos were provocations, articulated statements of intent. They probed and prodded the status quo with radical ideals and values, laying out ground rules for creative action and sounding a clarion call to the likeminded.

Manifestos usually have an "enemy," but the best ones are more than a hectoring list of dislikes. Karl Marx understood that the manifesto is a performance, crafted to resonate with its intended audience, provoking them to think and ask questions while also codifying and communicating a new set of ideals, beliefs and values. The best manifestos are utopian, not only identifying defects and flaws but proposing resolutions and ideals. The great manifesto is a vision of a better world as seen through the eyes of its creators. It highlights what is no longer good enough while suggesting a better way. It provokes, cajoles, encourages and changes. It becomes a guiding light.

Kick in the Eye

The Bauhaus was the most influential art school of the 20th century. It sought to reinvent art and design education by unifying art, craft and technology. The Bauhaus challenged the hierarchical orthodoxy that discriminated against "applied art" in favor of "fine art," that is, favoring the artist over the artisan. It embraced the machine age and the role of machines in making. The Bauhaus became the cradle of modernism that helped shape the visual culture of the century. And it started with a manifesto:

"Architects, sculptors, painters, we all must return to the crafts! For art is not a "profession." There is no essential difference between the artist and the craftsman. The artist is an exalted craftsman ... proficiency in a craft is essential to every artist. Therein lies the prime source of creative imagination. Let us then create a new guild of craftsmen without the class distinctions that raise an arrogant barrier between craftsman and artist!"

Walter Gropius
excerpt from The Bauhaus Manifesto (1919)

Walter Gropius was the founder of the Bauhaus. He believed his provocative yet utopian vision could be achieved by teaching "indispensable proficiencies" to students and embracing the machine. These proficiencies would include perception, form, materials, color theory and many others, enabling students to break down artificial barriers and collaborate on a "total work of art." The Bauhaus removed other obstacles, too. Women were encouraged to enroll. There were no teachers or pupils, only masters, journeymen and apprentices working toward the common purpose articulated in the manifesto. The school quickly became a cadre of the likeminded, where friendly relations were encouraged between members. There were plays, concerts, lectures and legendary parties that enabled free expression, constructed a creative community and further reinforced the sense of shared purpose. But like many radical provocations, this cadre often confused those on the outside:

"When we dared to go out on the streets—especially the girl weavers who wore trousers—there was always an uproar. 'Impossible!' people would say. When we came along with ponytails mothers warned daughters, 'Don't look! They're from the Bauhaus!'

We were seen as the punks of Dessau!"

Professor Kurt Kranz
Bauhaus Student (Bauhaus 1994)

The Bauhaus did not fully resolve its vision, partly as a result of its dissolution by the Nazis—it was far too radical for their mediocre minds—partly because complete resolution was always unachievable. But it is precisely because the manifesto set its sights and expectations so high that it became a rallying point for a community. The Bauhaus manifesto was an articulation that issued a visionary, radical and provocative challenge to the status quo. It gave creative mavericks something to cluster around and at times challenge. As a result the diaspora of "Bauhaus punks" who emigrated to England, the US, Israel and beyond after Hitler came to power would transform the visual and material culture of the 20th century, assuring the school a place in design history. A few decades later, a new generation of punks would cluster around a new manifesto to change culture again.

Itchy Knickers

"There are two rules I've always tried to live by: turn left if you're supposed to turn right; go through any door that you're not supposed to enter. It's the only way to fight your way through to any kind of authentic feeling in a world beset by fakery."

Malcolm McLaren
This Much I Know (2008)

Malcolm McLaren was an itinerant art student, rag trader, wannabe Svengali and consummate maverick. After years of government funded "study" at London's top art schools, he decided British music and culture of the early 1970s was terminally dull and arrogantly complacent. He wanted to shake things up. He wanted to make a mark. And so he became manager—or creator, depending who you talk to—of The Sex Pistols.

McLaren went outside music industry orthodoxy to make his band famous. And better than making The Sex Pistols famous, McLaren made them infamous. He and the band became "an itch in someone's knickers" (Wallington-Lloyd cited in Savage 1991, p.38). McLaren was inspired by anything he could approximate or appropriate, notably the playfully subversive ideas of the Situationists. In *Society of the Spectacle*, Guy Debord provocatively argued that society had become simply an accumulation of spectacles engineered by the mass media and capitalism, where everything once directly lived had retreated into representation (1967, p.7). This resonated with McLaren, who particularly liked the Situationist concept of *detournement*—where the spectacle was creatively hijacked and exposed through subversive pranks. Debord argued for this sub-version because "in a world that is really upside down, the true is a moment of the false" (1967, p.9).

McLaren engineered a series of stunts and pranks to gain a following for The Sex Pistols. He constantly irritated the mainstream to expose its complacency and hypocrisy. With then-girlfriend Vivienne Westwood, he created clothes adorned with provocative images and Situationist statements for the band to wear. He concocted fights and assaults at their gigs and encouraged foul-mouthed appearances on family television shows. He staged an infamous performance where the Pistols played *God Save the Queen*—a song that described the British monarchy as a fascist regime—on a boat called *Queen Elizabeth* sailing past the Palace of Westminster at the height of the Silver Jubilee celebrations. As you might imagine, this did not go down at all well with the British Establishment. Police launches were dispatched and the boat forced to dock. As the police approached, McLaren raised a fist and shouted: "You fucking fascist bastards." He and others were promptly arrested and taken to jail. But this was exactly the outcome McLaren wanted. He had filled the boat with journalists who would lovingly describe every moment in the music press and beyond. McLaren deliberately courted controversy instead of confirmation. You either loved or loathed The Sex Pistols. And that was fine with him.

The Sex Pistols became the seminal band of punk rock, if not the first or even the best. And with McLaren steering, their antics attracted a gang of outcasts and mavericks from every part of British society. These early punks creatively rejected the status quo with music, fashion, art and anything else at their disposal. This resonated with more young people across the nation and beyond, detonating a punk movement that continues to influence culture to this day. But although 1977 was perhaps the apogee of punk—it really began a few years earlier.

You're Gonna Wake Up One Morning

"I have been called many things: a charlatan, a con man, or, most flatteringly, the culprit responsible for turning British popular culture into nothing more than a cheap marketing gimmick. This is my chance to prove that these accusations are true."

Malcolm McLaren
interviewed in Classic Rock Magazine (2010)

The derogatory epithet "punk" had been around for years in the US. And there had been bands—MC5, The Stooges, The Modern Lovers, etc.—who created the sonic prototypes for punk from the late 1960s onward. But the catalyst for the punk rock explosion of 1976 and 1977 came two years earlier when Malcolm McLaren collaborated with Bernie Rhodes—later manager of The Clash—and Vivienne Westwood on a t-shirt–based manifesto. Called *You're Gonna Wake Up One Morning*, the manifesto was inclusive and exclusive at the same time, resonating with some, repulsing others, provoking all.

The manifesto was divided across the front of the t-shirt. On one side was a list of things McLaren and Rhodes hated about 1970s society and culture; on the other, the things they wanted to celebrate. It was a tongue-in-cheek reaction to the dull conformity and complacency of the time that sought to articulate another way. A utopian vision of a world where "imagination," Simone de Beauvoir, Joe Orton and John Coltrane would banish Leo Sayer, the National Front, grey skies and "all those fucking saints." Forever. No wonder it struck a chord.

Fittingly, "imagination" is the final thing celebrated on the shirt. And by imagining another reality, a road less traveled, McLaren was gambling his wearable articulation would provoke a strong enough reaction to attract more cultural mavericks and outcasts. If it could, it might just help him form a movement, gain momentum and change the culture around him. It did. The playful, sarcastic, disruptive t-shirt served as a rallying point for the avant-garde of punk. And it brought the act of manifestoing—which had become the preserve of politicians, artists and designers—into the realm of commercial popular culture. Today, both the punk spirit and the manifesto are alive, well and living in an eco-brewery just outside Aberdeen, Scotland.

Postmodern Punks

BrewDog is a self-defined "punk brewery." Founded by two friends bored with industrially brewed lagers and stuffy real ales, it shakes things up through provocations and controversies, sometimes articulated in the form of a product, sometimes as a stunt. BrewDog created a new movement of "beer punks," became the world's first crowdfunded brewery, achieved an annual turnover of £30 million in 2014 and by 2015 boasted the UK's bestselling craft beer, *Punk IPA* (BrewDog 2015a). Not bad for a company under a decade old, founded by two guys and a dog with virtually no capital, that had to scale up during the worst recession in 80 years.

What helped BrewDog was its manifesto for change. It classically identified an enemy to hate and a utopian vision of a time when that enemy is banished, a time when there would be:

"There will be nothing industrial or genneric in sight, nothing monolithic, nothing mass-produced."

BrewDog (2010a)

And BrewDog was clear what it wanted to achieve:

"To make other people as passionate about great craft beer as we are."

BrewDog (2010b)

BrewDog wears its punk influences on its sleeve, embracing playful subversion and engineering media storms to get its point across. It is the spiritual heir to both McLuhan and McLaren—with a healthy dose of Debord thrown in. BrewDog is an idea factory channeling an anti-establishment, anti-mediocrity ethos into one probing provocation or surreal stunt after another. Its first London bar opened to the sound of a BrewDog tank rumbling down the local high street. It brewed a series of super-strong beers—including the best-named beer ever: *Tactical Nuclear Penguin*—that enraged UK industry watchdogs. BrewDog then smartly responded with a weak beer cheekily titled *Nanny State*. BrewDog always upsets the applecart and is consistently an itch in someone's knickers. And its fans love that.

The BrewDog manifesto articulates its ideas and values, identifying what it deems meaningful. It communicates an ethos, attracts the likeminded, guides direction and represents the collective vision of everyone on the BrewDog team:

"We Bleed Craft Beer. This is our True North.

We Are Uncompromising. If we don't love it, we don't do it. Ever.

We Blow Shit Up. We are ambitious. We are relentless. We take risks.

We Are Geeks. Learn obsessively. Share evangelically.

Without Us, We Are Nothing. We are BrewDog."

BrewDog
The BrewDog Charter (2015)

This punk spirit both attracts and repels people. BrewDog is not for everyone. The values enshrined in the manifesto, the products the manifesto enables, the endless sensational stunts, all inspire fanatical devotion among likeminded beer lovers around the globe. People cluster around the anti-homogenization, anti-establishment, anti-pretension narrative to make a stand. It helps construct a meaningful identity and define what they believe, placing those beliefs in opposition to others. Of course, this is dichotomous—you're either BrewDog or you're not—and there are recent indications the company is softening this binary stance as it scales. But the BrewDog punk approach has resulted in such stratospheric success that if they haven't already, the beer punks will be invading a town near you soon.

Articulated Provocations

BrewDog is not the only creative organization harnessing the power of the manifesto to define itself and attract a loyal fan base. From brewers to clothes labels to high-end restaurants, creative people are probing culture and context with provocative statements of intent that resonate with the likeminded. Manifestoing is just one creative, effective and empowering "attract mode" that can make your ideals and values concrete, drawing people to you and providing foundations for entrepreneurship. However, provocations do not have to be articulated through pure writing, as McLaren's t-shirt or BrewDog's beers demonstrate. Provocations can be expressed as products, services, performances, playful experiences and much more. But before you start making any of those, first you need to wake up and know what side of the bed you're on.

Approximate Authenticity

*"History, it is easily perceived, is a picture-gallery
containing a host of copies and very few originals."*

Alexis de Tocqueville
The Old Regime and the Revolution (1856)

It's a Small World

Our world has been shrinking for hundreds of years—but recently the speed of contraction has accelerated. Globalization, ably abetted by electronically networked communications, has altered time and space. Trade and transactions between one side of the planet and the other now occur in milliseconds. Open Skies policies have led to low-cost flights, meaning we can radically change our physical realities on a weekend whim. Open borders have allowed us to change those realities more permanently, for professional advancement or that dream place in the sun. There has been an "intensification of worldwide social relations which link distant localities in such a way that local happenings are shaped by events occurring many miles away and vice versa" (Giddens 1991, p.64). As a result of this process, our cultural and political differences have been flattened and we have increasingly become global citizens.

Or have we? Recent events such as Brexit, the election of Trump and the rise of nationalism suggest a backlash in progress. Some people seem to feel that being a citizen of everywhere feels a lot like being from nowhere. More feel left behind and under threat. What feels like freedom to the highly educated and highly skilled feels like punishment to those with less to trade in the global marketplace. This phenomenon is what Bauman (2007, p.7) terms "negative globalization," a "selective globalization of trade and capital, surveillance and information, violence and weapons, crime and terrorism, all unanimous in their disdain of the principle of territorial sovereignty and their lack of respect for any state boundary." In light of this globalism run wild, protectionist narratives of "taking back control" become compelling. Under assault from cheap goods and cheap labor from abroad, plus the increased threat of terrorism, many nation states are adopting protectionist stances and closing their borders. So-called national values are hastily rediscovered and reasserted. We are turning inward.

Perhaps. But this is a strange and confused backlash. We want to safeguard jobs from cheap foreign labor, when the real threat comes from automation. We close our borders to global terrorism, ignoring the painful and disturbing reality that most terrorism is homegrown.

We satirize and stereotype other nations, while happily visiting them on weekend breaks and summer holidays. And we "Buy American" or "Buy British" without considering what that really means.

The German Job

In 2001, the new Mini was launched. Despite criticism by traditionalists, the car was an immediate success. By 2013, the Mini was not only a Top 10 seller in the UK but also a major success around the globe, accounting for 40% of all UK car exports (Love 2013). And in 2016, over 63,000 were sold in the UK alone. These not-so-mini offspring of the iconic car designed by Sir Alec Issigonis can be spotted whizzing around the UK, often with a Union Flag displayed prominently on the vehicle, sometimes right across the roof.

There are few cars on the road that want to be as authentically British as the Mini. The models are still called *Cooper*, *Clubman* and *Countryman*. Launch events feature Bulldogs named *Spike* and noted British historians celebrating the Mini as "a symbol of Britishness—lovable, cheeky, reliable, robust. A small car with big clout" (Sandbrook, quoted in Love 2013). Once you slap a Union Jack on the bodywork, these cars feel more authentically British than fish and chips (more on this later). But scratch the surface and you'll discover the Mini is not as British as it seems.

The Mini marque is now owned by BMW AG. Although the cars are mostly manufactured in Oxford, some models are made in Austria and the profits end up in Stuttgart. Parts are sourced from around the world—as with any other car-manufacturing supply chain—and the vehicle's designer was born in Morocco to an American father and Spanish mother. In short, the new Mini transcends nationalities and provides a snapshot of the globalized economy. Yet these cars still feel authentically British because BMW made a conscious decision to trade on that "Britishness" from the start. It positioned the new Mini as creative and slightly maverick, a car with a strong British heritage and "personality." This is aligned with a certain British underdog cheekiness that can be traced back to the Swinging Sixties, to John Lennon's impertinent wit and *The Italian Job* (Edensor 2006). The new Mini is that maverick creativity reinvented for a new century and embodied on four wheels, a perfect blend of crafted history and mechanical innovation.

Advertising experts like Sir Martin Sorrell argue that in a world of globalization "consumers are seeking out brands with genuine history and authenticity" (quoted in Hiscock 2002). It seems the more choice we're given, the more brands and culture transcend national borders, the more we want products to feel authentically of somewhere or embody something tangible. We want a Mini because of its British heritage and "cheeky chappy" personality. But knowing this four-wheeled maverick is underpinned by German quality doesn't hurt. Likewise, Jeep emphasizes its free-roaming pedigree and American roots with models called *Cherokee* and *Renegade*. Land Rover trades on British luxury and myths of off-road *Discovery*. Of course, both marques are mostly foreign owned—Jeep by Fiat Chrysler, Land Rover by Tata Motors of India—and many owners will never take them further off-road than the pavement outside their local deli. But none of this seems to matter. It is the exciting approximation of authenticity that makes these brands and products resonate, not quotidian realities or facts regarding who owns the modes and means of production.

100% Authentic

A mistake often made when discussing authenticity is to assume it resides in a product, service, or person. Nothing could be further from the truth. Authenticity is not an inherent quality; it is an ongoing multifaceted negotiation, fluid rather than solid. Richard Peterson identifies the fabrication necessary for artists to create and innovate in country music while maintaining a sense of heritage and tradition. In his book on authenticity and country, he describes how both the music and its attendant culture hinges on ideas of authenticity. But, he argues, this is not inherent in the song, artist, or event that is designated authentic; instead it is a socially agreed construct (1999, p.21). Peterson also states that as there is no authority to confer authenticity in country music, it is instead continually renegotiated, reworked and adapted through ongoing interactions between creators, audiences and commercial interests (1999, p.22). Often authenticity can be fabricated by adopting particular language, symbolism, identities, or conventions. If these are accepted, then a song or artist can be authentic. In short, songs and artists are only authentically "country" when enough people agree they are.

Peterson's argument applies equally across popular culture. The ancient Greek notion of *authentikos*—an authoritative text or sole authority that "fixes" authenticity—has disappeared over the past century or so. Yet strangely, we are increasingly surrounded by the rhetoric of the authentic. It is applied to food, clothing, songs, politicians, even indie game makers. Whether these things or people are accepted as authentic depends on how successfully their authenticity has been fabricated and performed and how well it can be sustained through ongoing negotiations. Our increasingly globalized world with its multiplicity of choice has not led to cultural flatness and complete homogenization. Instead it has caused antithetical reactions. Rather than destroying authenticity, globalization has led to an ever-increasing appetite for it. We are now constantly engaged in a search for something pure and authentically real, even when that authenticity is little more than a response to market demands (Cobb 2014).

100% Dynamite

"'The napalm sauce, sir?' asked Rashid. 'Yeah. The napalm sauce.' The first spoonful swiped a mustache of sweat on to Keith's upper lip and drew excited murmurs from the kitchen. 'Bit mild,' said Keith when he could talk again. Tears inched their way over his dry cheeks. 'Bland, Rashid,' said Keith, later, as he paid and under tipped. 'Bland. Dead bland.'"

Martin Amis
edited excerpt from London Fields (1989)

The Indian restaurant scenes Amis describes in *London Fields*—the postmodern pinnacle of his career—will resonate with anyone who has experienced the classic British "curry house" after the pubs shut. These restaurants fill with hordes of inebriated diners who plough through mountains of mouth-scorching Vindaloo or Madras curries, wash them down with liberal amounts of fire-quenching Indian lager, then stagger home. Since the 1950s, "going for an Indian" has been the eat-out experience of choice for many Brits, particularly those from the white working classes (Fielding 2014; Wilson 2017). Myriad Indian takeaways add a "grab it and go" option and Indian-themed ready meals can be found in every supermarket. This exotic import has become the fast food of choice, even supplanting fish and chips as the national dish. Britain is a nation of Indian food lovers.

But if we interrogate this phenomenon through a frame of authenticity, things become more complicated. Just as fish and chips is not "authentically" British—the idea of frying potatoes was most likely an import from the Low Countries, fried fish served with them a product of Sephardic Jews immigrating to London's East End in the late 19th century (Walton 1992)—the food served in the quintessential British curry house bears scant resemblance to authentic Indian food. One reason is that nearly 90% of "Indian" restaurants in the UK are actually owned and operated by Bangladeshis and Pakistanis, who have distinct regional food cultures and traditions that differ sharply from those of India (Khaleeli 2012: Wilson 2017). Another is the relationship between these restaurateurs and the expectations of their customers as negotiated through the marketplace.

What has occurred in the UK is a constant fabrication, negotiation and renegotiation of what constitutes "authentic" Indian food since the 1950s. As Bangladeshi restaurateurs worked to gain acceptability for their food within indigenous British society, they adapted their offer to conform to white working-class expectations. Meat was elevated over vegetables to more closely resemble the traditional British "meat and two veg" meal. Traditionally dry dishes were sauced to approximate gravy and starchy components were added to mimic potatoes. However, this was done carefully to ensure everything still felt exotic and authentically Indian. The food still had foreign names and was hyperspiced with unfamiliar ingredients, in the process inventing a scorchingly hot food that no Indian person would fully recognize as their own (Wilson 2017). Restaurants adopted names that reinforced their Indian credentials—The Raj, The Imperial Madras, Passage to India—but also resonated with echoes of the lost British Empire, foreign yet familiar, reassuring in their cultural hybridity. Inside were stereotypical images of the Taj Mahal, exotic music and other fabricated cues that could be recognized by their customers as "Indian." The British Indian restaurant became a space of fabrication, where authenticity was approximated and negotiated in response to the logic of market demand. Similar phenomena have occurred around the world. The Rijsttafel ubiquitous throughout the Netherlands is freely adapted from its Indonesian roots. The gloriously inauthentic General Tso's chicken—so popular in the US a full-length documentary was made about it—has no real analog in China. But none of this matters as long as you can keep approximating and renegotiating authenticity with your customers or audience. The extraordinary success of Indian food in the UK emphasizes the effectiveness of adaptability. Start with some base ingredients and a vision for what you're attempting to do, then learn and adapt your way to success. The trouble is, the minute you stop learning and adapting, things can go wrong.

Salaam Bombay!

"The British public have a love affair with Indian food. But the proposition offered to them was the tired stereotype of a curry house and lager."

Adash Radia
Co-founder of Dishoom (quoted in Featherstone 2016)

From only 300 in 1960, there were over 12,000 Indian restaurants in the UK by 2011. Politicians cited chicken tikka masala as "the national dish" and a distillation of the success of multicultural Britain (Cook 2001). But in recent years the quintessential curry house has entered a decline, with the Bangladeshi Caterers Association warning thousands could shut down over the next few years. There are many causal factors—the rise of other cuisines such as Thai, Japanese, Vietnamese, Korean, even American BBQ. The unwillingness of many third-generation British Asians to endure the long hours, backbreaking work and casual abuse that comes with running an Indian restaurant, opting for university and the professions instead. Government restrictions on immigration that have left chronic labor shortages in most restaurants. But perhaps most importantly, the expectations and knowledge base of customers have changed and many curry houses have failed to adapt to meet them. Due to cheaper air fares and the recent relaxation of visa requirements, Britons of all classes have been visiting India in record numbers (*Telegraph* 2015). To their surprise, they find little sign of the hybridized dishes served in the curry houses back home. There has also been increased criticism of "Banglish" food by Indian cooks and food critics such as Madhur Jaffrey, who described chicken tikka masala as "the dish without a home" (cited in Fielding 2014). All this has increasingly led to a failure in the renegotiation of authenticity, as more knowledgeable customers keen on searching out authentic Indian food realize it's unlikely to be found at The Imperial Madras. But this shift isn't the end for Indian food in Britain—it's a new beginning.

Dishoom opened in London's Covent Garden in 2010. It was an immediate success. More branches opened across the capital and by late 2016 it had expanded to Edinburgh. Dishoom takes its influences from the Irani cafés of 1930s Bombay, founded by Iranian immigrants to the city in the 19th century. These were highly democratic places that transcended class, caste and regional cuisine, breaking down social and cultural boundaries while serving great food. It was this ethos experienced first-hand that inspired the founders—all members of an extended Indian family—to open Dishoom. That and a deep desire to bring high-quality food rooted in India to the British public (Basu 2014; Featherstone 2016).

Like the curry house, authenticity at Dishoom is a construct. It is fabricated and negotiated. The restaurants are designed to evoke the "feel" of Bombay's century-old Irani cafés but experiencing this depends on a willing suspension of disbelief. Such willingness is manufactured by painstaking attention to detail, intelligent cues and references through interior and graphic design, menus that replicate dishes served in the "real" thing, cocktails that adapt classics with an Indian twist, a walk-up policy that creates a degree of controlled chaos that feels "authentically" Bombay. All reinforced by lots of workers and customers with South Asian roots. Dishoom fabricates and stages an "authentic" Indian experience through all these things, plus high-quality food that eschews hyperspiced neon-red sauces. The experience is so enjoyable that a Yelp list voted the original branch the best eatery in the UK in 2016 (Yelp, Inc 2016).

Dishoom is successful because it embraces the performative aspect of authenticity. The founders are perfectly aware Dishoom is not an Iranian cafe in 1930s Bombay, because "we are not Iranians and this is not the 1930s in Bombay" (Basu 2014). And they know you know that, too. No one is trying to con anyone. What Dishoom does is embrace its invented reality, instead approximating a feeling of authenticity to deliver a great experience: a couple of enjoyable hours where the diner is transported to a parallel Bombay-tinged reality filled with potent drinks and quality food. Dishoom is not the tired parody many curry houses have become but instead a playful and celebratory pastiche of Indian cuisine and culture. Its founders acknowledge it can never be truly authentic but just needs to feel authentic enough. They recognize the source material cafés as beautiful spaces led by powerful philosophies and see Dishoom primarily as a tribute to that (Basu 2014). Their restaurants are believable because they effectively pay that tribute, wearing influences proudly on sleeves and keeping tongues firmly in cheeks.

Don't Fight It, Feel It

"What I'm trying to do, as an amateur, is 'authentic approximation' ... I'm not trying to be original. If you sit in a studio all day trying to be original, you'll never do it."

Andrew Weatherall
(quoted in Gieben 2013)

You don't need to be a car maker or restaurateur to understand the power of approximating authenticity or the futility of constantly fretting about being 100% authentic and original. Andrew Weatherall—one of the most critically acclaimed DJs, remixers and music producers of the last 30 years—today describes himself as a gentleman amateur. His approach leans heavily on the idea of creativity as an additive process, believing "if you go into a studio and do an authentic approximation of the music you love, I think you end up becoming original without even trying" (quoted in Gieben 2013). Weatherall says his best work is done when his influences are unconscious, a product of extensive inductive learning and slow percolation. Clothing designer Nigel Cabourn has a similar approach. Celebrated for "authentic" garments based on his obsessively sourced collection of military and outdoor wear from the first half of the 20th century, Cabourn admits the perceived authenticity of his clothes is only ever an approximation. He candidly says "I Cabournise them. I mean … at some point I have to decide what fabrics, colours and textures to use. And I can't have the clothes fitting the way they did in 1950. But I do try to copy the little things when I can, trimmings and things like that" (quoted in Cronberg n.d.). Cabourn has also imbibed his influences over a protracted period, allowing them to percolate into his work. And he wears these influences on his sleeve—literally and figuratively—putting his source material front and center when telling the story of a collection and its garments. He also knows this is where the value is produced: "I could tell you stories about every little detail on a garment. People come up to me and ask me why my clothes are so expensive, so I tell them. The stories justify the price" (quoted in Cronberg n.d.).

The rhetoric of authenticity surrounds us. We are told to be authentic to ourselves—a narcissistic exhortation based on the nonsensical notion that we believe the same thing at all times—and that certain things are more authentic than others. But it is impossible for anything to be truly authoritative and authentic in a world where gatekeepers have become almost irrelevant. Who is to say what is genuine, real, true? What feels authentic to you seems plastic and fake to the next person. The best bet is not to worry so much. Approximate authenticity and embrace its performative aspects, just like Dishoom. Be believable, have integrity, but don't take yourself too seriously. Wear influences on your sleeve. Don't bury them, celebrate them. Don't let yourself stop learning, becoming a tired parody of something you no longer believe in. That really is fake. Instead, add a new personal twist to things that inspire you. Put new content through old processes. Put old content through new processes. You'll achieve something fresh and exciting by default.

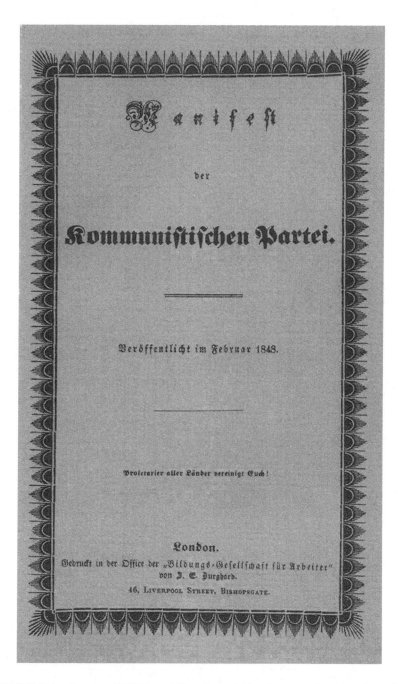

FIGURE 2.1 Cover of 1848 publication of *The Communist Manifesto* by Karl Marx and Friedrich Engels. (Courtesy of Wikimedia Commons, https://commons.wikimedia.org/wiki/File%3ACommunist-manifesto. png.)

FIGURE 2.2   The Spice of India Restaurant and Takeaway, Nelson, Lancashire. (Courtesy of Robert Ward, https://commons.wikimedia.org/wiki/File:Spice-of-India-Restaurant-Nelson-Lancashire.jpg.)

Bunker Busting

"In our increasingly complex and confusing world, we need all the help we can get from each distinct domain of our emotional and intellectual being."

Stephen Jay Gould
The Hedgehog, the Fox and the Magister's Pox (2004)

Industrialization led to a division of labor. Workers were deskilled and trained to do a single task, resulting in specialisms and knowledge silos. Art and the humanities concurrently became separated from science, forming the almost antithetical fields of knowledge CP Snow famously called the "two cultures." Each culture then developed a bunker mentality. But as we accelerate into an uncertain 21st century, this needs to change. Bunkers must be busted if we are to survive and thrive.

Art et Science

"It is a world in which the creative imagination of the artist is now needed by the men who handle computers."

Marshall McLuhan
(quoted in McLuhan and Zingrone 1997)

Our conception of art and science views each as a separate entity, possibly the binary opposite of the other. Science is measured and rational, the arts subjective and irrational. Science aims for truth, art for expression. Science is defined and procedural, art is loose and intuitive. Each domain appears to have separate goals and looks to be inhabited by different people. You only need conjure up a typical stereotype of an artist or scientist to know this is true. But it wasn't always this way.

During the early European Renaissance, the so-called polymath was king. Philosophies and principles of art, architecture, engineering and science were understood by all intelligent people (Ashley-Smith 2000). The Renaissance was a rebirth of scientific and artistic knowledge from the classical world that had been forgotten during the Dark Ages. The scientific discoveries of Copernicus and Galileo that culminated in the works of Leonardo da Vinci, Michelangelo and Rembrandt were rooted in the recovery of ancient wisdom (Gould 2004; Richmond 1984). But Copernicus was not simply a scientist; he was also a classics scholar and diplomat. Galileo was a philosopher as well as the "father of scientific method."

Likewise, Leonardo and Michelangelo were the embodiment of the "renaissance man" (and sadly, they were only men at this point). Even Rembrandt—considered one of the greatest artists in history—was highly knowledgeable of scientific principles and concepts. Indeed, many Renaissance artists belonged to science-related guilds because they knew how to mix ingredients—rather like a chemist or pharmacist—to produce paint, or understood the complex chemical processes required for etching. Increasingly artists also needed to understand the geometry that informed new theories of perspective and composition. And today it seems likely that many Renaissance artists integrated science even further into their work than was previously thought.

One of our most persistent artistic stereotypes is the "artist as genius." This myth depicts the penniless master ensconced in a drafty garret, making art for art's sake because their imagination and craft are so far ahead or apart from the mainstream that contemporaries do not appreciate—much less buy—their work. The artworld—art critics and historians, galleries and dealers—does little to dispel such romantic and misleading myths. But at the turn of the millennium, David Hockney did. In his book *Secret Knowledge*, Hockney advances a controversial thesis. He argues that, from the early 15th century onward, many great Western artists employed the science of optics—the branch of physics concerned with the behavior and properties of light—by using mirrors and lenses (or a combination of the two) to create living projections (2006, p.12). These projections were then used as tools and templates to enhance looking at and vividly representing, the material world (Hockney 2006, p.14).

Unsurprisingly, Hockney's thesis proved contentious and many in the artworld sought to dismiss it. But this has proved difficult. For not only is Hockney one of the most significant artists of the last 60 years—with a practitioner's intimate knowledge of making—he was also collaborating with respected physicist and optics expert Charles Falco. Consequently, the Hockney–Falco thesis has inspired a host of new research into the use of optics throughout the history of art. Analyzing the work of Rembrandt, one recent paper even concluded that the great artist used lens and mirror technology to help make his self-portraits (O'Neill and Palazzo-Corner 2016, p.9).

Each exploration of the Hockney–Falco thesis causes heated debate within the artworld. Some argue against it objectively, but most dispute the thesis out of a need for self-preservation. The strongest resistance comes from those who believe Hockney and Falco's argument devalues the genius of the artist and consequently the artist's work. Of course, these people usually have a vested professional or financial interest in keeping art values—both monetary and cultural—as high as possible. An example of such protectionism is the review of documentary *Tim's Vermeer* conducted by Jonathan Jones. The film follows inventor Tim Jenison's Hockney-inspired attempts to prove Johannes Vermeer painted with the help of optics. Jones—an art critic for *The Guardian*—rubbishes the film, claiming it fails to show "any sense of the greatness of art" and "is a depressing attempt to reduce genius to a trick" (2014). He laments the documentary "implies anyone can make a beautiful work of art with the right application of science. There is no need for mystical ideas like genius" (Jones 2014). Jones is brazenly peddling the artist-as-genius myth here. Worse, he is implicitly reinforcing a dichotomy between art and science: art is mystical and filled with genius, science merely the rational application of knowledge—perhaps even a trick. Either way, he is missing the point.

Hockney and Falco never argue that artists who used optics were in some way "cheating" or poor exponents of their craft. They do not suggest science invalidates artistry. If anything, Hockney believes the opposite, arguing that to "suggest ... artists used optical devices ... is not to diminish their achievements. For me, it only makes them all the more astounding" (2006, p.14). This stance echoes Marshall McLuhan's argument that artists are "navigators," often first to deploy or produce value with new thinking or technology (McLuhan and Zingrone 1997, p.278). In fact, the Hockney–Falco thesis is a celebration of the union of art and science and the ability of such a union to produce astounding work. Hockney is perfectly aware that Renaissance polymaths would be puzzled by our binary approach toward these two fields of knowledge. The question is: why do most of us now exist only in one domain or culture? How did we arrive at a point where a whole body of knowledge is closed to us and our endeavors?

The Division Bell

There is no precise moment when art and science became separate domains. Scholars mostly argue for a process that began in the late Renaissance. This was impeded temporarily by the unifying ideals of the early Enlightenment, before accelerating during the scientific revolution of the late 17th century, resulting in a yawning chasm by the middle of the 19th (Snow 1961; Wilson 1999; Gould 2003). Stephen Jay Gould (2003, loc.410) argued the opening of the divide in the 17th century resulted from a debate between Ancient and Moderns, where Aristotle and the Renaissance were pitted against Bacon and Descartes. It is worth remembering that science as we know it did not exist until this time and Gould believes the separation of domains was mostly the result of the new "scientists" staking a claim for their scientific methods in the face of entrenched institutions (2003). Whatever the exact causes, it is clear that by the middle of the industrialized

19th century, science and art (including the humanities) had divided into two distinct domains of knowledge with separate cultures.

The "two culture" theory was first articulated by CP Snow in his Rede Lectures of 1959. Snow believed "the intellectual life of the whole of Western society is increasingly being split into two polar groups" (1961). These groups had become unable to communicate or exchange knowledge with each other. Snow argued this had serious ramifications for "our creative, intellectual and, above all, our normal life ... leading us to interpret the past wrongly, to misjudge the present and to deny our hopes of the future ... making it difficult or impossible for us to take good action" (Snow 1961). Certainly, Snow had his private agenda, mostly rooted in experiences of cultural snobbery from the dominant arts and humanities academics at Cambridge. But the lecture was a sensation and his ideas resonated around the globe.

For Snow, the principal cause of the two cultures was a "fanatical belief" in specialization, particularly within education (1961, p.144). The trend toward specialized education began in the 19th century and accelerated throughout the 20th, possibly reaching a peak as Snow was writing in the 1950s and 1960s. No wonder he was worried. School, college and university curricula had made it nearly impossible to study art and science subjects simultaneously. Therefore success in either domain became dependent on specialization and people had to make hard choices (Ashely-Smith 2000). As a consequence, it became acceptable for specialists in one culture to be ignorant of issues in the other. As education was compartmentalized, we became increasingly monocultural, ignorant of both knowledge and imaginative experience outside our respective domains and subjects (Snow 1961). And although the peak of the two cultures may now have passed, there is no doubt we are still suffering from the fallout.

Here We Go Again

As constant uncertainty and disruption change the creative industries, the nature of business and work in these fields inevitably alters. To cope with this change, we must build adaptive capacity and resilience, drawing on all knowledge from all domains to navigate safely past the icebergs. Unfortunately, the dominant narrative for education is based not on adaptability and resilience but on plugging existing skills gaps for industry.

The STEM (science, technology, engineering and math) agenda seeks to correct perceived skills gaps in these crucial areas, touting economic disaster for any nation that fails. But STEM has something missing: the arts and humanities. By pushing STEM, we're again implicitly creating an art/science divide, following a path of domain-limited specialization instead of providing an interdisciplinary education for the leaders, innovators and creative entrepreneurs of the future—you know, the ones less likely to get replaced by artificial intelligence (AI). And to make matters worse, there is a good chance STEM skills shortages are fallacious.

According to respected demographer Michael S. Teitelbaum, the received wisdom claiming a shortage of STEM graduates is not so wise. Teitelbaum (2014) argues "there is little credible evidence of the claimed widespread shortages in the U.S. science and engineering workforce," citing extensive research from various sources to support this. And while agreeing that expertise in STEM is crucial, he argues that US higher education produces way more graduates in these areas than the nation needs. There is little evidence suggesting the situation is markedly different in other "developed" nations but the STEM shortage narrative persists. As a consequence, STEM occupations are increasingly an employer's market. Salaries are being driven down and careers in these areas are starting to look less attractive. The winners in the short term are the large tech companies who would rather not pay big salaries with extensive benefits (Dash 2016). Unsurprisingly, many of these companies are the most enthusiastic supporters of STEM. Now, we totally get the importance of the bottom line. We're not communists. But too much focus on short-term profit usually means things get missed—like lessons from history.

The Rad Lab

When the US entered the second world war, the way innovation happened changed dramatically. The most transformational change was the emergence of publicly funded collaborations between the military, private industry and academic institutions of a kind unknown before 1940 (Turner 2006). Unfortunately—due to President Eisenhower's 1961 farewell address, Oliver Stone's *JFK* and thousands of conspiracy theorists—this transformative military–industrial–academic complex is now held responsible for every abominable innovation or nefarious activity of the past 70 years. Of course, these collaborative projects were responsible for new and secret weapons, with the Manhattan Project the most infamous outcome. But if we stop staring at the conspiracy trees for just a moment, the forest comes into view. For not only did these collaborations innovate some of the most game-changing technologies of the war, but they also produced many of those that transformed the relative peace that followed, including the internet, GPS and video games. Even more importantly for this essay, they provide a historical model for how to overcome the limitations of siloed specialisms.

After the German invasion of Poland in 1939, Vannevar Bush arranged an urgent conversation with President Roosevelt. Bush, a former Massachusetts Institute of Technology (MIT) professor and administrator, persuaded FDR to create the National Defense Research Committee. Its goal would be to channel government funding to civilian contractors and research universities, enabling them to work together on innovative projects for the military. Renamed the Office of Scientific Research and Development, by the end of the war, Bush's organization had contributed over $450 million ($6 billion in 2017) to research new technologies, knitting together a fabric of military, industrial and academic cooperation at the same time (Turner 2006, p.18). At the heart of this were laboratories where innovation flourished in an environment of interdisciplinary and nonhierarchical collaboration, including Los Alamos, Oak Ridge National Laboratory and the groundbreaking Rad Lab at MIT.

Initially housed in a variety of buildings, the mostly Anglo-American–staffed Rad Lab moved to a new but temporary wooden structure known as Building 20 after 1943. And it was here the magic happened. The lab quickly became a site of flexible and collaborative work that brought multiple disciplines together. Engineers worked with designers, mathematicians with planners. Risk-taking and entrepreneurship became the norm in a permissive culture that eschewed hierarchy. Crucially, "formerly specialized scientists were encouraged to become generalists ... able not only to theorize but also to design and build new technologies" (Turner 2006, p.19). The Rad Lab culture encouraged crossing professional boundaries and shattering disciplinary silos and this culture was facilitated by Building 20 itself. Built out of wood with a horizontal layout, the "Plywood Palace" was highly adaptable, inherently nonhierarchical and conducive to serendipitous encounters. Courtyards between wings could be repurposed to house collaborative projects, walls cut down or put up at will and the horizontal floor plan "helped to encourage interaction between groups," according to lab veteran Henry Zimmerman (Brand 1995). The Rad Lab staff became joined together in a common search for technologies that would help win the war. They were less concerned with doing things right, more with doing the right thing, at the right time. And this they did. An MIT report estimated that in five intense war years, the Rad Lab achieved over 25 peacetime years' worth of innovation (Garfinkel 1987). The project was a model of effectiveness, demonstrating what can be achieved when specialisms were de-emphasized, knowledge bunkers busted and interdisciplinary bridges and networks built instead.

Come Together

"To be absolutely certain about something, one must know every-thing or nothing about it."

Henry Kissinger
(quoted in Ferguson 2015)

"Since we live in an age of innovation, a practical education must prepare a man [sic] for work that does not yet exist and cannot yet be clearly defined."

Peter Drucker
The New Realities (1989)

Perhaps one of the best arguments for going to college or university is to be part of a learning community where knowledge, creativity and critical thinking are valued and lasting social and cultural connections formed. These communities socialize young people. They support them to learn by providing a space to learn and experiment in. At their best they encourage a curious mind and learning mindset, personal growth, entrepreneurship and establish future networks that enable serendipitous collaboration—just like Building 20. Unfortunately, many colleges and universities have become obsessed with skills agendas and notions of employability. As a result, these institutions are hurtling backward into the future. They have forgotten that the experimental learning communities and spaces, and the serendipitous social encounters these enable, are what makes them valuable. Some universities have closed down social spaces, more are moving much of their delivery online, supposedly to help students learn but usually to help themselves fit ever-larger numbers of paying customers into cramped campuses. Both approaches negate serendipitous and interdisciplinary collaboration rather than encourage it.

We need education but we do not need an educational system that is reopening the divide between the two cultures and stuck in the industrial era. Specialized education is simply an industry training people for industry, mass-producing workers for mass-production work that is either being outsourced or teetering on the edge of AI-induced extinction. As the industrial age recedes further into the rearview mirror, we need a fresh and pragmatic approach to education. We must recognize that the domain-specific specialisms and knowledge silos of industrialization will no longer work in our postindustrial future. Instead of specializing we must connect and harness all knowledge—art, the humanities and science—to best equip us for uncertainty.

Do It Fluid

*"Fixation is the way to death, fluidity is the way to life.
This is something that should be well understood."*

Miyamoto Musashi
The Book of Five Rings (circa 1645, 2011)

Despite the plan to demolish Building 20 after the second world war, it continued to be used long after the Rad Lab was disbanded. For the next 50 years, it would house experimental projects, becoming known as the "Magic Incubator." Here would be born some of the most influential ideas and innovations of the late 20th century. In fact, had Building 20 not housed the Tech Model Railroad Club in the early 1960s, you probably wouldn't be reading this book. Its permissive culture empowered three members of that club to mess around with a DEC PDP-1 computer in their spare time. As a result, those friends created *SpaceWar!*—the fountainhead of modern video games. The key to Building 20's ongoing success was that it never became a knowledge silo; it was never assigned to any one school, department, or center; it was always a permissive space for beginning a project, a graduate student experiment, or interdisciplinary research (Brand 1995, p.114). The Rad Lab and Building 20 succeeded by busting bunkers of domain knowledge. They provided a setting—a physical environment—where an experimental, heuristic, entrepreneurial mindset could emerge and thrive. And this was achieved through principles that embraced domain fluidity, rejecting disciplinary division and bureaucratic rules to build a risk friendly, nonhierarchical, interdisciplinary culture. The great artists who used optics in their work also embraced domain fluidity, using new scientific knowledge and technologies to enhance their artistic skills. Fluidity enables great innovation; rigidity leads to obsolescence. We must reunite the "two cultures" and cross disciplines to bridge innovation gaps and ensure our future. A future where principles and philosophies of art, the humanities, technology, science, engineering and math are once again understood by all intelligent people.

FIGURE 2.3 *Spacewar!* running on the Computer History Museum's PDP-1. (Courtesy of Joi Ito, https://commons.wikimedia.org/wiki/File%3ASpacewar!-PDP-1-20070512.jpg.)

Monument Valley: A Case Study in Craftwork

Can a trendy East London design studio with no background or pedigree in making games create one of the best games of the modern era? Can a game use modern art as its muse and still find success with a mainstream audience? Can a game be so simple it needs no written instruction, yet still be a deep, emotive experience? Can a premium-priced game be short enough to be consumed within a single commute without alienating its paying customers? Can a premium app leave all of that free-to-play "money on the table" and still make a handsome profit?

Conventional wisdom says the answer to each of these questions is a resounding *no*. *Monument Valley* says: "Hell, yes!"

Whale Fail

Formed in 2011 as a self-funded, experimental team inside of ustwo—a digital design agency with clients including Sony, JP Morgan and Adidas—ustwo Games was an attempt to reinvest profits into the creation of original products and intellectual property. Its first title, *Whale Trail*, was a one-button arcade game inspired by Andreas Illiger's *Tiny Wings*. With vibrant visuals, engaging gameplay, a Gruff Rhys soundtrack and savvy marketing, *Whale Trail* generated over 38,000 downloads in its first week of release (Dredge 2011).

But despite its early promise, *Whale Trail* struggled to find a sustainable business model. The game took over two years—and 3.6 million downloads—to recoup a development budget of £250,000. Matt "Mills" Miller (2012), co-founder of ustwo, considered *Whale Trail*—and the process of making it—the "beta" for ustwo Games. In hindsight, it is more accurate to view the game as the alpha; the beta came next.

Just a Blip

Blip Blup represented a step change for ustwo Games. Responding to lessons of *Whale Trail*, it had a clarity of purpose and creative constraint from the start. The game—and the approach to making it—can be viewed as a proto-*Monument Valley*, where the principal ingredients of *Monument Valley*'s success were first explored and articulated. According to designer and programmer Manish Mistry (2013), instead of starting with a single idea the project began with the team asking itself a series of constraining yet provocative questions:

- How would it feel to tap on some squares and see light spread out from my finger?
- What if there were things that blocked the light?
- Can I create a puzzle from this?

Blip Blup was the answer to these questions. Quickly the concept evolved from a paper prototype into an engaging experience with a bold minimalist aesthetic and a clear, purposeful, set of guiding principles (Mistry 2013):

What it is:

- It's a game about thinking
- It's a game about stopping and taking your time
- It's a game about logic.

What it isn't:

- It's not a game about speed
- It's not a game about timing
- It's not a game about quick reflexes.

Inspired by the "fail fast" approach deployed in ustwo's corporate client projects, *Blip Blup* evolved inside a series of weeklong prototyping sprints, each ending with a company-wide show-and-tell presentation. These displays exposed progress to real players and ustwo co-workers; according to Mistry (2013), they became something of a compass for the team:

> If an idea was engaging, we'd take it further. If it didn't have a spark, we would shelf [sic] it and move on. It was an important lesson for us to learn how to say no to our own ideas if they simply weren't good enough.

To create levels that were visually stimulating, fun to play and requiring of mental ingenuity, the team meticulously handcrafted each one, an approach that demanded "many gruelling [sic] hours ... spent playing, tweaking and replaying levels" to find the right balance between difficulty and playability (Mistry 2013).

At a time when the majority of mobile games were migrating to a freemium business model, ustwo Games went against the grain by going premium. This decision reflected the desire for *Blip Blup* to be a "simple proposition—straightforward puzzling and nothing else," a game that eschewed mainstream gamers for a "niche audience of puzzlers" (Mistry 2013). *Blip Blup* would prove an enlightening experience for ustwo Games, prompting it to refine its mission of intent. According to soon-to-be-hired executive producer Daniel Gray, there was a renewed ambition to "do something that has meaning, that has something to say to players" (2014). As *Blip Blup* launched in May 2013, this grand plan was already in motion—but first ustwo Games needed to assemble its A-team.

A Product of Its Creative Environment

Ed Catmull (2008), president of Walt Disney and co-founder/president of Pixar Animation Studios, has long argued that ideas are overrated:

> A few years ago, I had lunch with the head of a major motion picture studio, who declared that his central problem was not finding good people—it was finding good ideas. Since then, when giving talks, I've asked audiences whether they agree with him. Almost always there's a 50/50 split, which has astounded me because I couldn't disagree more with the studio executive. His belief is rooted in a misguided view of creativity that exaggerates the importance of the initial idea in creating an original product. And it reflects a profound misunderstanding of how to manage the large risks inherent in producing breakthroughs.

Instead of idolizing ideas, Catmull (2008) suggests four guiding principles for creative projects: Empower your creatives. Create a peer culture. Craft a learning environment. Stimulate meaningful postmortems. Through exploration, experimentation and critical self-reflection, ustwo Games reached similar conclusions: if your purpose is to create experiences that push a medium forward, then you do not just need good ideas or people, you need the right team within the right creative environment.

In late 2012, Miller set about remodeling ustwo Games, assembling a team "built on tight relationships between talented people" that was capable of realizing his ambitions (2013). The original *Whale Trail* team had come from inside the agency—app developers and graphic designers—with no direct game making experience. This naivety had its advantages, but Miller now wanted to "blend our own home grown skills with those of the games world thoroughbreds" to realize his vision for ustwo Games (2013). Key hires made during this period included Daniel Gray and designer Ken Wong.

With the right team assembled, Miller took a leaf out of the Pixar playbook and empowered it to think and act independently. He set no goals, budgets, or timeframes, instead giving the team complete ownership of the decisions it made and the games it produced. Miller's only stipulation was that the team "make something we can all be proud of" (quoted by Bernstein 2014). Expectations set, the team began exploring its next big thing, spending the next three months prototyping in all shapes and forms. It met weekly to see what resonated and every week the answer seemed to be the same: "the pencil sketch on the wall" (Gray 2014).

What If … ?

The question of "how one might design a game where the architecture was the central character?" had intrigued Ken Wong for years (Wong 2014). Inspired by sacred architecture and its ability to concurrently convey artistry, mystery and innate playfulness, Wong (2014) kept returning to the question of "how to make an interactive experience out of this?" Everything clicked into place when Wong rediscovered *Ascending and Descending* by MC Escher, an artwork he had never previously considered through the lens of game design. Wong (2015) asked himself:

> What if you had to guide a figure to enter the building, solve some puzzles hidden in the interior rooms, with the goal of getting to the highest tower? Rather than following the character with a first-person or third-person camera, we could keep the emphasis on the environment by retaining the bird's eye view and this enclosed framing that Escher had used.

His answers would become the seed for *Monument Valley*.

With Wong preferring to pitch concepts in the form of posters, the first prototype of *Monument Valley* was a simple pencil sketch created in March 2013. Daniel Gray (2014) remembers that it drew "a lot of curiosity and enthusiasm" from the rest of the team, studio and passing visitors. It gained so much attention Gray began probing interested parties, asking them, "how would you play with a game like that?" (Gray 2014). The innate playfulness and mystery in architecture revealed that even as a simple sketch, *Monument Valley* could capture the imagination and start playing in a person's head; it was already a place where people wanted to spend time.

Through a series of rapid digital prototypes, the team explored and identified the core mechanics of play before turning their attention to the wider experience: How would the core mechanics evolve through play? How would the tactile experience feel? What secondary and tertiary activities were needed to support the core mechanics? How would they add a greater depth to the experience? How long would the experience be? (Gray 2014). By May 2013, ustwo Games felt that they had enough of the necessary answers to repeat the approach of *Blip Blup* and pitch *Monument Valley* to the entire company (Gray 2014).

An interesting side-effect to operating inside an agency—rather than an orthodox game-development silo—was that none of the team's studio colleagues were game makers. Instead, the early champions of *Monument Valley* were "animators, graphic and user interface designers and programmers, people with a broad cultural palette and a deep understanding of the way people use mobile devices," according to Gray (quoted by Bernstein 2014). These people did not obsess about game mechanics or gaming exceptionalism: they just wanted to be surprised and delighted. Even in its earliest prototyping phase, *Monument Valley*—shaped by its surroundings, sensibilities and supporters—had developed principles.

A Line in the Sand

With *Monument Valley*, Ken Wong (2014a) set out to "create a piece of interactive art worth hanging on a wall." Not the typical goal of your average game maker. Wong and the team intended to "rethink what a video game is and why people play them" and discard many of the "popular elements of traditional video games that often frustrate less hardcore players and leave them excluded" (Wong 2014a). He understood that games were surprisingly difficult for the non-gaming majority: too challenging and dexterous, too demanding of a person's time and often thematically unappealing. Wong (2014a) observed:

> Other games exclude large groups of players because of their content or aesthetics. Although some of the finest games ever made include graphic violence, poor gender representation and endless dank corridors of blue and brown metal, their great moments often prove inaccessible to all but the most dedicated gamers.

Such observations helped the team shape what *Monument Valley* stood for and against—an understanding Wong (2014a) formalized in a set of design principles used to guide development:

> The game would be so simple it needed almost no instruction.

> The game would appear friendly and engaging. If Escher could make artwork that was both beautiful to behold and

geometrically fascinating to a wide audience, perhaps we could achieve a similar feat in the interactive medium.

Players will appreciate quality play time over quantity of play time. Instead of creating as many levels as possible, we would only add levels when we had something new and unique to say. Keeping the experience short would allow more players to see the story through to the end.

Challenge is not the focus of the game and difficulty is not the central arc. The feeling of discovery and the joy of exploring a new world can be just as powerful and stimulating.

[The game] would earn the player's emotional engagement. The art, sound, text and animation are restrained and subtle, designed to permit empathy, not force it.

Turning Fantasy into Reality

The desire to make a selfish experience posed a unique set of challenges for the team. Each chapter—or level—had to work harmoniously as a playful interactive experience, a piece of architecture and a graphic design composition. Each also had to feel unique and contain a "distinct and separate theme, gameplay mechanic or story beat" worth articulating (Wong 2014b). Once again placing emphasis on quality rather than quantity, Wong and the team reprised the handcrafted design approach of *Blip Blup*, significantly increasing the physical, mental and financial investment required to "achieve an elegant balance of interaction, beauty and storytelling" (Wong 2014b). This approach was inefficient but effective. "All killer, no filler. We like to handcraft, not mass-produce" was Daniel Gray's mantra (2014). Such was the painstaking, often impractical, adherence to these design principles, it would be December 2013—nine months after the original concept sketch—before the team was ready to start showing the game off.

Showing Off

Few game makers appreciate the importance of exposing their work early and often. Fewer still incorporate it into their workflow. But *Monument Valley* proactively used play-testing to see "what made [people] smile and what made them frustrated" (Wong quoted by Bernstein 2014). Rather than treat early access and promotion as an afterthought, ustwo Games worked as hard at attracting and building a relationship with fans and the press as it did making the game. Because of this, months before its release

Daniel Gray already sensed that *Monument Valley* was something "bigger than the team"; it was a unique "shared experience in which everyone —team, fans, press" was invested (2013).

The game was introduced to the world in a flurry of blog posts in December 2013. A carefully curated combination of words, visuals and videos introduced the concept, building interest and anticipation. Forty-eight hours after release, the teaser trailer had 18,000 views. Gray (2013) initially estimated the team would receive 100 responses to its beta-testing invitation. When it received 1,200, he received the clearest indication yet that ustwo Games "might just be onto something." At the end of 2013, the first public beta rolled out and the team spent the next four months leveraging their army of play-testers to turn a good game into a great experience.

A Luxury Experience

In May 2013, Miller sent an email to the *Monument Valley* team, challenging it to "unleash on a level never seen." Using the recent success of the *Superbrothers: Sword & Sworcery EP* as impetus, Miller (quoted by Wong 2014c) outlined his aspirations for *Monument Valley*:

- win apple [sic] iPad game of the year 2013 as the very least
- get awards from being the most wonderful experience from a magic point of view and design
- must be the type of art you need to put on your wall, must be so so iconic
- must sell for super premium
- must engage apple [sic] with progressive builds from today
- must excite the whole studio with charm, delight and wow
- must sell 200,000 copies in year 1!!!
- must engage industry cool kids, so they want to talk about it socially ... ie be so hot they can't ignore
- must make you cry ...
- must make me say, i wish ustwo made that
- must do more, this is 1% of what this project must mean
- this is the one ...
- no pressure ...

The game made good on its promise when it was named iPad Game of the Year 2014—although this was a year later than Miller dreamed due to the length of development. There were thousands of decisions that took *Monument Valley* from concept sketch to prestigious award but two stand out from Miller's email: selling for super premium and engaging with Apple—the platform gatekeeper and kingmaker—long before the game was due for release. The decision to go super premium was contrarian and risky. The conventional thinking of the time held that premium mobile games were dead, but the team wanted to lead rather than follow. It had scant regard for "what the rest of the industry is doing" (Wong quoted by Sheffield 2014). Instead, the team's interest was in creating something valuable for a small, discerning audience. For Wong (quoted by Sheffield 2014), premium best communicated inherent value:

> Price communicates value, in ordinary life; it's thought that high-quality goods are worth spending money on. We wanted to communicate that our game was a premium experience, like staying in a five-star hotel, or driving an Audi, or owning an iPhone. The rationale was simple—and, again, artisanal— "What is the quality of those hours?" We think that 90 minutes of only our best work can be worth more than hundreds of hours of doing the same thing over and over again.

In an App Store dominated by free games and freeloading gamers, ustwo Games appeared crazy to reject the traditional "industry standard" gaming product for a "compact yet bespoke" curated interactive experience (Gray 2014). In particular, the extremely short length of the experience raised eyebrows, but Gray (2014) was happy to argue that length does not equal value:

> My favourite movie of all time is *Enter the Dragon* and I don't believe it would have been improved by watching Bruce Lee one-inch punching henchmen repeatedly for a further five hours. The only way *Monument Valley* could truly realize its grand vision was to go premium and avoid modern tropes such as leaderboards, pay walls and heavy social integration.

And it wasn't just Gray or Wong that held this view. The director of games at ustwo Games, Neil McFarland (quoted by Kollar 2014), was just as critical of this arbitrary, unfounded industry assumption:

> There's a weird mirror between the use of the player's time and the use of our time as developers. We want to give the player as much as we can with the time they've got and it's the same for us as developers.

> We want to make sure we're spending our time doing stuff that we really love—not grinding on making loads of padding to fill out a fixed, desired time for the game.

Where the decision to curate a luxury experience confounded industry expectations, it delighted Apple. When awarding the 2014 Apple Design Award, judges described *Monument Valley* as "a game that set out to do something big and it succeeds" (quoted by Dormehl 2014). That award—and the iPad Game of the Year accolade that followed six months later—were the culmination of a long and deliberate courtship. A courtship that began with the team asking themselves, "If Apple were to make an internal first-party game, what would it look like?" and ending with an experience that was as uncompromising on design, user experience and seamless usability as something designed by Apple in California (Gray quoted by Bradley 2017; McFarland 2015). For Gray (quoted by Bradley 2017) the logic was simple: game makers are a slave to the tastes and cultures of the platforms they publish, so if ustwo Games could make *Monument Valley* look and feel as good as a first-party experience, then "of course Apple are going to pick up on it!"

ustwo Games first previewed *Monument Valley* to Apple in June 2013 and as development progressed Apple received updates of increasing quality on a regular basis. Like their newfound fans and the press, Apple was made to feel part of the shared experience (Gray 2014). The reward came on April 4, 2014, when *Monument Valley* launched with a massive marketing push from Apple, featuring on the front page of the App Store in 155 countries (Wong 2014e). This editorial sway helped propel the game to the top of the paid app charts in more than 30 countries in just four days. A week after launch, it had recouped development costs and become profitable; a milestone *Whale Trail* took two years to achieve. In under six weeks, *Monument Valley* sold over 500,000 copies (Wong 2014d) and earned universal acclaim from the gaming press and the industry itself.

> *"Monument Valley is the most elegant game I've ever played. Every aspect—the presentation, the puzzles, the UI—amazingly elegant. Play it!"*
>
> **Tim Schafer**
> *President, Double Fine* (2014)

But at the same time it gathered patronage from its peers, something far more interesting was happening. *Monument Valley* was crossing over into wider popular culture.

Crossing the Cultural Chasm

Miller's fantasy of creating "the type of art you need to put on your wall" became a reality when *Monument Valley* screen prints went on sale shortly after the game's release (Wong 2014f). Beyond the obvious commercialization, it indicated the game was moving beyond the initial sense of shared experience and taking on a life of its own. The game's screenshot-sharing feature introduced a convenient, compelling way for fans to collect and share their newly acquired digital works of art. A modern twist on the arcade attract mode—the prerecorded demonstration displayed for the purpose of enticing passersby—over 600,000 screenshots were saved in the first year of release with 60,000 shared across email, Facebook, Twitter and Instagram (Gray 2015). The game also spawned a popular Tumblr fan art gallery—with over 200,000 submissions—and a range of handcrafted wooden toys sold via the artisanal marketplace, Etsy (naturally). But the best was yet to come.

In mid-2015, *House of Cards* featured the game in its third season, with President Frank Underwood not just playing the game but eulogizing it:

> *"Whoever you're, whoever you think you're, believe also you're a silent princess. Your name is Ida, your journey is one through a forgotten landscape of twisting staircases and morphing castles, atop floating stones defiantly crossing an angry sea, within dimly lit caverns cobwebbed with ruins, MC Escher could only grasp at in a dream state."*
>
> **President Francis J Underwood**
> *House of Cards, Chapter 31* (2015)

When the episode was broadcast in February 2015, the impact was "insane," according to Gray, generating eight times the typical number of weekly downloads and highlighting "the amount of people that don't know about games unless they see it in another medium" (Gray quoted by Blake 2015). The team had succeeded not only in making "every screen worthy of being framed and hung on a wall" but deserving of the presidential seal of approval.

Punk Provocations
- What if you gathered 10 interesting photos or sketches, then asked, "how would you play with a game like that?"
- What if you identified five reductive gaming tropes and directly contradicted them?
- What if you reduced your game down to its most interesting, inspiring five-minute experience?

FIGURE 2.4 Early sketches of what would become *Monument Valley*. (Reprinted with permission from ustwo games,

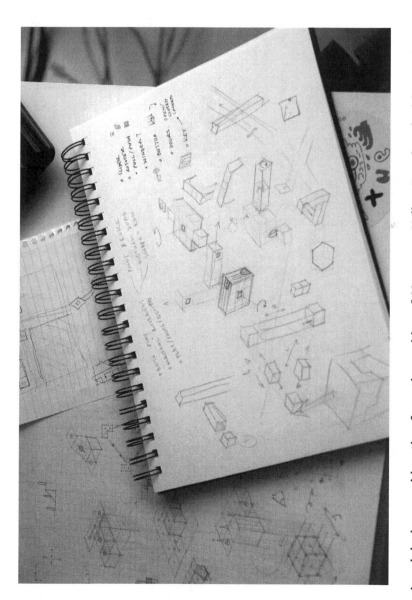

FIGURE 2.5 Level design consideration from the making of *Monument Valley*. (Reprinted with permission from ustwo games, ©ustwo Games 2014. All rights reserved.)

FIGURE 2.6 A screenshot from *Monument Valley*. (Reprinted with permission from ustwo games, ©ustwo Games 2014. All rights reserved.)

Chapter **3**

Remake/Remodel

Abstract

The demise of the traditional publisher model, the democratization of making and an increasingly oversaturated market have left the game sector in a state of flux. To remain relevant, game makers must reevaluate and reimagine the cultural inputs and creative outputs that shape their experiences and the experiences they create.

This chapter suggests that game makers must accelerate the sector's deindustrialization and disregard premature incorporation, prescriptive processes and commoditization for the masses. Instead, game makers should embrace adaptability and curiosity in order to curate meaningful, playful experiences that surprise and delight audiences.

Into the Unknown

"As an architect, you design for the present, with an awareness of the past, for a future which is essentially unknown."

Norman Foster
My Green Agenda for Architecture (2008)

Unknown Unknowns

February 2002, five months after the tragic events of 9/11. US Secretary of Defense Donald Rumsfeld is hosting his regular Pentagon press conference. NBC correspondent Jim Miklaszewski poses a question about the reported lack of hard evidence linking Saddam Hussein's Iraqi regime with the supply of weapons of mass destruction to terrorist organizations. Rumsfeld (2002) provides a typically evasive answer:

> Reports that say that something hasn't happened are always interesting to me, because as we know, there are known knowns; there are things we know we know. We also know there are known unknowns; that is to say we know there are some things we do not know. But there are also unknown unknowns—the ones we don't know we don't know.

The comment was met with bemusement by the White House press corps and widely mocked in popular culture. But reflecting on the quote today—regardless of Rumsfeld's motivation—it makes a valid point: context matters in a complex world.

By the Book

At the time of the infamous quip, Rumsfeld was serving President George W Bush. The path to the White House is familiar to the Bush family. George W's father, George HW Bush, served as the 41st president of the US just a decade before him. So when Jeb Bush, George W's younger brother, launched his campaign for the 2016 Republican presidential nomination, he brought out "the playbook," the tried-and-tested, "play-by-play" Bush blueprint for winning the race to the White House (Stokols 2016).

The Playbook—a real document stored in a binder—had been successfully deployed in the election of both Jeb's father and elder brother and his campaign team saw no reason to deviate from a winning plan. Bidding to become the third Bush in three decades to hold the most powerful office in the world, Jeb's team knew "cash, organization and a Republican electorate ultimately committed to an electable centre-right candidate" typically decided the nomination (Stokols 2016). Unfortunately for Bush, the 2016 race was anything but typical.

> *"When you're the son and brother of former presidents, the grandson of a U.S. senator, how do you run in a year like this? It is just a year of personality, not message. All of a sudden, there was no path for him. They just kept falling back on his record as governor, which is all he has—and no one gives a shit."*

Anonymous Republican operative "close to the Bush family"
(quoted in Stokols 2016)

In more predictable times, Jeb Bush's decade-long record of conservative accomplishment as governor of Florida would have probably swayed voters. But in 2016 there was little appetite among a disillusioned electorate to pay deference to the political establishment. The race became a battle of personality rather than policy and the playbook had made no provision for the biggest personality in the race: Donald J Trump. By the time Bush suspended his campaign in February 2016, Trump had eviscerated him in the press, in the polls, in live debates and at the ballot box. As Trump confounded experts to emerge as the prospective nominee, the Bush campaign was impotent. It was incapable of adapting to circumstances, adjusting its risk-averse positioning, or reacting to unforeseen, unorthodox campaigning.

> *"You cannot run a political campaign and not have the ability to adapt, to pivot. To sit there and say 'We have a book' just shows immaturity."*

Anonymous, longtime Bush family donor and supporter
(quoted in Stokols 2016)

The Playbook presumed a campaign that played out on Bush's terms, a campaign where political record and policy details were vote-winning plays. There was no plan to counter the man *Slate* called "the best bully American politics has ever seen" (Parton 2016). When Trump's popularity grew, Bush—unable to adapt or improvise—was left holding a binder of rational predictions and orderly plans that bore no resemblance to reality. It's what Donald Rumsfeld refers to as a "failure of imagination" (quoted in Larivé 2014).

In the Loop

So how did Trump manage to overcome an experienced politician like Jeb Bush? According to the *Atlantic*, *Politico* and several prominent political commentators, he got inside his OODA loop (Fallows 2016; Shafer 2016). As the establishment figure and frontrunner in the polls, Bush and his meticulously planned campaign had everything to lose. Operating at a quicker tempo than his rival, Trump was able to seize the initiative and shape the unfolding race and its narrative, forcing Bush to react to unpredictable, unfolding circumstances rather than execute his planned prescriptions. Trump is a populist, his politics are ambiguous, his intentions unpredictable and his actions adaptive and largely improvised. Winning is more important than ideological virtue, political correctness, or sticking to a plan. This was populist theater and Trump was the director. Outmaneuvered and disorientated, by the time Bush had finally prepared his reaction—filtered through a bureaucratic stream of political consultants, policy wonks and pollsters—Trump had again shifted the narrative and reality of the race (McLaughlin 2015).

Whether Trump explicitly deployed the OODA loop as his political strategy is debatable. For the record, we think not. Doing so credits him as some Machiavellian political chess master rather than the astute opportunist and spellbinding showman we see. Regardless, there is merit in the consideration and value in understanding the credited OODA loop. The work of Colonel John Boyd—the Korean War fighter pilot who grew into "arguably the most important military thinker" of the 20th century (Ford 2010, loc.11)—the OODA loop is a mental model consisting of four main elements: Observe, Orient, Decide, Act.

The first stage of the loop is observation: using contextual awareness, data and judgment to understand reality as it is, rather than what we assume or wish it to be. The second is orientation: the analysis and synthesis of assumptions, observations and existing paradigms to form clear perspectives. The third stage is decision: moving forward with purpose, informed by intentions, best guesses and reoriented perspectives. The fourth is action: the high-tempo testing of decisions. Boyd's model is often portrayed as a glib four-step linear process cycle, but in reality it is considerably more dynamic, recursive and messy (see Figure 3.1). An OODA loop—and everything that emerges from it—is informed by its circumstantial, environmental and cultural inputs and its dynamic outputs. As Boyd highlighted in his military briefing *The Essence of Winning and Losing*, the entire loop is an "ongoing many-sided implicit cross-referencing process of projection, empathy, correlation and rejection" (Boyd 1996).

Coming from the mind of a man nicknamed "40-Second Boyd" in the US Air Force—based on a standing bet he could "wax" any opponent's tail in under 40 seconds or he'd pay $40—who later helped design the F-16 jet fighter and personally advised Dick Cheney on military strategy during the 1991 Gulf War, it is unsurprising discussions around the OODA loop are often wrapped up in tales of conflict and machismo. But Boyd was really a *bricoleur*, his mental model as much influenced by Gödel's incompleteness theorems, Heisenberg's uncertainty principle and the second law of thermodynamics as it was by great military minds like Sun Tzu, TE Lawrence and Carl von Clausewitz (Ford 2010). Tellingly, Boyd never formalized the model, preferring to practice what he preached and maintain the OODA loop as an ever-evolving verbal concept, presented and tested in military briefings and subjected to the same "whirl of reorientation, mismatches, analyses/synthesis" he believed everything else should be (Boyd quoted by Hammonds 2002).

The New Rules of Engagement

By the end of 2004, attacks on American forces in Iraq averaged 87 per day and the American death toll had passed 1,000 McChrystal (2015, p.4). Al-Qaida Iraq (AQI) were poorly trained and ill-equipped, yet the US Joint Special Operations Task Force (the Task Force) was struggling to overcome its threat. AQI had got inside the Task Force's OODA loop. Writing about his experience as head of the Task Force, General Stanley McChrystal (2015, p.4) recalls:

> Although lavishly resourced and exquisitely trained, we found ourselves losing to an enemy that, by traditional calculus, we should have dominated. Over time we came to realize that more than our foe, we were actually struggling to cope with an environment that was fundamentally different from anything we'd planned or trained for. The speed and interdependence of events had produced new dynamics that threatened to overwhelm the time-honoured processes and culture we'd built.

McChrystal and the Task Force incorrectly assumed that AQI was a traditional insurgency that could be outthought and outfought with robust military planning and a tried-and-tested tactical playbook. Very quickly they realized AQI was actually a hyper-connected, decentralized network and not the rigid, prototypical military structure they had assumed. AQI was dogmatic and offensive in its ideology but agile and improvised in its actions. It was able to strike at disorientating speed with devastating effect. It was entirely unpredictable and irrational.

To overcome AQI, McChrystal had to dismantle the "awesome machine," the efficient "military assembly line" that had become "too slow, too static and too specialized—too efficient—to deal with volatility" (2015, p.90). In its place, McChrystal (2015, p.4) embraced the uncomfortable truth that "a problem has different solutions on different days" by shifting to an operating rhythm that favored intuition, heuristic learning and improvisation over predictive planning and efficiency of execution. In the dynamic swirl of an uncertain environment, the impactfulness of *doing the right things* become more important than the efficiency of *doing things right*.

By the time the Task Force eliminated AQI leader Abu Musab al-Zarqawi in June 2006, it was "learning and adapting quicker than the enemy and—finally—hitting them faster than they could regenerate" McChrystal (2015, p.251). Central to this resurgence were three guiding principles: common purpose, shared consciousness and empowered execution. Common purpose afforded all of the Task Force's contributing forces a genuine sense of clarity and focus. Shared consciousness broke down silos and introduced lateral transparency, intelligence and insight across the operational environment. Empowered execution trusted the teams and individuals closest to the problem with authority to adapt and respond to emergent threats and opportunities, regardless of rank, permission, or status.

Replacing predictable processes with adaptive frameworks enabled McChrystal and the Task Force to confront and overcome, the complexity of unknown unknowns. McChrystal (2015, p.23) explains:

> The pursuit of "efficiency"—getting the most with the least investment of energy, time, or money—was once a laudable goal, but being effective in today's world is less a question of optimizing for a known (and relatively stable) set of variables than responsiveness to a constantly shifting environment. Adaptability, not efficiency, must become our central competency.

Don't Trust the Process

The misguided pursuit of efficiency and predictability is not limited to the political and military landscapes. It is also a recurring blight on the creative process, blunting the effectiveness and diluting the impact of artists and creators. Even Pixar.

In the afterglow of *Toy Story*, two defining creative principles emerged: "Story Is King" and "Trust the Process." Story Is King articulated the *why* of Pixar: nothing—not technology or commercial opportunity—would be permitted to get in the way of telling the greatest story possible. Pixar president Ed Catmull took immense pride in the way people spoke of how *Toy Story* made them feel, rather than obsessing over the computer wizardry that brought it to the big screen (2014, loc.1060). Trust the Process articulated the *how* of Pixar: the working practice that allowed it to navigate the inevitable "difficulties and missteps in any creative endeavor" (Catmull 2014, loc.1060). Ordinarily skeptical of well-intentioned but ultimately hollow maxims, Catmull convinced himself Pixar's principles were the exception due to the studio's enlightened culture.

More than two years into production—12 months before the film was scheduled to be released into theaters—*Toy Story 2* was in deep trouble. Catmull had been disturbed by "varying degrees of bad" in early cuts of the film but assumed "the process will fix things for us" (2014, loc.1088, loc.1254). The root of the problem was the misguided assumption that because *Toy Story 2* was a sequel, Pixar could assign inexperienced directors and simply have them follow "the process" to replicate the inspiration, innovation and contextual serendipity of the original, a film that "changed movie history" (Catmull 2014, loc.1254; Zorthian 2015). Despite their best intentions, the directors—lacking experience and creative conviction—had only succeeded in telling a story that was hollow and predictable (Catmull 2014, loc.1102). Upon viewing a rough cut, *Toy Story* director John Lasseter declared the planned sequel a "disaster" (quoted in Catmull 2014, loc.1101).

Only months before *Toy Story 2* was due to open in theaters, the project hung in the balance. For a young company with one box-office hit behind it, the stakes were extremely high. Pixar chairman Steve Jobs told the entire staff that *Toy Story 2*'s failure would be "game over" for the company (quoted in Jacobs 2011). Provoked into action, Pixar rebooted the project—trading blind faith in an abstract process for trust in inspired, empowered people. The incumbent directors were replaced by Lasseter and a creative core team that would be guided by only one principle: Story Is King. The next nine months would prove the most intensive, exhausting period in Pixar's history—Catmull refers to it as the "cinematic equivalent of a heart transplant"—but a Pixar-quality *Toy Story 2* would hit its deadline and be released to great acclaim, even outperforming the original at the box office (2014, loc.1131, loc.1171).

Reflecting on the experience, Catmull (2014, loc.1253) recognizes that trusting a process bred an unintended complacency:

> We should trust in people, I told them, not processes. The error we'd made was forgetting that "the process" has no agenda and doesn't have taste. It is just a tool—a framework. We needed to take more responsibility and ownership of our own work, our need for self-discipline and our goals.

Talkin' All That Jazz

"Anybody can play. The note is only 20 percent.
The attitude of the motherfucker who plays it is 80 percent."

Miles Davis
(quoted in Tingen 2001)

Game making is fraught with unknown unknowns yet continually undermined by reductive assumptions and failures of imagination. There is not only a need to embrace uncertainty but, as Boyd suggests, to continually revise, adapt, destroy and recreate our theories and systems to confront it (Ford 2010, loc.655). As the OODA loop illustrates, there are too many unique contextual variables—ideals, ideas, unfolding circumstances, unfolding interactions with environment, outside information, implicit guidance, cultural traditions, genetic heritage, newly discovered information, heuristic learning, past experiences, collaborator composition, analysis and synthesis—to place your faith in prescriptive playbooks, efficient assembly lines, or abstract processes.

Consider Simogo, the Swedish game making duo of Simon Flesser and Magnus "Gordon" Gardebäck. They reject onerous documentation, precision planning and the cult of productivity. Instead, they improvise, starting out with a bold intention and feeling their way to the final experience. Flesser is unapologetic: "The way we make games is like jazz music; we improvise and put in new stuff as we go along ... you know where you're going with it, but you never know how long the improvisations will last" (quoted in Nicholson 2012). The improvisation only stops when Flesser and Gardebäck have captured their definitive, distinctive experience: "much like a recording artist we want our games to feel Simogo. It should feel like something only we could make" (quoted by Nicholson 2012). It all sounds gloriously inefficient.

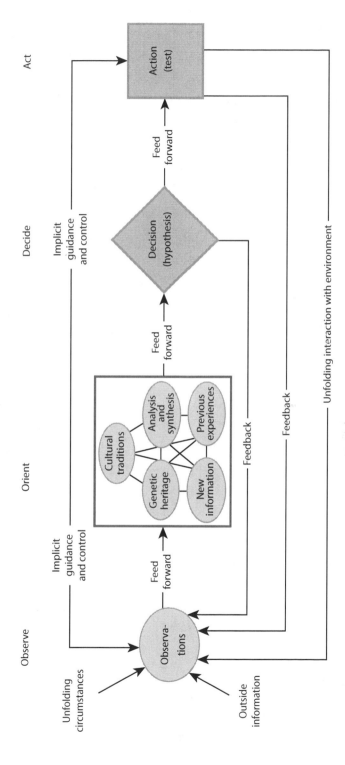

FIGURE 3.1 John Boyd's OODA Loop by author Sean Taylor. (Adapted from a diagram by Patrick Edwin Moran. Licensed under Creative Commons Attribution 2.0 Generic via Wikimedia Commons, https://commons.wikimedia.org/wiki/File:OODA.gif.)

After the Gold Rush

"There was a shopping mall. Now it's all covered with flowers.
If this is paradise. I wish I had a lawnmower."

Talking Heads
(Nothing But) Flowers (1988)

The Age of Abundance

It has never been easier to make a game. There are currently more than 7,500 indie games on Steam alone (Steam Spy 2017). And it has never been easier to turn professional game maker. Even in a relatively small country like the UK, there are over 2,000 active video game companies (Ukie 2016, p.12).

The Age of Uncertainty

Between April 2015 and April 2016, the number of indie-tagged games on Steam increased by over 50% (Jarvis 2016). In the same period, the median average number of copies sold per "indie" game fell by roughly the same amount (Jarvis 2016). There might well be more indie games but each game is selling less. Much less.

According to a report by The Independent Game Developers' Association (TIGA), 65% of game studios in the UK are "microstudios" employing four or fewer people (2016). The same report revealed that these microstudios are currently closing down at a rate of nearly 100 per year.

It is not just microstudios that are feeling the squeeze. A sector survey revealed that the average salary for a solo independent game developer was just $11,812—around $7,000 less than the mean annual wage of a US fast-food worker (Chalabi 2014; Gamasutra 2014). The same survey—published by *Gamasutra*—revealed that 57% of indie game developers (both solo and collectives) recoup less than $500 in game sales.

Getting High on Your Supply

The chances of a comedy–drama about two transgender prostitutes—shot exclusively on an iPhone—finding success at the box office seems unlikely. But that is exactly what Sean Baker's

2015 film *Tangerine* achieved. Baker's "exuberantly raw and up-close portrait of one of Los Angeles' more distinctive sex-trade sub-cultures" was produced on a budget of just $100,000, yet it went on to gross over $700,000 at the US domestic box office (Chang 2015; Wikipedia 2016).

And if that seems unlikely, what about a horror film shot for just $20 on an iPhone that earned its creator more than $20,000 and attracted over half a million viewers on Amazon's video-streaming platform? Just a few years ago, that would have been ridiculous to contemplate. But it's exactly what Justin Doescher achieved with his 2016 film, *The Break-In* (Economist 2017).

In reality, however, *Tangerine* and *The Break-In* are outliers. Both are comforting and deceptive tales of survivorship bias told at a time when "the median box-office return for low-budget films in America is a measly 25 cents on the dollar" (Economist 2017). What the films demonstrate is that modern tools and technology have democratized film production and distribution to the point where anyone can make a movie on their own terms. The down-side of such democratization is, according to screenwriter and producer Beanie Barnes, a supply-heavy indie film industry that is "cannibalizing itself" (2014). Too many films are flooding into an ecosystem at a time when the amount of money made from indie films has decreased significantly. As Janet Pierson, head of South by Southwest Film Festival, observes: "the impulse to make a film has far outrun the impulse to go out and watch one in a theater" (quoted by Ball and Menon 2014).

Heads You Don't Win, Tails You Lose

The Long Tail theory asserts that the cultural and economic shifts of the past two decades have dramatically altered the shape of the demand curve, reducing the importance of the mass market—and mass marketed—hits at the head of the curve and amplifying the commercial potential of the infinite number of low-demand niches at the tail (see Figure 3.2).

Commercial viability used to be constrained by the physical limitations of the traditional retail, publishing and broadcast sectors. But in the internet era, constraints such as physical manufacturing overheads, distribution logistics and brick-and-mortar shelf space no longer apply. In a digital economy, the need to "lump products and consumers into one-size-fits-all containers" inside a single mass market is no longer necessary—supply can almost always scale to meet demand—so the focus shifts away from winner-takes-all ecosystems fixated on blockbuster products and services (Anderson n.d.).

Popularized by then–*Wired* editor-in-chief Chris Anderson, the long tail describes a world where "narrowly-targeted goods and services can be as economically attractive as mainstream fare" (n.d.). A world where physical scarcity is replaced by digital abundance, creating an infinite number of viable niche markets, each with their own enthusiastic audience, online distribution channels and extended half-life. Obscure interests and subcultures—previously rejected as unsustainable, unworkable, or unacceptable—are now thriving hubs of community and economy.

In the games sector, the long tail removes the need for publishing and distribution intermediaries, with creators free to self-publish their work and zoom into microscale, niche markets that were not previously economically viable. Without the requirement for physical manufacturing, logistics, or shelf space, game makers can sell directly to consumers via low-cost digital distribution mechanisms.

While the long tail might have changed the rules of the game, it is wrong to suggest that the balance of power has tipped in favor of makers. The primary beneficiaries of long tail economics are platform holders and aggregators operating at scale—Amazon, Spotify, Netflix, Steam, etc.—consumers and ironically, hit makers. In 2016, the top five performers at the box office were all made by Disney. Combined, its releases for that year accounted for one-fifth of total film revenue worldwide (Epstein 2017).

Within a long tail ecosystem, "it turns out … the hits get bigger," according to David Edery (2009). Formerly worldwide games portfolio manager for the Xbox Live Arcade platform and now CEO of the independent studio, Spry Fox, Edery is well placed to offer a perspective from both sides of the distribution divide. In his opinion, current ecosystems are even more top-heavy than those of the PS3 and Xbox 360 console generation—a period "long-derided for its hit-driven nature" (2009).

By solving the distribution problem for creative enterprises, the long tail introduced a new one: discovery. The "tyranny of limited inventory" still exists but with eyeballs and attention replacing physical retail space as the limiting constraint (Koster 2009). For game makers, this issue is compounded not just by an extremely oversaturated, low-barrier-to-entry ecosystem but also by a lack of differentiation regarding genres, mechanics and audio-visual aesthetics among self-identifying "indie games."

Direct Action

Independents lacking an established fanbase who launch work into long tail ecosystems cede control of their destiny. Their choices are to wait patiently—possibly forever—to be picked and promoted by the platform holder, hope to be the "needle in the haystack" that is discovered organically by enough customers, or partner with a traditional publisher and outsource their hopes and dreams to an intermediary. Each option is a game of chance with the odds stacked against the maker.

The alternative is to stop playing by the rules and instead cultivate a meaningful direct relationship with a small but passionate fanbase. As *Wired* founder Kevin Kelly astutely observes in his cult essay *1,000 True Fans,* publishers, studios, labels, aggregators and intermediaries are very much a 20th century phenomenon—a consequence of industrialization and the retail trends of the era (2016). In contrast, patronage and direct audience relationships are timeless concepts.

Kelly (2016) argues traditional corporations, publishers and intermediaries are "under equipped and ill-suited" to return to the implicit artisanship of the long tail; they are "institutionally unable" to find and function within inefficient, unscalable niche markets. For example, labels and publishers can retain more than 85% of payouts made by music-streaming sites such as Spotify. In 2015, the average payout to labels and publishers from Spotify was between $0.006 and $0.0084 per stream, yet as little as $0.001128 found its way to the artist (Dredge 2015). Such behavior is not personal; it's just business. And not particularly good business either. The economics of niche products make little sense for traditional intermediaries incompatible with the long tail economy. The effort required to find, understand and connect with obscure interest groups outweighs the modest reward. You need mass to make millions and most subcultures simply do not scale to that size. Kelly (2010) identifies this as "The Shirky Principle," where "institutions will try to preserve the problem to which they are the solution."

Direct relationships with your community—conversational, emotional and transactional—can be transformative. Take *Minecraft.* In the summer of 2009, Markus "Notch" Persson wrote the basic game over a weekend and began sharing progress on *TIGSource,* an independent community for game makers and players. One month later, he charged people €10 to download a primitive version and sold 40 copies in the first weekend (Cheshire 2014). From there Persson cultivated a passionate *Minecraft* fanbase and began releasing updates for the community every Friday. It would not be until the summer of 2010—20,000 sales of a "work-in-progress" *Minecraft* later—that he would quit his day job and start up Mojang to develop the game full time (Persson 2010). When sales hit 200,000 later that year, PayPal suspended Persson's account, suspecting fraud (Cheshire 2014).

Not everyone can be *Minecraft*. It's another outlier example. But with time, patience and sincerity, anyone can capture the attention of 241 passionate, like-minded individuals, the average number of supporters for a successful Kickstarter campaign according to Kelly (2016). Similarly, only a small number of creators can afford to quit their day job thanks to the passion and generosity of their Patreon patrons. But thousands can make a meaningful connection with a small but delighted audience and be rewarded for their craft.

Direct relationships are neither a panacea or a one-size-fits-all solution. But they are an opportunity to regain ownership from centralized hubs of long tail publishing and aggregation. Instead of being subjected to popular fads and fashions, oversaturation and the tyranny of discovery, they afford the opportunity to find, grow and lead a tribe of like-minded people and get rewarded for doing so.

Don't Quit the Day Job

Digital distribution—and the subsequent rise of long tail economics and its dominant centralized aggregators—has radically changed the rules of game making. In contrast to previous eras, independent game developers are overabundant and ever-increasing. Similarly, games themselves are no longer scarce or ephemeral. Instead, they exist forever on an overcrowded virtual shelf. Daniel Cook, Edery's Spry Fox co-founder, asks: "What happens when demand is fixed and supply is high?" (2016). In his view, a fallow period of consolidation and conservatism that precipitates standardized demand, heightened competition, winner-takes-all markets, escalating development costs and a culture of risk aversion across the games sector. Sound familiar?

According to Cook, to survive as an independent in this harsh new reality, game makers must do one of three things: become a genre king, dominate a niche market, or develop and manage a brand. But "not everyone can stay independent"—unsustainable game making enterprises will be left with the choice of becoming either hobbyists with day jobs who make games for love not money, externally-funded "independent" game makers who get paid to make their games for the profit of others, or hired guns who perform specialized labor for mega studios and publishers (Cook 2016). The only other alternative is extinction.

Of those three options, becoming a hobbyist is undoubtedly the most appealing to the truly independent of mind. And it's in step with Kelly's *1,000 True Fans* hypothesis. Being a hobbyist is not about quitting game making but rejecting an oversupplied mainstream marketplace and the institutionalized assumption that independent game making is a right rather than a privilege. Cook's advice to up-and-coming creators is to "expect a situation closer to what we see with writers, painters and musicians" (2016).

Pride and Provenance

In 2016, Ken Wong returned home to Australia to set up Mountains, a "craft games studio." Why "craft" and not "indie"? Well, for Wong (2016), craft is a statement against video game monoculture and mass-market homogeneity:

> You're not trying to mass produce things that are disposable, you're trying to craft beautiful, bespoke things that are maybe a bit more meaningful, or more lovingly made.

With Mountains, Wong intends to explore more human themes and craft flawed, vulnerable experiences for the discerning few, rather than safe, sanitized games for the masses. Critical of how repressed game makers can be in their creative expression, Wong wants to challenge the institutional fear of making playful experiences "about life and death and love and sex and sadness" (2016).

Conscious of his privileged position as creator of *Monument Valley* and the security and agency that affords him, Wong shares Cook's view that supply has outstripped demand, that we are "witnessing the democratization of an artform" (2015). As a hobby and mode of meaningful self-expression, game making has never been more accessible or more necessary. But as Wong (2015) highlights, just because a medium is accessible, does not mean it owes you a living:

> It's a mistake to assume that an artform is only validated by its commercial viability, or that being able to create something somehow entitles one to income. Making a living by

writing poetry, drawing comics, playing the oboe or skate-
boarding is only possible for a few. This only forces the best
to strive for ever greater heights, while the rest can enjoy
expression and experimentation without the distraction of
monetizing their work.

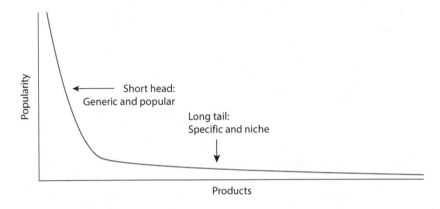

FIGURE 3.2   The long tail. (Reprinted with permission by Sean Taylor.)

Start a Band, Not a Business

"It's better to be a pirate than join the navy."

Steve Jobs
(quoted by Hertzfeld n.d.)

How to Survive an Indiepocalypse

When the game industries speak of the "indiepocalypse," they tend to be referring to an impending extinction event for the indie game making subculture. Andy Baio, ex-Kickstarter Chief Technical Officer and co-founder of the XOXO Festival, has a wholly different interpretation. For Baio, an indiepocalypse is a "global shift in how culture is made" (2013). Catalyzed by the democratization of creator tools, the means of production and digital distribution, the indiepocalypse is a liberating force for "hackers and makers across every form of art" that enables them to find, cultivate and monetize a direct, meaningful relationship with a niche fanbase. A fascinating collision of artisanal sensibilities and a DIY punk attitude.

Of course, punk is a term loaded with assumptions and pejorative connotations. Like the hipster and the artisan, the punk has become a lazy caricature. Like craft, punk as a noun draws on careless nostalgic myths, this time of three-chord thrashing performed by angry young white men kitted out in a uniform of comedy Mohawks, safety pins and Doc Martens boots. But we are not interested in punk as a noun, only as a verb. The idea of doing it yourself, grabbing whatever is at your disposal and expressing yourself. We share Malcolm McLaren's (2008) interpretation of punk:

> I always said punk was an attitude. It was never about having a Mohican haircut or wearing a ripped T-shirt. It was all about destruction and the creative potential within that.

Digging Your Scene

As an active participant in the alternative music scene since 1978, Shellac guitarist and Nirvana producer Steve Albini draws a distinction between the state of the music industry and the health of the music community. Albini (2014) argues the music industry experts speak of is "essentially the record industry." When these experts warn "pretty soon nobody will be making music anymore because there's no money in it," they do so with the selfish assumption that the same old mass-market institutions, processes, distribution pipelines and income streams that used to make the industry money must be restored to their former glories (Albini 2014).

While the music industry—labels, ghost songwriters, promoters, publicists, lawyers, accountants, advertising agencies, radio, MTV, journalists, big record store owners—were busy manufacturing the mainstream, the alternative music communities were doing it themselves. Independent bands did not enjoy the "luxuries" of mainstream middlemen, so they had to be inclusive and resourceful, clustering into local subcultural scenes and forming recording collectives, cooperative labels, independent clubs and fanzines. Albini grew up within this kind of culture. And it was here his punk sensibilities—a desire to make his own records, conduct his own business and control his own career—were forged. Alternative bands were living out Kelly's theory of *1,000 True Fans* before it was conceived, building a direct relationship with their fans and patrons. Albini (2014) reckons that by the mid-1990s, Shellac was returning a 50% net profit on every record it self-published, earning a better per-piece royalty than Michael Jackson, Bruce Springsteen, Prince, or Madonna. And so, says Albini, were thousands of other bands with a similar punk attitude.

The internet amplifies the potential of the punk. No longer constrained by the local maximum, bands are free to indulge themselves and develop direct, emotional connections with like-minded people around the globe. The music community is now an infinite peer-to-peer network of esoteric subcultures and niche markets. Or, in Albini's (2014) words:

> Imagine a great hall of fetishes where whatever you felt like fucking or being fucked by, however often your tastes might change, no matter what hardware or harnesses were required, you could open the gates and have it at a comfy mattress at any time of the day. That's what the internet has become for music fans. Plus bleacher seats for a cheering section.

Inherent Vice

"It's what we called punk rock capitalism. Just be really aggressive, really ambitious and you can't have debt."

Suroosh Alvi (2016)

In 1994, a recovering heroin addict launched a free cultural magazine, *Voice of Montreal*. This publication was to be Suroosh Alvi's way of shining a light on the "depraved underground culture" he obsessed over but felt was ignored by the local media (Alvi 2016). The *Voice of Montreal* made no economic sense. Alvi had zero experience as a journalist and was launching into a "shrinking English market in an economically depressed city" (Alvi quoted in Dunlevy 2016). There was barely enough advertising demand to sustain the two incumbent alternative publications of the time, the *Montreal Mirror* and *Montreal Hour*.

The *Voice of Montreal* was "a laughing stock" but thanks to a Canadian Government welfare program, rational economics were not a consideration and Alvi believed the cultural conversation he could stimulate was more necessary than ever (2016). Nobody was inherently curious about "punkish indiscretion, skater culture, sex, drugs and music" or the seedy subcultures where they flourished (Yakowicz 2014). Nobody was expressing themselves with wonky approximations of gonzo journalism and provocative design. Nobody was unapologetically speaking directly to and for, Alvi's (2016) generation:

> We hadn't been to journalism school, so the way to do that is to get as close to the source as possible. If we are going to write about the prostitution community in Montreal, let's get the prostitutes to write that story.

Adopting a punk approach, *Voice of Montreal* spent the next two years bootstrapping itself while Alvi and his co-founders, Gavin McInnes and Shane Smith, lived off welfare. Smith played a pivotal role in the rise of the magazine. A raconteur who, in Alvi's words, could "sell rattlesnake boots to a rattlesnake," Smith secured valuable, credible advertising from Californian skateboard companies and expanded the magazine's distribution into international markets (Alvi 2016). His most audacious act of tricksterism was engineering the magazine's divorce from its nonprofit parent company, achieved by planting a story in the local press that *Village Voice* was about to launch a trade-mark lawsuit over the use of "Voice." It wasn't. But, suitably panicked, the parent company folded *Voice of Montreal*. Almost immediately, Alvi, McInnes and Smith started the magazine up again under a new name. Only this time it was independently owned by themselves and operated for profit (Alvi 2016). Bigger, glossier and boosted by $10,000 (CAD) in family loans, Alvi (2016) recalls the magazine became more culturally potent, if not more professional:

> We created this really raw magazine. There were a lot of typos but it really jumped off the page and it was kind of shocking

stuff ... this weird little take on American culture that was coming from Montreal and we were sending this magazine to San Francisco, Chicago, LA and New York and the Americans were eating it up.

In 1998, they sold a percentage of the company in exchange for what Alvi describes as a "big fat cheque" (quoted in Dunlevy 2016). Conscious that the magazine had plateaued and needed to get beyond bootstrapping if it wanted to realize its potential, the founders courted the interest of Montreal technology entrepreneur Richard Szalwinski, persuading him to part with $250,000 (CAD) for 25% of the company. The self-perpetuated legend goes that the deal concluded in a single meeting, without any due diligence and based on an arbitrary valuation "pulled from thin air" (Alvi 2016). Szalwinski used his investment to convince the team to move operations to New York City and scale beyond its simple print magazine to create a multichannel online media platform.

Of course, the simple print magazine in question was *Vice*, now one of the world's largest and leading digital media and broadcasting companies. Valued at $4 billion (USD) in 2015, Vice Media now boasts Disney as investors, HBO as broadcasting partners and a multimedia empire spanning magazines, books, record labels, film production companies, bars, online video channels, cable network stations, online web series, television shows and award-winning documentaries (Dunlevy 2016). But despite its meteoric—and often crass and controversial— rise, Smith's grand vision for Vice Media's future is as unprofessional as its past: "We're trying not to be shitty" (quoted in Rose 2016).

Skivers and Strivers

Fate did not bring Stuart David and Stuart Murdoch together to form Belle and Sebastian; the Scottish band emerged out of the "botched capitalism" of 1990s Britain (Taylor 2004). Like most musicians of the time, David had been using unemployment benefit as an "unofficial artist's bursary in the absence of anything more legitimate" (2015, p.4). But in 1994 the Conservative government began to crack down on "abuses" of the welfare system, coercing long-term benefit claimants into training for work programs. David (2015, p.4) had been claiming for eight years—ever since his high school teacher taught him how to attend school and claim unemployment benefit—and knew he was on thin ice.

Initially resistant, David came round to the idea of joining a training program when he discovered Beatbox, a Glasgow-based music

industry course for out-of-work musicians. The idea of daily exposure to fellow artists and free access to a recording studio appealed
and the news that joining the course would "pay" him an additional
£10 per week benefits, plus travel allowance, only sweetened the deal.

Beatbox was botched capitalism in action. Housed in a warehouse
in Glasgow's Finnieston district—a decaying industrial area in the
west of the city—Beatbox only existed because its organizers could
not access government funding to set up their personal recording
studio without even using the space to run a training course for
unemployed musicians. An afterthought to the recording and promotion of bands the organizers managed, the course was a "total
shambles" recalls David, with "scores of unemployed musicians sitting around in a dark, airless labyrinth, doing nothing" (2015, p.10).
Regardless, David found a kindred spirit in the shy but stylized
Stuart Murdoch—a songwriter slowly getting back to normality
after spending years unable to work due to chronic fatigue syndrome. Bonding over a mutual dislike for blues music, machismo,
drugs, cigarettes and alcohol, the duo were soon performing at
open mic spots across the city and recording Murdoch's songs at
Beatbox.

The key to writing a great song is, according to Murdoch, "knowing what the song's about before you start" (quoted in David 2015,
p.43). The same approach extended to the creation of Belle and
Sebastian itself. This, unlike the making of most of bands, was an
unorthodox process of curation rather than creation. The band
existed in its own little universe, shaped as much by Murdoch's
ideals as his ideas. He was uninterested in putting together any old
band to secure a record contract. He wanted to assemble a group
of like-minded individuals who believed in his songs enough to
want to be part of Belle and Sebastian. Gradually, over the course
of a year, the imaginary band in Murdoch's head came together in
reality. Stevie Jackson (guitar) asked to join after seeing Murdoch
and David perform at an open mic show he compèred. Isobel
Campbell (cello) and Chris Geddes (keyboards) were persuaded to
join after chance social meetings with Murdoch. The final piece of
the puzzle was David's flatmate, Richard Colborn (drummer), who
had recently moved to Glasgow to study music business at Stow
College.

Every year, the students of Stow College's HND Music Business
course choose a local band and invite them to record a single.
The class then produce, release and promote the single under the
tutelage of Alan Rankine, 1980s new wave popstar turned record
producer. In 1996, the class chose Belle and Sebastian, offering

to fund five days of studio time to record a CD single that would be released and promoted by the college's record label, Electric Honey. True to form, where others would have snatched at the opportunity, Murdoch parlayed the offer into something better suited to his grand vision. Murdoch thought CDs were a commodity, so he insisted the single be released on vinyl. Then he dropped the bombshell that the band would not be recording a single but an entire album. Rankine was skeptical a whole album could be recorded in a week—if The Beatles could do it, so can we, was Murdoch's counter—but agreed to the demands (quoted by David 2015, p.98). He remarked that Murdoch's stubborn vision reminded him of his ex-bandmate in The Associates, the late, great, Billy McKenzie:

> *"Bill always knew what he wanted. Great artists usually do. You have to give them room to follow their vision."*

In March 1996, the band entered the legendary CaVa Sound studio in Glasgow's West End to record their debut album. Despite only playing one concert as a full band before this session, Murdoch's idealistic approach to sculpting his band—rather than forming any old band—created a unique chemistry. In David's words, a "slightly shambolic magic" enabled the band to record the 10 songs that would make up *Tigermilk* in just three days (2015, p.148).

Four months later at the same location, Electric Honey hosted a party to launch the album. A mixture of excited record executives, Glaswegian indie kids and curious art students were treated to a live performance from Belle and Sebastian and a free vinyl copy of *Tigermilk*. The next day, some of the less-appreciated complimentary copies began appearing in local charity shops for £1. But within months, the record would be changing hands for up to £850 as fans scrambled to get their hands on one of only 1,000 pressed copies (David 2015, p.199). In 1999, *Tigermilk* was rereleased on Jeepster Records to give the band's growing fanbase a chance to own it. Jeepster was a London-based independent label bankrolled, ironically, by the wealth of a stock market trader. Botched capitalism indeed.

Premature Incorporation

Simon Parkin argues that the all-too-rapid industrialization of games has robbed them of the kind of self-indulgent, experimental inception periods that provoked the cultural breadth and diversity of other artistic mediums. For games, "the cultural conversation has always been secondary to the industrial question: how do we monetize this?" (Parkin 2014).

Games *can* be as culturally enriching and credible as any work of music, literature, or cinema. Yet game makers censor themselves by prioritizing premature incorporation and fiscal sustainability ahead of curiosity and cultural expression. Starting a business should be the consequence of successful entrepreneurship and demonstrable market demand not a vain reaction to a vague idea. The opposite of play is work.

Steve Albini believes that bands starting out should accept that external assistance or intervention will not be forthcoming and consequently learn to make do with the raw materials and opportunities at hand. It is Albini's belief that if you're doing something pleasurable in its own right—singing, acting, painting, game making—you have to "expect that society will undercompensate you for that on a professional level" (Albini quoted by Friedman 2015). For every person that wants to be fully compensated, hundreds will willingly do it for nothing.

Operating as an artist who does business but does not believe their art owes them a living—as opposed to operating as a business who does art to make payroll—is liberating. Starting a band deals with the world as it is: game making does not owe you a living but it does allow you to explore your indulgences and express yourself on your own terms. But prematurely starting a business only sees the world as you would like it to be: your idea is amazing, its production will be flawless and everyone is going to instantly discover, love and buy it. It is worth quitting the day job for, going into debt for, even assuming fiscal responsibility for.

The world has enough games and professional game development studios. What it needs now is more dilettantes and delinquents questioning systemic assumptions, subverting institutions and building their own esoteric communities. Avoid premature incorporation; bureaucracy is always the enemy of creativity. Start a band, not a business.

Stop Just Making Stuff

"Any survivor of a Sixties art school will tell you that the idea of making a product was anathema. That meant commodification."

Malcolm McLaren (2008)

Objectified

At the end of 2016, there were more than 3 million active apps on the App Store and around 80% of them were free (Chapple 2016). Studies show that one in four people abandon a mobile app after just one use (O'Connell 2016). More stuff, less attention.

You have to ask yourself a question. Do you want to craft meaningful experiences or do you just want to make more stuff, more vapid products to toss into the digital landfill?

Are You Experienced?

Robert Hughes placed little financial or aesthetic value on the work of Jean-Michel Basquiat. Considered by many "the greatest art critic of our time" (Jones 2012), Hughes reckoned Basquiat to be not only limited in talent but complicit in his "manufactured" role as the "wild child ... curiosity ... noble urban savage" of the 1980s New York art scene (1988). For Hughes, the rise of Basquiat was the story of a "small, untrained talent caught in the buzzsaw of artworld promotion," elevated to absurdly overrated heights by the dealers, collectors and critics of the time. Basquiat's seed of unformed, unrefined talent required the "boot camp of four years in art school" to develop the "real drawing abilities ... disciplines and skills without which good art cannot be made" (Hughes 1988).

Following Basquiat's untimely death, Hughes (1988) wrote a thoughtful yet thought-provoking obituary, identifying the "cluster of toxic vulgarities" that, in his opinion, Basquiat's career appealed to:

"First, to the racist idea of the black as naif or as rhythmic innocent and to the idea of the black artist as 'instinctual,' outside 'mainstream' culture and therefore not to be judged by it: a wild pet for the recently cultivated white. Second, to a fetish about the infallible freshness of youth, blooming amid the discos of the Downtown Scene. Third, to an obsession with novelty— the husk of what used to be called the avant-garde, now only serving the need for new ephemeral models each year to stoke

the market. Fourth, to the slide of art criticism into promo-
tion and of art into fashion. Fifth, to the art-investment mania,
which abolished the time for reflection on a 'hot' artist's actual
merits; never were critics and collectors more scared of missing
the bus than in the early' 1980s. And sixth, to the audience's
goggling appetite for self-destructive talent (Pollock, Hendrix,
Montgomery Clift)."

All this "gunk," as Hughes (1988) framed it, "rolled into a sticky ball around Basquiat's tiny talent and produced a reputation."

Brian Eno likes the work of Robert Hughes and Jean-Michel Basquiat. In the essay *Miraculous Cures and the Canonisation of Basquiat*, Eno counters the opinion Hughes held of Basquiat, contemplating whether a narrow focus on the intrinsic value of Basquiat's paintings was the reason Hughes "doesn't get him at all?" (1996, p.366). Eno argues that criticisms put forward by Hughes were founded on three false assumptions: that Basquiat was performing the traditional, art-schooled role of artist; that the art world should not indulge in myth-making or conspire to construct "genius"; that Basquiat's co-conspiracy in such acts—"to project himself and make himself projectible [sic]"—is out of bounds for the artist (1996, p.366). But what if, Eno asks, the job of the artist is not to create venerated objects but to instead create situations where an audience can enjoy art experiences? Suppose that art is not defined by something inherently inside of "it," but instead, something that happens inside of "you" [the eager audience]? If this were true, then we should "stop thinking about art as objects and start thinking about them as triggers for experiences" (Eno 1996, p.368). Suddenly, Eno (1996, p.368) has given art and its inherent aesthetic value has a wholly different interpretation:

> The value of the work lies in the degree to which it can help
> you have the kind of experience that you call art. It is then
> possible, within the context of the right experiences, for a
> test tone to become a qualified musical experience. It is also
> possible for you to have quite different experiences from me,
> which says nothing about the test tone and everything about
> our separate perceptions of it, our different expectations and
> cultural predispositions. What we could then agree is that
> there is nothing absolute about the aesthetic value or non-
> value of a test tone and that we don't even have to consider
> the question of aesthetic value with a view to arriving at any
> single answer: it could have one value for you and another
> value for me and different ones for both of us at another time.
> It can change value for each of us. More interestingly, we can

also say that there is nothing absolute about the aesthetic value of a Rembrandt or a Mozart to a Basquiat.

By shifting attention from the intrinsic value of the object to the extrinsic value of the subjective experience, art becomes "something that happens," a process rather than a quality (Eno 1996, p.369). A process whereby the definition of art is diffuse and different: art experiences are triggered for different people by different art of all shapes, sizes and sensations:

> *"So I think there's a whole lot of things that we do which you might just call stylization. But what I want to persuade you is that they are actually part of this very broad definition of art as I'm using it. I made a list of things that I would put under that umbrella. Symphonies, perfume, sports cars, graffiti, needlepoint, monuments, tattoos, slang, Ming vases, doodles, poodles, apple strudels. Still life, Second Life, bed knobs and boob jobs.*
>
> *All of those things are sort of unnecessary in the sense that we could all survive without doing any of them, but in fact, we don't."*
>
> **Brian Eno**
> *BBC Music John Peel Lecture* (2015)

What then, does all of this have to do with making games? Well, it challenges us to think of games not as strictly defined objects but as triggers for experiences, little machines that "feed us sensations to keep us from the gloom of everyday existence" (Eno 1996, p.367).

What If …

Innovation is simultaneously everywhere and nowhere. As a word it has lost its meaning. As a practice it has lost its purpose. Anthropologist Grant McCracken suggests that corporate adoption of innovation has led to its domestication. Once-wild explorations have been tamed by the "tyranny of closed management" and the commodification of the "innovation economy" (2012, loc.109). Corporations have spent the past decade trying to make innovation systematic and processed, the unintended consequence of which has been the delivery of less genuine innovation, not more. To counter this creative stagnation, McCracken suggests a return to something "a little more practical and a lot more curious": the "culturematic" (2012, loc.105). In his book of the same name, McCracken describes culturematics as "a little machine for making culture ... designed to do three things: test the world, discover meaning and unleash value" (2012, loc.59). Rejecting the theater of corporate innovation, culturematics are cheap and cheerful experiments rather than precisely constructed prototype products or quantifiable initiatives. Designed to playfully provoke the world, culturematics start by asking: "What if...?" For example, by asking "What if I ate all my meals at McDonald's for a month?" documentary maker Morgan Spurlock created *Super Size Me*—an entertaining and affecting alternative to the dry academic studies into the nutritional impact of fast food. Similarly, by asking "What if I made my made my own content for *Saturday Night Live*?" Andy Samberg subverted a comedy institution (McCracken 2012, loc.165).

Typically, when a new comedian joins *Saturday Night Live* (*SNL*), they enter a ruthless production process where "no one invests so much as a second in something that might not work because the clock is ticking" (McCracken 2012, loc.71). Struggling for airtime, Samberg and *SNL* writers Akiva Schaffer and Jorma Taccone reached a conclusion that "some of these weirder concepts [rejected sketches] were things we just needed to film and present because that was the way to show people that it was potentially good" (Taccone quoted in Fox 2016). Borrowing a camera, Samberg, Schaffer and Taccone—longtime friends who wrote and performed under the name The Lonely Island—started writing, shooting and producing their own *SNL* Digital Shorts. On December 3, 2005, *SNL* premiered *Lettuce*, a surreal sketch starring Samberg and Will Forte that cost The Lonely Island just $20 to make (Fox 2016).

A culturematic probe is a value detection device that sometimes "phones home with data, sometimes with cash" (McCracken 2012, loc.195). In the case of The Lonely Island, the culturematic "phoned home" with Emmy wins, Grammy nominations and more than 1.7 billion views on YouTube (Fox 2016). By adopting a playful approach, The Lonely Island created a low-budget, high-value *SNL* laboratory where they could test the world, discover meaning and unleash value outside of the competitive, costly, time-sensitive production process of a live weekly television show. By assuming all of the creative and financial risks, they were able to gain enough leverage to probe "places and do things out of range of the *SNL* players [the ensemble cast]" (McCracken 2012, loc.70). As Schaffer (quoted in Fox 2016) explains:

> If we made a video for free on our own time and then it comes out badly, there's no embarrassment there. Whereas if we asked for a big budget and did it in the system and then it turned out stinky, maybe we'd never get another shot.

McCracken's culturematic framework is pure punk. It rejects the corporate template of betting big on the shiny singular idea and instead embraces curious exploration and naive DIY productions. Culturematics do not rely on market research or offer corporate certainty; they are neither functional nor innovative. Culturematics are just triggers for playful experiences, often-futile provocations of questionable utility that seek, as Eno might say, to "feed us sensations that keep us from the gloom of everyday existence" (1996, p.368).

Skål

In 2006, Mikkel Borg Bjergsø was a science teacher with a passion for the US craft beer scene and a dislike for the boring industrial beers of his Danish homeland. What if, Bjergsø wondered, he started releasing the beers he was brewing in his apartment?

His first release was *Beer Geek Breakfast,* an oatmeal stout brewed using a French-press coffee maker. The beer won international acclaim on the tasting circuit and brought Bjergsø's fledgling brewery, Mikkeller, to the attention of leading US craft beer distributors. Since that debut brew, Mikkeller has launched over 650 different beers and exported to more than 50 countries as part of Bjergsø's mission to "show people ... what beer can be and, for me, actually is" (2014).

Unlike most brewers, Mikkeller does not have its own brewery. As a "gypsy brewer" it carefully crafts its recipes then outsources actual brewing to other facilities around the world (Weiner 2014). Sidestepping the distraction of physical brewing allows Bjergsø to concentrate on pushing the boundaries of good taste with culturematic questions such as: What quality of fattiness would a beer obtain if you sprinkled popcorn into the mash? What would happen if you dumped a load of mouth-numbing Sichuan peppercorns in during brewing? How much fresh seaweed would lend a beer the right umami jolt? (Weiner 2014).

Possessing little commonality with the traditional beer industry and its industrially processed beers, Bjergsø draws inspiration from "people who have different ways of thinking about flavors and aromas. Winemakers, coffee-makers, chefs, other brewers" (quoted by Weiner 2014). And when a diversity of influence collides with outsourced brewing, happy accidents can occur. Due to a typographical error in Bjergsø's supplied recipe, one brewery ended up adding 100 times more vanilla sugar to a Mikkeller Imperial Stout. The result was 10,000 "spoiled" bottles that Bjergsø elected to release regardless. "People went crazy" for *Beer Geek Vanilla Shake*, which became one of Mikkeller's most popular ever beers (Bjergsø quoted by Weiner 2014). By delegating the rote production process, Mikkeller keeps overheads low, creating more space for serendipity and the freedom to pursue its self-sufficient, self-indulgent manifesto (2016):

WE AIM TO …
… brew beer that challenges the concept of good beer and moves people. We do this by using the best ingredients and work with the most talented and creative minds around the world.

… make quality beers a serious alternative to wine and champagne when having gourmet food.

WE FAIL TO …
… calm down. We are always thinking in new ways and ideas, always working on the next project. Sometimes it's hard for people to keep up…

… make beer that is watery and tasteless. In our world beer challenges people's taste buds – whether it's in a bitter, spicy, sour or fruity manner.

WE LOVE TO …
… explore the existing beer genres by using the best raw material available. The refined product is the aim – not to keep down costs. This leads to very special brews by Mikkeller: Stouts with Vietnamese Kopi Luwak coffee, chipotle chili, lychee fruits – just to name a few.

… cooperate with other breweries around the world, who inspires us and teach us new ways of doing things …

WE HATE TO …
…work with people that don't give a damn. There are so many wonderful, passionate and honest people in the beer world, why spend time on the rest?

The physical production process may be just a commodity to Bjergsø—"you can train a monkey to brew beer" he told the *New York Times*—but aesthetic value is not (quoted by Weiner 2014). Playful and iconic, Mikkeller succeeds in being "anomalously cool" in a sea of boring beer labels (Weiner 2014). Bjergsø understands that look, feel and storytelling are important contributors to the *experience* of beer: "never put a good beer in a bottle that looked bad … the beer wouldn't be good anymore" (quoted by Weiner 2014).

Reinventing Records

*"My role models are artists, merchants.
There's less than ten that I can name in history.
Truman. Ford. Hughes. Disney. Jobs. West."*

Kanye West
(quoted by Eleftheriou-Smith 2016)

"'Art is never finished, only abandoned' is an over-familiar phrase. Originally attributed to Leonardo da Vinci, it has been the subject of numerous cultural remixes through the ages:

A poem is never finished, only abandoned."

Paul Valéry
(quoted in Keyes 2006)

"Movies aren't finished, only abandoned."

David Fincher (2014)

"A painting is never finished, only abandoned."

Pablo Picasso
(quoted in Keyes 2006)

Each time, the underlying principle remains the same: perfection is an impossible goal; better to draw a line under your work and release it into the world. It's a sentiment we agree with, but what does such abandonment mean in a hyper-connected world?

The Life of Pablo was a watershed moment for Kanye West and the mainstream music industry, an "exemplar of modern celebrity music making," according to the *New York Times* (Caramanica 2016). West did not release his seventh album on February 14, 2016; he launched its first iteration and began probing the ongoing relevance and validity of the packaged product and the rigid release process. Describing the album as a "living breathing changing creative expression," West (2016) released two further iterations of *The Life of Pablo* within the first month of release, alongside warnings of more to come. Instead of abandoning his work, West turned it into a piece of emergent transmedia performance art, played out on Twitter, YouTube, Tidal, Spotify, Madison Square Garden, Saturday Night Live, Periscope and at pop-up fashion shows.

To claim, as *Pitchfork* did, that the record contained "no major state-ments, no reinventions, no zeitgeist wheelie-popping" as it emerged from its "protracted and often chaotic roll-out," is to view *The Life of Pablo* as a commodity instead of an ever-evolving experience (Greene 2016). Similarly, to label the record the "first SaaS" album, as *TechCrunch* did, or liken it to video game patching, like *Kill Screen*, exposes a similar lack of imagination (Tzuo 2016; Solberg 2016). *The Life of Pablo* is far from perfect; it is not West's best work and will likely never be. But to judge it by traditional measures ignores the theatrical experience West wrapped around it. At a point where the foundations of the mainstream music industry are crumbling, Kanye West challenges orthodoxy, probing what exactly it means to release a record and curating an experience in which, perhaps, the medium is the message.

Shit Happens

"We need to make games that people care about so much, they can't not play them."

Jonathan Blow (2006)

Entrepreneur Joshua Topolsky warns that gimmicks and token digitization will not save mainstream media organizations. Root problems, Topolsky suggests, are not solved by the superficial application of "bots, newsletters, a 'morning briefing' app, a 'lean back' iPad experience, Slack integration, a Snapchat channel, or a great partnership with Twitter" (2016). The media's tried-and-tested model built on the concept of scarcity and geographic local-ity is gone. No longer can a few conglomerates control the majority of what we read, watch, listen to and play. At the emergence of digital, media organizations ceded control to people who did not understand or have the best interests of media at heart. The result was a media actively trading quality of experience for quantity of eyeballs, a deliberate dilution undertaken in the belief that the prize was not to be the "best" of something, but to have the "most" of something.

This approach, Topolsky believes, is unsustainable in the long term. The "best and most important" media is not made to reach the "*most* people … [but] made to reach the *right* people" (Topolsky 2016). For all our faults Topolsky argues, we are humans not "content con-sumption machines," and the current uncertain landscape repre-sents an "incredible opportunity for the smart people in media to hit the reset button and start doing interesting things for discernable audiences again" (2016). Whether that is achieved through brewing coffee-flavored beers in your kitchen, filming $20 comedy sketches, or cultivating the myth of genius around your "tiny talent," it is clear there is a ready and willing discernable audience waiting impatiently for experiences to be triggered. Your choice is either to go and delight them, or to continue to shovel shit to the always-distracted, ever-decreasing masses.

> *"Your problem is that you make shit. A lot of shit. Cheap shit. And no one cares about you or your cheap shit. And an increasingly aware, connected and mutable audience is onto your cheap shit. They don't want your cheap shit. They want the good shit. And they will go to find it somewhere. Hell, they'll even pay for it."*

> **Joshua Topolsky**
> *Your Media Business Will Not Be Saved* (2016)

FIGURE 3.3   Author Chris Lowthorpe enjoys a beer in Mikkeller Bar, Copenhagen. (Reprinted with permission from Chris Lowthorpe.)

The Work of Play in the Age of Digital Reproduction

"Gifts must affect the receiver to the point of shock."

Walter Benjamin (2009)

The Rational Anthem

In sociology, *rationalization* refers to the process of replacing societal traditions, customs and emotions as behavioral motivators with efficiency, predictability and calculation. Rooted in Max Weber's 1905 essay collection, *The Protestant Ethic and the Spirit of Capitalism*, the most visible manifestations of rationalization are seen in the rise of 20th century industrialization and bureaucracy.

A more contemporary term is "McDonaldization," coined by sociologist George Ritzer to not only describe a pervasive, rationalized fast-food culture but also the homogeneity of globalization. Ritzer (n.d.) identified four pillars of McDonaldization: efficiency, the optimization of process, time and human capital; calculability, the objective quantification of sales and services performance; predictability, the consistent and formal application of discipline, order, systemization, routine and methodology; and control, the standardization and automation of practice, process and product.

They Call Me the Seeker

Economist David Galenson identifies two types of artistic innovator: conceptual and experimental. Conceptual innovators are "finders," working with methodical certainty toward their goal with a "clarity of intent and confidence in their ability" (Galenson 2004). In contrast, experimental innovators are "seekers," who, Galenson notes, are characterized by "persistent uncertainty about their methods and goals" and an inherent, unarticulated dissatisfaction with their work (2004). It is this uncertainty and dissatisfaction that provokes experimental innovators to explore and probe their way toward their imperfectly perceived objectives, embracing trial, error and serendipitous discovery as they go.

We all like to think of ourselves as conceptual innovators, bringing sparks of genius to life with methodical precision. But the truth is that most of us just aren't that talented. Conceptual innovators—such as Pablo Picasso, F Scott Fitzgerald, Bob Dylan, Orson Welles and TS Eliot (Galenson 2010)—are the outliers. The rest of us must accept the complexities and frustrations of inefficient, inconsistent, imperfect experimentation.

We do not do enough to debunk the myth of conceptual innovation within game making. We fetishize stories of inspired genius and bury the ugly truth of uncertainty and experimentation. From the outside, *Portal* looks, feels and plays like a work of genius, an experience like no other that is so tight, refined and wonderfully articulated. In truth, the making of this masterpiece was considerably more uncertain, serendipitous and iterative.

Before *Portal* came its predecessor, *Narbacular Drop*, a senior-year game project from a team of students attending DigiPen Institute of Technology. The team—led by designer Kim Swift—set out to create an experience that was simple yet unique. Simple because the team understood through previous projects that "there are never enough hours in a day to do what you'd like" (Barnett et al. 2008). Unique because every member of the student team needed an attention-grabbing game to put on their resumes. And grab attention it did. Valve hired the team to remake the game using their *Source* engine just 15 minutes into a demo for Gabe Newell.

Very quickly after joining Valve, the team were introduced to and immersed in, a culture of play-testing and iterative design. Where *Narbacular Drop* had followed a linear development process that reserved play-testing for the final month of development, *Portal* adopted play-testing as a regular habit. From the very first week of development, Swift and her team used play-testing as a means of challenging perceived progress and questioning their conceptual design assumptions. The insights and observations gathered in play-tests fueled sprints of rapid iteration, which in turn created the context for the next round of play-testing.

A particular highlight of *Portal* was its innovative approach to narrative. Through GLaDOS—"part instructor, part antagonist, total fruit-loop" (Bramwell 2007)—*Portal* demonstrated that less narrative could be more. The game rejected exposition for a more subtle, sophisticated brand of storytelling closer to Marshall McLuhan's notion of "cool" media: turning the audience into an active constituent of the experience, responsible for filling in the gaps themselves. This approach is all the more interesting because too often games typecast themselves as McLuhan's "hot" media: reducing audience participation in the story by feeding them a high definition, high exposition narrative (McLuhan 1969).

But the creation of GLaDOS was not inspired genius. It was the result of exploration, iteration and constraint. Through play-testing it became apparent that *Portal* was "a little dry" and in need of more "flavor and ... entertaining narrative" (Barnett et al. 2008). The orthodox response would have been to add more nonplayable characters and cut-scenes, but the team had neither the time or resources for such "an impressive amount of animation work and scene choreography" (Barnett et al. 2008). Instead, they enlisted Valve staff writer Erik Wolpaw (*Psychonauts*, *Half-Life 2*) to construct a compelling narrative through audio alone. Just a week later, Wolpaw returned with prototype sample dialog recorded using a simple text-to-speech program (Barnett et al. 2008):

> It was a series of announcements that played over the newly-christened "relaxation vault" that appears in *Portal's* first room. Everyone on the team liked the funny, sinister tone of the writing and so Erik continued to write and record announcements for other chambers, while still searching for the story proper.

During testing, it became apparent these announcements were not only incentivizing player progression but providing entertainment and amusement. What was intended as a short-term placeholder solution was, in fact, the narrative voice *Portal* had been seeking all along. By juxtaposing the sterile environments and logical problem-solving with a surprising, playful narrative, much-needed personality had been injected into the experience (Barnett et al. 2008):

> The guide, now named GLaDOS, would simply talk to players throughout their experience—praising them, taunting them and, whenever possible, trying to make them feel guilty for the nonstop acts of defiance and mayhem that game players are conditioned to commit routinely in game environments.

> Our hope was that by the end of the *Portal*, players would know GLaDOS better than any boss monster in the history of gaming. Though we knew at some point the player would have to meet and destroy her, we thought it would be even more satisfying if players got a chance to cause her some emotional pain along the way.

Oscillate Wildly

Powers of Ten takes us on a mesmerizing journey through scale and shifting perspectives. This classic short film by Charles and Ray Eames illustrates the universe "as an arena for both continuity and change, of everyday picnics and cosmic mystery" (Eames Office 2013). Beginning with a closeup shot of a picnic in a Chicago park, the camera steadily moves out to reveal the edge of the known universe and then back toward Earth, eventually down to molecular level in the hand of a man sleeping at the picnic. Selected for preservation by the Library of Congress for being "culturally, historically, or aesthetically significant," *Powers of Ten* is a simple yet compelling illustration of the power of scale and perspective (Eames Office 2013). It is also completely unrelated but perfectly illustrative of how shifting scales and perspectives can inform game making.

Too often game makers are distracted by the design detail of the product to the detriment of the experience's wider cultural context. As Dan Hill (2012, loc.432) explains in *Dark Matter and Trojan Horses: A Strategic Design Vocabulary*, there is a need for designers to continually shift perspectives, to "deliver definition of and insight into, the question as much as the solution, the context as much as the artefact, service or product." Hill labels the context "the meta" and the artifact "the matter." He urges continual oscillation between the two. That *Portal* emerged from the deliberate practice of such emergent and contextual iteration is unsurprising. As a company, Valve places a cultural premium on "highly collaborative people" with the capability to "deconstruct problems on the fly and talk to others as they do so, simultaneously being inventive, iterative, creative, talkative and reactive" (Valve 2012). Purposeful innovation does not occur in a vacuum. It is an ongoing dialog between the maker and the player, an ever-shifting perspective focusing upon both the matter—and its necessary attention to detail—and the meta: the wider cultural context.

Delicious

Cooking in front of customers changed the way David Chang looked at food. Short on money and space in its formative years, Chang's Momofuku Noodle Bar had an open kitchen that meant Chang spent his days not only cooking for his diners but watching them experience his food. Because of this he instantly knew what worked and what did not and would be reimagining and remixing his food every day in search of great dishes.

What is a great dish? For Chang (2016), it "hits you like a Whip-It: there's a momentary elation, a brief ripple of pure pleasure in the spacetime continuum." The first dish to consistently taste this delicious was his Momofuku pork bun. A "slapped together" impromptu addition to the menu, the dish saw Chang take some pork belly, top it with hoisin sauce, scallions and cucumber and put it all inside some steamed bread. It was Chang's interpretation of Peking duck buns and was an instant hit: "People went crazy for them. Their faces melted. Word spread and soon people were lining up for these buns" (2016).

A mediocre cook but a brilliant chef, Chang compensates for his lack of rational technique or conceptual genius with a genuine love of food, a sense of purpose and an innate curiosity that extends beyond the monocultural boundaries of haute cuisine. It is this curiosity that led him to his "unified theory of deliciousness"—a riff on Douglas R Hofstadter's theory of strange loops—a mathematical notion of systems that "shift from one level of abstraction (or structure) to another" before they unexpectedly fold back upon themselves, despite feeling like they are "departing ever further from one's origin" (Hofstadter 2007, pp.101–102). A strange loop provokes a *Powers of Ten*-like journey of shifting scales and perspectives. And for Chang, his unified theory of deliciousness contextualizes that journey: delivering taste sensations to the diner in the moment while simultaneously, unexpectedly, transporting them back to a past experience or emotion. This deliciousness can be easily achieved by serving up something explicitly nostalgic, but Chang argues what separates "good dishes from the truly slap-yourself-on-the-forehead ones" is the ability to evoke this sort of sensation with a dish that looks and smells different but tastes overwhelmingly familiar. That is his—delicious—strange loop. In the case of the Momofuku pork bun, Chang took the American love of the BLT sandwich and filtered it through his love and understanding of Peking duck buns to create something seemingly exotic and unknown yet completely familiar and comforting to the Western palate. Steamed bread + fatty meat + cool crunch = transcultural blockbuster (Chang 2016).

Cultural Consumption

The answer to the needlessly complicated question of what we should eat is, in fact, so simple Michael Pollan (2009, loc.108) believes it can be explained in seven words:

Eat food. Not too much. Mostly plants.

A food journalist, Pollan came to this realization while researching his 2008 book, *In Defense of Food*. In the follow-up, *Food Rules*,

Pollan states (2009, loc.80) there are only three things you need to know about diet and nutrition:

1. Populations that eat a "Western diet"—lots of processed "foods," additive fats and sugars and refined (modified) grains—are more likely to suffer from "Western diseases" like type 2 diabetes, obesity and cancer.
2. Populations that eat a culturally contextual, natural diet—regardless of geographic location or nutritional composition—are much less likely to suffer from chronic diseases.
3. Those who quit the industrialized Western diet see dramatic health improvements.

But if it is that simple, why has this harmful industrial rationalization of our diet been allowed to happen? Because it is more efficient, argues Pollan, "the more you process any food, the more profitable it becomes" (2009, loc.105). By way of demonstration, Pollan (2009, loc.459) highlights that it was not until "industry took over the jobs of washing, peeling, cutting and frying the potatoes—and cleaning up the mess" that the French fry achieved ubiquity.

Food Rules presents 64 simple guiding principles for eating healthy and happily. For example, rule number 19 states: "If it came from a plant, eat it; if it was made in a plant, don't." This principle helps make a case for eating as a cultural experience, rather than the efficient consumption of "industrial novelties" and heavily processed "edible food-like substances" (Pollan 2009, loc.142). In the latter part of the book, Pollan develops the theory that "why" and "how" you eat—the unspoken rituals that govern a person's (and a culture's) relationship with food and eating—have as much bearing on your health as "what" you eat. To illustrate the point, Pollan cites the French paradox: the nutritional mystery of a population that consumes "all sorts of fatty foods and washes them down with red wine" but is "healthier, slimmer and slightly longer lived" than consumers of a typical Western diet (2009, loc.524). For the French, Pollan argues, eating is not a rational necessity but a cultural experience consisting of languid communal meals, small portions, small plates, no second helpings and no snacking. No doubt Pollan's rule 43 (2009, loc.508) also helps: "Have a glass of wine with dinner."

A Certain Ratio

Formed in resistance to the opening of Italy's first McDonald's, the Slow Food movement is a literal reaction to McDonaldization. A self-styled "avant-garde's riposte" to the industrialized "fast life," the movement seeks to shift society away from the fast-food culture it has become accustomed to with the promotion of three interconnected principles: good—quality, flavorsome and healthy food; clean—production that does not harm the environment; fair—accessible prices for consumers and fair conditions and pay for producers.

In the original *Slow Food Manifesto* (1989), the movement argued that producing food must be considered a gastronomic act. Extending this notion to game making begs the question: what if we considered producing games to be a playful act, as opposed to a rational procedure? How would such a contextual shift reframe the process of game making? Would efficiency remain a worthy pursuit? Would iteration become a natural consequence of deliberate co-creation? Would we still feel compelled to make rationalized games instead of delicious playthings?

Experiences such as *Monument Valley*, *Dear Esther*, *Threes*, *Hotline Miami* and *Journey* provide a glimpse of an answer. With more in common than simply being case studies in this book, each embodies an alternative way of making and selling games in the postindustrial era by:

- Starting out with bold, visionary ideals but much looser ideas of how exactly the experience would look, sound and feel
- Rejecting mainstream conformity for something more experiential
- Embarking on an inefficient but highly effective journey of experimental innovation
- Using iteration to craft a holistic experience that obsessed as much about the wider cultural context as it did its attention to design detail
- Developing their own theory of deliciousness that confounds expectations and provokes playful, perspective-shifting experiences that resonate deeper than the average game.

Threes: A Case Study in Itinerant Iteration

In early December 2012, Asher Vollmer, *Puzzlejuice* creator and University of Southern California alumnus, opened up Microsoft Word and began writing a story. But the page remained blank; he just couldn't get the words out. Frustrated—"it didn't come easy to me, which was annoying because games have always come easy to me" (Volmer quoted by Kerr 2014)—he began playing with the arrow keys on the keyboard and watching the cursor move around the screen.

Inspired by this simple, playful interaction, Volmer prototyped *Threes* the same night and shared it with his *Puzzlejuice* collaborator, Greg Wohlwend. Provoked into action, Wohlwend began visualizing how this simple yet delightful functional prototype could look and feel as an iPhone game. Within a day, Volmer and Wohlwend had captured the substance (core gameplay) and style (visual look and feel) of *Threes*. In their own words, they were "fairly close to the final product" (Vollmer and Wohlwend 2014).

So, why did it take them another 423 days to release the game? And even longer to curate the experience in a way that appealed to the widest possible audience?

The Long, Hard, Stupid Way

Designer and illustrator Frank Chimero (2011) speaks of the surprisingly difficult time he had writing his first book and his attempts to turn this struggle into a positive lesson instead of "a thing to be down about." To illustrate, Chimero references a scene in the HBO show *Treme* where David Chang—playing himself in a cameo role—criticizes his Momofuku sous-chef for trying to cut a corner, telling him: "We don't work like that here. We do things the long, hard, stupid way" (quoted by Chimero 2011).

In other words: we don't optimize for efficiency; we do whatever it takes to communicate the intended experience best. Chimero (2011) explains:

> I think that, from the perspective of someone who makes things—and I bet that a lot of people out there are also folks who make things in some capacity—when you work the long, hard, stupid way, it looks a lot like toiling and worrying and starting over and scratching good ideas to look for better ones. It's staying up late; it's waking up early; it's all of those

sort of romanticized things. All of those actions are inspired by just caring a lot. That's not to say that you can't be efficient and care about your work: I think that's totally possible. But I don't know how to do that, because I have to do things the long, hard, stupid way.

Propelled by the progress of its first 24 hours, *Threes* set off on its own long, hard, stupid way. Vollmer's original prototype was—unapologetically—a slide puzzle with numbers. Over the next year, its simplicity was diluted with gameplay features such as holes, mouths, flags, planets, atoms, arrows and walls (Vanhemert 2014). At the same time, its elegance was obfuscated by contrived visual metaphors that saw the numbers replaced with rolls of sushi, broccoli and "The Argoyles," argyle-patterned monsters who fed off number tiles (Vanhemert 2014).

Vollmer and Wohlwend were always searching for that one thing to enrich an experience that was engaging in the moment but lacking the timeless "easy to learn, a lifetime to master" quality of a great puzzle game. This search proved challenging and other commitments—coupled with diminishing iteration returns—slowed momentum. Three months after the highs of the first prototype, weighed down with extra rules, features and noise, Vollmer concluded "*Threes*, in its current state, is not worth releasing" (Vollmer and Wohlwend 2014). The project was put on hold indefinitely and lay abandoned for the next four months.

In June 2013, Vollmer was sitting in a coffee shop when he had a random thought: "What if you're just combining/upgrading Argoyles?" (quoted by Vanhemert 2014). This breakthrough—later known as "merge mode"—stripped the game back to its playful core: slide the like-numbered tiles together to combine. Repeat for high score. By stripping away all of the extraneous details accrued over months of experimentation, Vollmer had stumbled upon a game that was even simpler, tighter, purer, more intuitive than his original prototype. He had found *Threes* as we know it today: a tiny game that you can "play over and over again and constantly get better at" (quoted by Vanhemert 2014).

This newfound simplicity and clarity of purpose came at a significant cost to the charm and character of the experience. Wohlwend found it "soulless" (Vollmer and Wohlwend 2014). Stubbornly, the duo wanted to deliver a game with "more personality than just numbers" and was determined to make the monsters work (Vollmer and Wohlwend 2014). Instinctively, Wohlwend believed the game needed warmth and charm to "balance out the harshness of the rules and gameplay mechanics," yet the pair struggled to find the right balance between visual form—monsters—and visual function—merge mode (Vollmer and Wohlwend 2014). If players could not read the numbers on the tiles, then the game was unplayable. But Wohlwend could not find the elusive harmony between personality and legibility.

You've Got a Friend in Me

Months passed before Zach Gage—Wohlwend's *Ridiculous Fishing* collaborator and early *Threes* champion—prompted the visual breakthrough (Vollmer and Wohlwend 2014). Why, Gage wondered, did the personality of the monsters and the legibility of the numbers have to compete against each other on the tile face? What if the monsters were displayed on the bottom edge of the tile, freeing up the tile's face to display its number? After months of wrong turns and dead ends, Gage's fresh perspective proved the key to balancing form and function. This subtle yet significant breakthrough enabled Wohlwend to hone in on the final—now iconic—look and feel of *Threes* in a couple of days. After almost a year of hard work—and harder thinking—*Threes* had mutated into the game Vollmer and Wohlwend had always been—sometimes unknowingly—striving for. They were almost there. Almost ...

In early December 2013, Adam Saltsman (*Canabalt*) identified an exploit. Employing a "corner strategy"—exploiting the corners of the game board to cheat the game system—Saltsman could achieve ridiculously high scores with little thought or effort. It was a fringe strategy but nevertheless a design flaw that undermined the game's potential for meaningful strategy and mastery. After brainstorming with Wohlwend, Saltsman and Gage, Vollmer was able to patch the exploit by "finding the delicate balance between randomness and the tools the players have to mitigate it" (quoted by Vanhemert 2014).

The importance of negating the corner strategy would only become apparent in the months after release. For now, with this final tweak, *Threes* had arrived at a "beautiful place" (Vollmer quoted by Vanhemert 2014). Less than two months later, 423 long days after the initial prototype, *Threes*—"the perfect mobile game ... one of the most elegantly designed games since *Tetris*" according to Ken Wong (quoted by Dormehl 2014)—was unleashed upon the public.

Subtraction and Sensibilities

Upon release, *Eurogamer* compared *Threes* to "one of those hipster restaurants ... delightful food ... terrifyingly smug surroundings" (Sorrell 2014). In an otherwise glowing review, it criticized the game for its "inevitable" and "profoundly and offensively banal" aesthetic (Sorrell 2014).

From the outside, it's an easy—if lazy—assumption to make. Even Wohlwend admits, "it looks like the entire time we were striving for simplicity and minimalism" (quoted by Kuchera 2014). But the truth was very different. For the majority of the game's production, Vollmer and Wohlwend rejected simplicity and minimalism and aimed for something grander. It was not the makers but *Threes* itself that resisted complexity, determined to be nothing more than a "cold mathematical brain game" (Vollmer quoted by Webster 2014). As Vollmer (quoted by Kuchera 2014) explained when discussing *Threes* release with *Polygon*:

> Every time I added anything like that [new concepts, new mechanics, new themes], it always felt unwieldy and unnatural. It just didn't want to be there. Every time I took that stuff out it felt like a good game again.

This tension between the game and its makers is what makes *Threes* so expressive, comfortable and confident in its skin. When Vollmer and Wohlwend finally accepted *Threes* for what it was, they did so with a tremendous clarity of purpose. To get to their desired destination, they had taken an extremely long, hard, stupid way. Vollmer himself admits that he would not have been confident enough to craft *Threes* as we know it "with just a week of working on it" (quoted by Kuchera 2014).

It's Ain't What You Do (It's the Way that You Do It)

In the preface to *How Music Works*, David Byrne (2012, loc.54) discusses how the same piece of music can be either "an annoying intrusion, abrasive and assaulting, or you could find yourself dancing to it." For Byrne, it all depends on "where you hear it—in a concert hall or on the street—or what the intention is." The colliding actions, interactions and reactions of the artist, audience, venue, medium and mood not only determine if a piece of music delivers in its intention but "what it is" (Byrne 2012, loc.56).

The same theory can be applied to games. A playful experience is not defined solely by play itself but by the curated microcosm it exists within: How is it distributed and sold? Who is it for? How should it make them feel? Where should they experience it? How should they perform? What will they see and hear? How will they feel? Is it a solo or collective experience?

Typically, game makers avoid such hard questions, rejecting deliberate curation for the familiar "make first, think later" approach. That's why many gaming experiences feel disjointed and underwhelming within the context they are experienced. It speaks to the courage and conviction of Vollmer and Wohlwend that *Threes*—the experience rather than the "packaged product"—and all its contributing inputs and outputs were a constant consideration throughout development.

Soon after the launch of *Threes*, Greg Wohlwend (2014) wrote a short essay lamenting that a lot of independent game makers use their dislike of marketing—"a bad word and a shitty thing"—to abdicate all responsibility for connecting with and selling to their intended audience. Dismissing the use of traditional marketing and disconnected marketing specialists to raise awareness—"old and weird and they don't work for us anyhow"—Wohlwend encouraged makers to start *showing* their work—and stories of how this work came to be—as an extension of *doing* their work.

For *Threes*, Vollmer and Wohlwend searched for the single sentence that would perfectly describe the game—that is, "a tiny puzzle that you can play forever"—for eight months. They agonized over every screenshot, icon, tagline and tutorial for aesthetic context. According to Wohlwend (2014), such decisions were afforded as much energy and attention as making the game itself and the result was they "managed to make our game that much richer outside of the space it resides in." In 2015, Vollmer (Vollmer and Wohlwend 2015) elaborated on this process:

> To spread the word about Threes! we kept everything small … That's essentially all we do, though we do it with a lot of heart and thought:
>
> - The emails that we send out to people had our custom animated gif explaining the game (you can see it on our Threesgame.com website).
> - The website that we put together went through about 5 revisions.
> - The tagline "a tiny game you can play forever" went through hundreds of revisions. We were changing it from the time we decided on Threes! as a name (about 6? months before launch) until the night before launch.

We kept things small and understated. Not adding too many messages, reviews or images. Nothing flashy. Just Threes!. It's tiny. So we stuck to that and stayed true to it.

Attack of the Clones

Just 21 days after *Threes* was released, a game called *1024* appeared. The same tactile interface, game mechanics and visual minimalism that characterized *Threes* were all present. There were some subtle differences—superficial oversimplifications and misinterpretations—but it was undoubtedly a clone. It was also "not very fun" in the opinion of Vollmer and Wohlwend (2014).

Shortly after, *2048* appeared, an iteration of *1024*. Freely available and open source, *2048* quickly gained mainstream popularity. In its first two months, more than 23 million people would play the game (Cirulli 2014). Initially, many people used the *2048* source code to create "throwaway" remixes. As a pop culture project, it was fascinating, spawning weird and wonderful mutations such as *Numberwang 2048*, *Large Hadron Collider 2048* and *Tetris 2048*. All flippant, fun, playful memes. But the spirit of the commons soon gave way to commerce. Soon app stores were flooded with *2048* clones and straight-up counterfeit versions of *Threes*, all carrying their own monetization model, typically in-app advertising or microtransactions. One counterfeit product even launched six days before *Threes* on the Google Play Store, causing *Threes* to be later dismissed by players as a clone of *2048*. For Vollmer and Wohlwend, "that all stung pretty bad" (2014).

Subsequently, Vollmer and Wohlwend (2014) have spoken of their concern that due to the speed of counterfeiting today, "it seems tiny games like *Threes* are destined to be lost in the underbrush of copycats, me-toos and iterators." A pessimistic view that, perhaps, ignores the unfair competitive advantage that mitigated the impact *2048* had on *Threes* and its long-term position. *Threes* is an experience with an aesthetic confidence and context, designed for a very discerning audience. It was a beautiful, lovingly crafted "gift" for its audience, as Frank Chimero would say. Where *2048* is easily beatable due to the presence of the aforementioned "corner strategy" exploit, *Threes* carries an unmatched level of personality and potential for mastery. *2048* is a dumbed-down derivative that did not take the long, hard, stupid road; as a result, it severely lacks contextual awareness. By taking the shortcut, its creator had no way of knowing the thousands of tiny decisions that gave *Threes* its simple veneer, hidden depth and timeless quality of experience.

Frees!

The stellar success of *2048* left a bitter taste in the mouths of Vollmer and Wohlwend. Not only because it could not exist without *Threes*—and all of the inspiration, energy and iteration that went into making it—but also because it served as "a constant, overwhelming reminder of our mistake" (Vollmer and Wohlwend 2015). Confounding their own modest expectations, *Threes* was a stellar success. In the year following its release, the game won numerous awards and was downloaded more than a million times. No mean feat for a $2.99 paid app in the App Store. But successful as *Threes* was, there was the inescapable feeling that it had not fulfilled its potential. For Vollmer, the greater success of their "bastard offspring" exposed the "potential for *Threes* and the potential audience and how big it could be" (quoted by Cameron 2015). Being behind a paywall had the greatest impact on audience size for both *Threes* ($2.99) and *2048* (free); it was the critical factor that "allowed *2048* to eat our lunch" (Vollmer and Wohlwend 2015).

Despite the download disparity, Vollmer believed *Threes* to be the better experience: "the original, the best and the game that will stick" (Webster 2015). The challenge was to figure out how best to find the "right solution for how to bring *Threes* to a wider audience" in a free-to-play model that upheld its style and sensibilities rather than just copied the banner advertising model of *2048* (Vollmer quoted by Webster 2015).

Along with its brilliant gameplay and beautiful style, a significant part of the game's appeal amongt Apple connoisseurs like John Gruber was that it had "no in-app purchase shenanigans" (Gruber 2014). The challenge Vollmer and Wohlwend faced was how to set *Threes* free without cheapening the aesthetic or undermining the experience they had worked so long and hard to establish. Vollmer considered a lot of traditional free-to-play games to be "super toxic," encouraging players to avoid supporting or respecting the makers of the games they play (quoted by Webster 2015). At the other end of the spectrum, he felt games that tried to pursue an ethical free-to-play model failed because they gave too much of their experience away for free.

To deliver the nicest possible free-to-play experience for *Threes*, both in-app purchases and banner ads were explored then discarded because they represented "the worst experience ... cheap" (Vollmer quoted by Cameron 2015). In the end, Vollmer elected to remix one of oldest free-to-play models around: "you earn credits by watching [video] ads and then spend them on rounds of *Threes*, sort of like an arcade machine" (quoted by Webster 2015).

One month after the release of *Threes Free*, the game had doubled its daily income and once again iterated itself toward success (Vollmer 2015). For Vollmer (quoted by Cameron 2015), it was a victory for the craftsman over the copycat:

> I would like [mobile game development] to get nicer and less antagonistic. The incredibly positive response that we've received makes it very clear that players are aware of how terrible most of these models are, even if they still generate a lot of money for a lot of people. Players are now becoming more educated about how bad that could be. The more we pursue player positive revenue models, the more people will be happy to engage with it and the better it will be for the industry as a whole.

Punk Provocations

- What if you stopped indulging yourself and listened to what your game wanted instead?
- What if you stripped your game back to its first playful principles?
- What single adjective describes the experience you're trying to create?

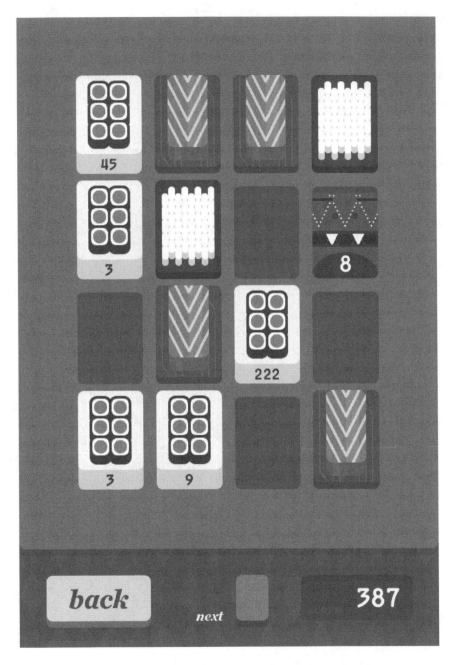

FIGURE 3.4 Sushi-themed tiles mock-up from the development of *Threes*. **(Courtesy of Greg Wohlwend,** *Threes Artist*, **https://commons. wikimedia.org/wiki/File%3AThrees_development_process_art_ mockup_10.png.)**

FIGURE 3.5   Final version, with tiny faces beneath the tiles, mock-up from the development of *Threes*. (Courtesy of Greg Wohlwend, *Threes Artist*,   https://commons.wikimedia.org/wiki/File%3AThrees_development_process_art_mockup_26.png.)

Dear Esther: A Case Study in Challenging Assumptions

When a professor usually receives a speculative research grant from the UK Arts & Humanities Research Council, the assumption is that their findings will be captured in a dry academic paper. Dan Pinchbeck made a game.

Dear Esther—the game—is a provocative story about love, loss, guilt and redemption.

Dear Esther—the production—is a provocative story about challenging assumptions of what games are, how they are made and who can make them.

What if ...

In *Dear Esther*, Pinchbeck explored both the limits and the limitations of the first-person shooter (FPS) genre. In a medium dominated by descriptive, procedural storytelling, how would a game feel if its story made no logical sense? In a genre characterized by twitch mechanics and visceral machismo, how would a FPS feel when stripped of its understood gameplay loops and preconceptions (Briscoe and Pinchbeck 2012a)?

Storytelling in games can be heavy on exposition; gamers expect everything to immediately make sense and makers are only too happy to explain. Such conservatism, in Pinchbeck's opinion (Briscoe and Pinchbeck 2012b), consistently reduces story to the "weakest point of the game":

> It's really quite an artificial thing. If you look at other art forms, if you look at something like a Jackson Pollock painting, it's not important which paint dribble came first or which order you should be looking at; it's just a whole experience.

Do It Yourself

Games research raises questions that usually "fall outside the kinds of media produced by the industry" (Pinchbeck 2008). Consequently, researchers have two choices: "discuss these questions theoretically" or "take advantage of the rich culture of modding and availability of game engines and try and build media ourselves to tackle them" (Pinchbeck 2008). Dan Pinchbeck chose the latter approach—labelling it "development-led research"—and set about creating a *Half-Life 2* mod. Keenly aware of the research team's "lack of skills and know-how in terms of the reality of making games," Pinchbeck (2014b) felt the hobbyist, remix-like approach of modding would allow his team to bypass technical distraction and focus on the storytelling experience. And the DIY ethic went beyond self-awareness and tools of choice. Rather than jump straight into working inside *Source*—Valve's *Half-Life 2* engine used by the modding community—the first design of *Dear Esther's* Hebridean island was simply a "massive lump of clay on a desk in a disused University office" that Pinchbeck carved paths and bored tunnels in to figure out the experience (Pinchbeck 2014a). Music would play a significant part in the storytelling experience, so Pinchbeck enlisted longtime collaborator Jessica Curry to score *Dear Esther*. Rather than retrofit the soundtrack at the end of development, Curry wrote parts of the score at the very outset; these tracks were then used to inspire and inform prototyping, design and storytelling (Pinchbeck 2014a).

Dear Esther's story is deliberately cryptic. Influenced by William S Burroughs, Pinchbeck wanted players to be intrigued and immersed within an emotional experience, not engaged in a literal, linear one. To subvert the assumptions of an FPS the game was stripped of explicit interactivity, forcing the players to immerse themselves in the environment and experience rather than directly play with it. The result is a "game" where the only (implicit) objective is to "explore a Hebridean Island, listening to a troubled man read a series of letters to a woman named Esther" (Wikipedia 2016). No tasks, no puzzles, no sense of progression, no rewards. Most importantly, no fun.

> *"If you're looking for fun—I've no idea why you're playing Dear Esther in the first place."*
>
> **Lewis Denby**
> *Touched By the Hand of Mod: Dear Esther* (2009)

Writing in *Rock, Paper, Shotgun*, Lewis Denby praised *Dear Esther* for exploring an emotion "few games dare to touch"—unhappiness—and challenging a gaming monoculture that had become "a little too comfortable with enjoying everything we play" (2009).

Who Remixes the Remix?

The release of *Dear Esther* inspired longtime modder Rob Briscoe. An environment artist at EA DICE, Briscoe (2009) had just shipped *Mirror's Edge* and was looking for a hobby project to occupy the six-month sabbatical he had planned to recover from the "crazy burnout" of an 18-month AAA crunch. As well as exhaustion, working on *Mirror's Edge* had "spawned some interesting ideas about how environmental design could be used to tell a story" and to "connect to the player on an emotional level" (Briscoe 2012a).

Briscoe (2009) likened the original rendition of *Dear Esther* to an "interactive painting or story" rather than *just* another game but felt the environment art detracted from the immersive experience. This was a weakness that—with his *Source* engine experience, passion for the modding community, AAA production standards and desire to tell stories through environmental design—Briscoe (2012a) was uniquely positioned to address:

> I realized that this was the perfect side-project for me; with an overhaul of the visuals and some polish to the design it could be something really special and it would also allow me to experiment with all of the ideas I'd had stewing in my head.

Briscoe's intention was to take the groundwork of the original rendition and remake it as a fully fledged, production-quality mod, a notion that Dan Pinchbeck was fully supportive of when Briscoe pitched the idea.

The Long and Winding Road

Briscoe initially estimated it would take only a matter of months to remake *Dear Esther*. Free from his EA commitments and with enough savings to support himself, Briscoe began exploring environmental design ideas, finding visual direction and stress testing the limitations of the engine in earnest. By the summer of 2009, Briscoe (2012a) was "happy with how it was shaping up" but increasingly aware his initial time estimation was unrealistic. Conscious of dwindling savings, Briscoe briefly considered abandoning the project and returning to full-time employment but was persuaded to continue by the enthusiasm and excitement shown by the modding community. They were not the only people impressed with his work-in-progress; it was around this time Briscoe (2012a) rejected an unsolicited job offer from Valve:

> On the flight home [from Valve] it began to dawn on me that there was something really special about this project, in a short time it had managed to rally together a large community of really passionate people and caught the attention of a company I had long since admired. As tempting as it was to take the job, I found my curiosity to see what the project

could grow into was much stronger. I'd never felt as passionate about a project than I did at this point it time and I was determined to finish it, no matter what.

Re-energized and reassured that his savings could stretch to 12 months of full-time focus—maybe 18 months if he really tightened his belt—Briscoe continued building out his remake. By June 2010, he had added a lot of his "ideas, designs and interpretations" into the game and reached out to Dan Pinchbeck for reassurance that the remake was not "drifting too far from his [Pinchbeck's] original vision" (Briscoe 2012a). Pinchbeck was not only supportive of the iterations but now convinced that the remake was too good to ignore and suggested licensing *Source* outright and releasing the remake as a standalone title rather than a mod. Briscoe was apprehensive. He saw the remake as a hobbyist project, deliberately free from commercial pressures, distractions and considerations. Did he want—or need—the heightened expectations and formal obligations? How would the supportive modding community react if *Dear Esther* abandoned them to turn professional?

"In my next development update, I floated the question of what the communities' thoughts would be on Dear Esther going indie, with the intention of making my final decision based on that feedback. Overall, the response that came back was resoundingly positive; almost everyone was in favour of it and some even vigilantly demanding it!"

Rob Briscoe (2012a)

The community response convinced Briscoe. The Chinese Room—the notional "studio" moniker Pinchbeck used to release his development-led research projects—was formalized and *Dear Esther* was suddenly a "real" project. Pinchbeck—still working full-time at the University of Portsmouth—handled the "licensing, funding, paperwork, etc.," which in turn freed Briscoe to concentrate on finishing the remake. If everything went to plan, *Dear Esther* would be released before the end of 2010 with a small amount of Briscoe's savings still intact (Briscoe 2012a).

Things did not go to plan.

Please, Release Me

At the start of 2011, things were "not looking good" (Briscoe 2012a). Pinchbeck had secured funding through the University of Portsmouth—who would retain the intellectual property—but

Dear Esther still did not have a commercial *Source* engine license. Valve rarely licenses its engine for standalone games, so negotiations were not a priority and painfully slow. The software giant was sympathetic to The Chinese Room's independent—professional hobbyist—status, but arriving at a mutually agreeable licensing fee took a long time (Briscoe 2012a). Eventually, Valve and the university reached an agreement. All that remained was for the contract to be "stamped and paid for by the university" (Briscoe 2012a). Confident, The Chinese Room went ahead and announced the forthcoming standalone release of *Dear Esther* to the press and their community, unaware of what was to follow:

> *"In March we were hit with a devastating blow; we'd lost our funding. To cut a long story short, the University's legal department had some issues with some of the standard liability clauses in the Engine License and refused to sign it. Basically, if there was a chance that someone, somewhere, could sue them over the game, they didn't want to take the risk and after weeks of Dan trying to cut through all of the bureaucratic red tape, they eventually pulled out completely."*

> **Rob Briscoe (2012a)**

After two years of hard work, *Dear Esther* was in limbo. Briscoe's savings had dwindled to almost nothing and he was forced to sell his possessions and live out of a single room in his apartment to save on heating and electricity. Just as it began to look like game over, Pinchbeck executed his Plan B. Already in discussions with the Indie Fund about investment for a separate project when the university deal collapsed, he decided to pitch them *Dear Esther* (Briscoe 2012a).

The Indie Fund is a benevolent collective of successful game makers on a mission to "support the growth of games as a medium by helping indie developers get financially independent and stay financially independent" (Indie Fund 2017). Members of the collective include Kellee Santiago, Jonathan Blow and Rami Ismail. According to Briscoe, the Indie Fund was reluctant at first—concerned by the potential commercial value of a mod remake—but were won over when given a chance to play *Dear Esther*. Just a few weeks later, the paperwork was signed and the monies transferred. By summer 2011, The Chinese Room not only had a full *Source* license but enough remaining funds to commission Jessica Curry to remaster the original soundtrack. Pinchbeck even persuaded the University of Portsmouth to transfer over *Dear Esther*'s intellectual property rights to The Chinese Room. All that remained was for Briscoe to port the game over to the latest *Source* engine code. But moving from the *Orange Box* to the *Portal 2* version of the engine left *Dear Esther* "completely broken" and Briscoe had no choice but to start living off an extended overdraft and credit card debt while he restored the project to working order (2012a).

Pinchbeck (2013) estimated *Dear Esther* would need to sell around 20,000 copies to return the Indie Fund investment and modestly compensate Briscoe and Curry. But if the game were less successful, Briscoe (2012a) would be left in serious debt:

> In retrospect it was the stupidest thing I've ever done, at the time I had no income and if the game failed, no way of paying it off. It was irrational, but at the time, all I could think about was finishing the game and keeping a roof over my head in the meantime.

Feeling the pressure, Briscoe began working 18-hour shifts, seven days a week to finish the game as quickly as possible. By October, *Dear Esther* had been submitted for consideration at the 2012 International Games Festival (IGF) and by November it was in beta. In February 2012—three years after Briscoe began his remake—*Dear Esther* was finally released on Steam. It became profitable in just five hours, much to Briscoe's (2012a) surprise and relief:

> It finally felt like all of the hard work, blood, sweat and tears had been worthwhile, but most importantly, that the instinct I'd felt all along that there was something special about *Dear Esther* was proving to be true.

One month later, *Dear Esther* won the prize for Excellence in Visual Arts at the IGF ceremony during the Games Developer Conference in San Francisco.

> *"No-one got paid for Dear Esther until release. Rob lived off ASDA pot noodles, Jess and I were both holding down other jobs. We paid our freelance coder and Nigel, but if the game hadn't sold, we'd have sunk two years into it for nothing. Doing it for the money is always a bad reason for doing it, but watching the figures on the first night of sales and realizing that the risk had paid off was one of the most amazing feelings ever. We still can't quite believe how many units it sold in that first 24 hours."*
>
> **Dan Pinchbeck (2014a)**

Ascension

When setting out to remake *Dear Esther*, Briscoe (2012b) assumed that to "really draw people into the visuals" the environment would have to be as photorealistic as possible. But the practical constraints of the engine—the photorealistic approach was a performance killer—provoked him into experimenting with a more illustrative style. Drawing inspiration from impressionism and its captivating mix of reality and surreality, Briscoe (2012b) developed a naturalistic and painterly style that concentrated on immersion and perception rather than "HDR, motion blur or JJ Abrams lens flare" and other photorealistic tropes. Briscoe even coined the phrase "emotional signposting" to emphasize that the job of the environment design went beyond conveying orientation and information. Its purpose was to "create a framework of feeling for the playing," subtly steering how the experience feels and making the player feel in the moment (Pinchbeck 2014a).

Just as integral to this emotional signposting was Jessica Curry's music. Its sparse and pastoral otherworldliness juxtaposed wonderfully with Briscoe's picturesque landscapes and Pinchbeck's ambiguous storytelling. Curry's work—which would go on to win a host of awards—was remarkable. First, the choral compositions were at odds with Curry's spiritual outlook: "I am an atheist who absolutely loves church music (try and unpick that one!). They say that the devil gets all the best tunes—well, I would disagree" (quoted by Smal 2016). Second, it emerged from a position of blissful ignorance. A graduate of the National Film and Television School, Curry had never scored a video game before *Dear Esther*, so unknowingly broke a host of game soundtrack "best practices." Third, Curry's arrangements were entirely interpretive—provoked by her personal experiences of playing the game—rather than a response to explicit direction from Pinchbeck. Curry did not even visit the Hebrides to research the game, instead expressing an imagined psychogeographic interpretation of the island.

> *"Jessica's work with the music has really brought the whole game together in a way I never thought possible. She's done some amazing things with the music to help portray the atmosphere and emotions throughout the journey across the island. I don't think I've ever seen music establish such a symbiotic relationship with the environment and story before, so for me it's really groundbreaking stuff. The music is no longer just a backdrop, but an integral part of the storytelling process."*

Briscoe and Pinchbeck (2012b)

Players Are People Too

Dear Esther stands accused of many things and pretentiousness is often one of them. But is that a negative? Games are often too eager to fit neatly into a box and signpost their supposed authenticity. Already stripped of the assumptive machismo and mechanics of an FPS, Pinchbeck (2014b) saw no reason for *Dear Esther* to underestimate its players: "gamers are smart and you shouldn't talk down to them. They can take big ideas and complex stories and they are hungry for interesting, new experiences."

Working to the mantra that "if it is for everyone, then it is for no-one," The Chinese Room did not assume their players were morons but trusted them to be smart, curious and imaginative people seeking out uncompromising emotional experiences (Curry 2012). This trust manifested not just in the high concept but in the brevity of interactivity and the pace of storytelling. An intimate experience, *Dear Esther* enables players to relate to the story and its characters "on a human level rather than as agents of action" (Stuart 2016).

> *"We think this is one of the key reasons why Dear Esther flew. You could feel the passion in the game and it didn't make concessions. For every person throwing their toys out of the pram about some weird 'is it a game or not?' debate, which I honestly, genuinely, still find utterly baffling, there was a building crowd of fans who took Dear Esther for what it was, a story told with heart and conviction."*
>
> **Dan Pinchbeck (2014b)**

But Is It a Game?

Dear Esther has enjoyed widespread critical and commercial success, receiving several prestigious awards and selling over a million copies. Yet one question, playfully summarized by the *Guardian*'s Keith Stuart (2016), persists:

> Stripped of traditional ludic elements, walking sims like *Dear Esther* give the player room to really investigate the feel of every location.

> There are no puzzles, no enemies. You're alone on a remote Hebridean island with little evidence of life beyond the cawing gulls and the odd glimpse of a shadowy figure on the horizon. There is one path to follow, which guides you over the dunes and into caves lit by phosphorescent flora. The story unravels,

not through the completion of tasks, but through a pondering, poetic narration and scattered letters.

Are you playing a game?

For Pinchbeck (2013), the answer is a resounding *yes*; his argument being games are "architectures for an emotional experience" and not spoonfed "exercise[s] in mechanics, in pattern manipulation, in goals and solutions." Pinchbeck (2016) argues it is reductive to equate a lack of visceral stimulation or overt interactivity with a lesser experience:

> I think it's one of those things that once you start unpicking it, it starts coming apart at the seams. If it's all about a game has to have mechanics well then you start to go, well, *Space Invaders*, is that less of a game than *Far Cry* because it's got fewer mechanics? Or, if a game is about having a fail state then does that mean that a game that doesn't punish you for dying, like a *Far Cry* game where it happens really trivially, does that make it less of a game than *Bloodborne* where the stakes for death are higher? Whichever way you come at it, you start unpicking those strands and it doesn't really make sense apart from the "feeling" of what a game ought to do.

The success of *Dear Esther* and the flurry of thought-provoking "walking sims" that followed in its wake—*Proteus*, *The Stanley Parable*, *Firewatch*, et al.—has not provided a definitive answer to Stuart's loaded question. But it has highlighted the absurdity of the argument. The failure to question the assumptions of what constitutes "playing a game" is a failure of imagination. Eclectic skeptics like The Chinese Room not only look at the diverse world around them and see the opportunity to bring interesting, previously unexplored, playful experiences to life, they also challenge gaming orthodoxy and exceptionalism in the process. Genuinely emotional playful experiences are not about mechanistic doing but resonant feeling. You can only love what you feel.

Practical Provocations
- What if you stripped an established genre of its game mechanics and preconceptions?
- What if you remixed rather than reinvented the wheel?
- What if you told a story through your environment and ambiance?

FIGURE 3.6 *Dear Esther* concept art by Ben Andrews. (Reprinted with permission from The Chinese Room, ©thechine-seroom 2017. All rights reserved.)

FIGURE 3.7 A screenshot from *Dear Esther*. (Reprinted with permission from The Chinese Room, ©thechineseroom 2017. All rights reserved.)

Chapter 4

Success Doesn't Suck

Abstract

Be a sellout! The modern game maker must simultaneously be the playful provocateur, the sincere trickster, the spellbinding story-teller, the community builder and the artisanal merchant. Being just one out of five—the isolated, stubborn maker—is no longer enough. Define yourself by vision and purpose rather than rigid business models or orthodox corporatism; prioritize building networks of passionate patrons over mindlessly building more games. Cultivate and curate on-demand, in-demand playful experiences.

This chapter argues that there is nothing glamorous in the clichés of the starving artist or the incorruptible, unsullied indie dev. We *do* live in a post-McLuhan world and the stories of how your things get made and how people find them *are* as significant to the experience as the game itself (Temkin n.d.).

It's Just a Business Model

"Our challenges seem complex. It will always be this way. But as long as we remember our first principles and believe in ourselves, the future will always be ours."

Ronald Reagan
Farewell Address to the Nation (1989)

Be singular about your purpose, not your business model. Business models are impermanent, based on assumptions that may or may not be true. Remember, today's truths are tomorrow's fallacies. Don't get too attached and set in your ways. Test assumptions and explore new options. Keep your eye on the ball. Be nimble and adaptable. Try different models for different projects. Be the disruptor, not the disrupted. Purpose and principles give the flexibility to overcome uncertainty. Best practice is the last refuge of the soon-to-be extinct.

Imagine

"A journey is like marriage. The certain way to be wrong is to think you control it."

John Steinbeck
Travels with Charley (1962)

All successful enterprises need a business model. According to Lean practitioner and author Ash Maurya, developing the right business model is initially more important than developing the right product or service. For Maurya, the business model *is* the product (2012, p.7). Even so, widespread misconceptions persist about the nature of business models. The antidote to such confusion might be to identify what a business model is *not*. For example, it is not a complex mathematical formula plotted on a whiteboard or spreadsheet that dictates all future action; it is instead a compelling story that describes how an enterprise works (Magretta 2002). A business model also should not be confused with a strategy. A competitive strategy outlines how your business will outperform the competition; a business model is a set of principles describing what your business is and how it will run (Magretta 2002). Businesses need to know who their customers are and what they value; they must know what they will get paid for and what economic logic will underpin how they deliver value to customers at an appropriate cost (Drucker 1994; Magretta 2002). A successful business model identifies a better way of doing this than existing alternatives and tells a more compelling story in the process. And like the best stories, great business models are a product of the human imagination.

Peter Drucker identified that business models—or "theories of business" as he called them—are based on assumptions. He argued these fall into three categories: assumptions about the environment or context a business exists in define what it gets paid for; assumptions about the specific mission of the business determine what success looks like; assumptions about the competencies needed to achieve this mission identify where a business must excel to become successful (1994). All these assumptions must integrate successfully to work. But assumptions can be mistaken or invalidated by environmental change. That's why Steve Blank's *The Four Steps to the Epiphany*, Alexander Osterwalder's *Business Model Canvas*, Eric Ries's *Lean Startup* and Ash Maurya's *Running Lean* have become so popular. These approaches recognize the importance of business models and advocate identifying and testing assumptions to give an enterprise the best chance of success. But even if you find the right model at startup, all theories of business are perishable and eventually become obsolete (Drucker 1994). To become successful then maintain success and avoid disruption, businesses must continually monitor and test their assumptions. You must be willing to iterate or even abandon your approach when circumstances dictate, or use alternative approaches for new products or services. If you diagnose problems early, you might sustain a business through incremental innovations. But if these innovations end up delivering smaller and smaller returns, you might need to do something more drastic. The most important thing is always to be clear about your central purpose and principles. If you know your destination, you can always adapt the route or change the mode of transport to get there.

In and Out The Eagle

"We never wrote a manifesto but we had one. The Eagle would be the sort of place where you could get a decent pint and a decent steak sandwich. There would be no bullshit. No optics. No tabs. No tips. And we would never forget it's a pub. It was fairly simple."

Michael Belben
Co-founder of The Eagle (2017)

Michael Belben and David Eyre were fed up. After working in high-end restaurants in London's Covent Garden throughout the 1980s, they now wanted a restaurant of their own, but rents were prohibitively high. They were also fed up with the dire food mostly available in London, particularly in the pubs they loved (Belben 2017). Unless you could afford upmarket restaurants like Alistair Little, Kensington Place, or The River Cafe (infamously known for "peasant food at plutocrat prices"), the choice was poor in those days. Belben and Eyre worked in good restaurants but couldn't afford to eat in them. Frustrated, the two friends decided they would open somewhere they—and people like them—would want to go. It would have food similar to The River Cafe but prices would be considerably lower. It would be a place where you could get simple but intelligent food without the frills. And it would have to be in a cheap area of London. In 1990, they found where.

Standing stoically on the corner of Farringdon Road and Baker's Row in Clerkenwell, The Eagle is an attractive but relatively unremarkable London pub. Unless you know its history, you could almost be forgiven for walking past without a second glance. When Belben and Eyre discovered it, the pub was struggling to keep the doors open. At that time many London pubs were doing the same. The damage was often self-inflicted. Pubs could be unwelcoming places then, especially if you were female. They ran mostly on cigarette smoke, stale beer fumes and unbridled testosterone. And even if you could get food, it was usually terrible. Bangers and mash featuring sausages of unknown origin and congealed gravy, or a ploughman's lunch of processed ham, third-rate cheddar and a solitary pickled onion exhibiting signs of rot. Belben and Eyre were not the only ones fed up. Something had to change.

And change it did. In 1989, the UK Monopolies and Mergers Commission ordered the big breweries to sell over 14,000 "tied" pubs to increase competition (Slade 1998). Belben and Eyre knew this was their opportunity. If they could find a decent pub with a cheap lease, maybe they could afford to open their restaurant. They heard about The Eagle and headed to Clerkenwell to investigate. Now one of London's most desirable and expensive areas, in 1990, Clerkenwell was seriously down at heel. Belben recalls the reason they chose that pub in that area was simply economics: "It was all we could afford. It was cheap because this area was desolate then" (Belben 2017). This was a risky approach. Not only would Belben and Eyre be opening a restaurant in a pub, but they would be doing it in the middle of a recession, in the middle of a gastronomic wasteland, miles from the bright lights of the West End.

The two friends were under no illusions it would be easy. With little capital, they had to do everything on the cheap. Friends helped clean the place up and do some basic decorating. The crockery and cutlery came from car boot sales. The furniture came from similar sources, with 40 church chairs sourced from a British Legion sale Belben drove past while in the Peak District. None of it matched. Belben (2017) recalls that what became The Eagle's much-copied aesthetic was simply a creative response to financial restrictions: "It was deliberate. I'd always been a great believer in making do but doing it in a stylish way." There would be no tablecloths, no credit cards, no reservations, no jukebox, no tabs and no tips. Staff would receive a decent wage—Belben and Eyre had both experienced the horrors of surviving solely on tips—but service would be paired back and upselling banned: "We didn't want it to get expensive. We didn't do starters. We didn't do puddings. It was the concept ... we called it 'one plate dining.' You want a pint or a nice glass of wine and a plate of great food. And any other selling traditionally done by waiters was out" (Belben 2017).

Eyre would initially produce the food—soups, hearty dishes with proper sausages from the Italian deli next door, Bife Ana (the signature marinated steak sandwich that remains on the menu today) and fresh salads—from the kitchen in a tiny room behind the bar. Stews and casseroles would be cooked in the upstairs flat (Belben 2017). Instead of menus, chalkboards would announce the food. The offer would also be adapted for each service to minimize waste; if Eyre ran out of an ingredient for one dish, he would reimagine what he had left into something else. Olive oil would replace butter on the tables, sea salt and freshly ground pepper would oust industrial condiments in sachets. A short, satisfying and affordable wine list—plus a couple of good rums—would augment a few decent beers. In January 1991, the two friends emptied out their pockets to put some small change in the till, then opened the doors.

The Eagle was an immediate success. Belben had started an "informal campaign" a few months earlier by sending friends and journalists a Christmas card in comic form, announcing The Eagle as a futuristic antidote to bad pubs and their bad food. Then he made a flyer and spent days pounding the streets of Clerkenwell. He visited the *Guardian* newspaper and every other office he could find, encouraging receptionists to come for lunch and bring their workmates (Belben 2017). He also tirelessly phoned food critics, cajoling them to visit an area they had probably never been to, professionally or otherwise. There was no formal advertising, only dedicated hustling. But it paid off. The receptionists came and brought their colleagues. And in February, Emily Green from *The Independent* ventured to Farringdon Road and wrote the pub's first review, describing "voguish Italian food" and quality ingredients (Green 1991). This enticed more critics and regular customers through the doors. And the former loved the place almost as much as the latter. Soon it became noticeable how many women were regulars, rare in pubs at the time. The great food, reasonable prices, utilitarian service, casual atmosphere and stripped-back aesthetic made The Eagle both affordable and welcoming to everyone.

The Eagle was the antithesis of snobby, expensive fine dining. Here people could see "all of the costs were on the plate, so they knew they were getting value for money" (Belben 2017). This was crucial in the middle of a deep recession when expense accounts were slashed and lunch became funded from the personal pocket. Just three months after opening, the pub had banked more money than had been predicted for a year. Belben and Eyre now extended the kitchen into the bar to allow everything to be cooked in the pub. This also added a bit of theatre as flames flashed and meat sizzled from the grills. More food critics arrived, including Jonathan Meades from *The Times*. Meades praised The Eagle for its "big flavours and rough edges"—later the title of its seminal cookbook—and quickly perceived that it heralded a revolution in eating out. He thought it was "certain to be copied sooner or later ... ineptly copied, of course, with no understanding of what makes it tick. It is not a former pub, it still is a pub—but one whose owners have written the rules" (Meades 1991). He could not have known how prescient his words were. A few short years on, critic Charles Campion reviewed The Eagle for the London *Evening Standard* magazine, where he infamously described it with a hyphenated portmanteau: "gastro-pub." A business model had been born.

The term *gastropub* is today redundant, sometimes even used pejoratively. It is often perceived as an embarrassing hangover from the 1990s, on a par with Britpop, the "Rachel cut," and Jamie Oliver. But the redundancy of the term is a result of The Eagle's innovations. In the years following its opening, new food-focused pubs proliferated across London. All of them looked to The Eagle as a conceptual template and business model. First, a rundown pub with character would be found. Then it was given a lick of paint, filled with mismatched furniture, plates and cutlery, plus a couple of old standard lamps with judiciously tilted shades. Chalkboards went up, good, uncomplicated food was cooked and the customers flooded in, thrilled they could eat and drink well for a fair price in a casual atmosphere. Many of these initial gastropubs were founded by people who "apprenticed" at The Eagle. In fact, David Eyre has described The Eagle as a "stud farm for chefs," due to the influence its entrepreneurial alumni exercised on London's food scene. The pub was also copied—as Jonathan Meades predicted—by corporate chains, including 1990s favorite All Bar One. Belben was inadvertently complicit in this: "the guy who was [All Bar One] brand manager came in and took me out for dinner. I explained about the church chairs and the blackboard menu, of course, he was writing away. All Bar One was basically the chain interpretation of The Eagle. And what a horrible thing that was" (2017). But despite this bastardization—maybe even because of it—the gastropub concept continued to spread; today thousands are found not only across the UK but also in Europe, North America and beyond.

Belben doesn't mind the "g-word" but Eyre is not so keen: "You don't have gastro-hotels. You don't have gastro-bars. It sounds like a belch" (Mesure 2016). Whatever their feelings, the term has come to define a particular business model. But this was not the result of any complex mathematical modeling. It was a product of the imagination of two entrepreneurs with a clear and simple purpose: "to open somewhere we wanted to go where you could get a decent pint and a decent steak sandwich" (Belben 2017). This purpose was supplemented by a set of principles based on honesty. Belben says: "Honesty is the thing that sums it up. You can apply it to everything. The idea itself is honest. The deal that you have with the customer is honest. You don't try and sell them more food than they need. There's an honesty in that. The style is genuine" (2017). The two friends combined their purpose and principles with a series of assumptions that understood their business context and environment—a recession, a cheap area with no reputation for food but lots of journalists and creatives; the existing pub offer, their lack of capital—and informed the no-frills, low-touch economic logic that underpinned the enterprise. They created a compelling story that resonated throughout the culture and helped transform London's gastronomic landscape.

The Eagle has now transcended the gastropub—probably because it never was one in the first place; it was simply a pub with great food. And that pub has survived hundreds of imitators, celebrating its quarter century in 2016. This is a real achievement in a challenging industry increasingly subject to fads, trends and sky-high costs. Chris has been visiting The Eagle since the mid-1990s, becoming highly skilled in poaching a table the second its occupants make the slightest indication of departure. For him and many others, The Eagle is a beloved constant. Of course, things have changed. David Eyre sold his share to Mike Belben after seven years, when life at The Eagle got too busy. Belben has continually reevaluated his assumptions and made incremental innovations where necessary. The Eagle now takes credit cards and you can reserve a table if there are more than six of you; it opens for Sunday lunch, has a website and even an Instagram account. New additions pop up on the menu from time to time and the wine list refreshes. But that's about it. The atmosphere is as relaxed as ever, the food as good. And as economic uncertainty hovers on the immediate horizon, The Eagle's honest, quality without the frills business model seems more relevant than ever. Clerkenwell has changed almost beyond recognition, becoming one of London's coolest areas and a gastronomic heartland. Much of that is down to two young guys, who 26 years ago had the crazy idea to serve great food with big flavors in a pub with rough edges.

Don't Leave Luck to Heaven

"Cats like me have become extinct. Cannae adapt, so cannae survive."

Daniel "Spud" Murphy
Porno by Irvine Welsh (2002)

Video games would not be the same without Nintendo. The company has been an innovator many times over, not only with consoles, peripherals and game content but also with its business models. As a result, there has been widespread discussion of the company's nongame origins and the way it transitioned to extraordinary success in the video game market. But although the company was not always in the business of games, it has always been in the business of play.

When people discover Nintendo was founded in 1889—and that clearly video games were not its original offer—they are often astonished. They shouldn't be. Video games are simply an evolutionary stage in a much longer history of games and play. That Nintendo Koppai began by handcrafting decorative playing cards called *hanafuda* (flower cards)—used in popular games based mostly on image association—is not particularly astonishing. Neither is the much lauded "conceptual leap" from cards and toys to video games that Nintendo executed in the 1980s. Games were a new and increasingly popular form of playful entertainments and Nintendo had a long history of making playful and entertaining products. Join up the dots and the video game pivot clearly makes sense. But what is astonishing is the way Nintendo went about entering the video game market. It combined unwavering purpose with hard-nosed business realism and a promiscuously adaptable approach to business models. And a little creative genius.

Hiroshi Yamauchi became president of Nintendo in 1949, after a series of complicated successions. In the mid-1950s, after a trip to meet Walt Disney executives in the US, he developed a single-minded vision to transform the playing card company he inherited into a global entertainment giant (Ryan 2013). Hiroshi controlled Nintendo with an imperial hand, seldom praising success and always criticizing mistakes; he was ruthlessly ambitious (Kent 2001; Donovan 2010). In the early years, he implemented innovations such as the first plastic coated playing cards in Japan, a partnership with Disney to reproduce its characters on Nintendo's cards and a successful expansion into making and selling toys. There were also failures, including "love hotels" and an instant rice product. But Hiroshi learned from these, realizing he had strayed too far from his competencies and those of his company. Nintendo's strengths were its excellent distribution network and retail stores across Japan, plus its expertise in designing and making playful entertainments. By the mid-1970s, Hiroshi's learning made him confident these competencies would help him conquer the new video games market.

Japan had been slow embracing video games, particularly in the home. Nintendo first entered the market with the coin-op arcade game *EVR Race*. It was a failure, mostly because it used unreliable technology. But by 1977, the *Pong* phenomenon had hit Japan and various manufacturers launched a succession of *Pong* home consoles. These included the Color TV Game console by Nintendo, which shipped over a million units. This initial success sent a strong signal that the company could make money from games, but still the Japanese market remained insular until 1978, when Taito's *Space Invaders* became a global sensation. Hiroshi observed this and realized how much money Taito had made. So he decided Nintendo must start making coin-op arcade games again. But that was not all. *Space Invaders* also confirmed Hiroshi's hunch that the real future of Nintendo lay in video games. He issued orders for workers to stop everything and concentrate on making the best video game products on the market (Donovan 2010, p.154).

Nintendo's first major success, Game and Watch, was the product of a business model underpinned by the "lateral thinking of withered technology." Espoused by Gunpei Yokoi, Nintendo's chief toymaker, this philosophy involved shunning the latest technology and finding new, innovative uses for mature technologies that could be mass-produced cheaply (Donovan 2010, p.155). Yokoi had spotted a "salaryman" playing with his LCD pocket calculator on the commute home and realized it would be possible to make a portable game using similar technology. Because LCD was a mature technology, it would be cheap to make and therefore affordable to buy, presenting lower barriers to entry. Incorporating the functionality of a watch and alarm clock would also attract customers and add value.

Yamauchi had defined Nintendo's purpose: to dominate the global video game market. After the success of its *Pong* console, he knew the company was competent at making, distributing and selling playful entertainments in the form of video games. Yokoi had now identified assumptions about context and environment—who the customer was and what they wanted—plus discovered what Nintendo would get paid for. In other words, he had identified the problem and the solution. And as part of that solution, Yokoi had also identified an economic logic that underpinned how Nintendo would deliver value to the customer at an appropriate cost. The company had developed its first business model for video games.

Game and Watch was an instant success. Launching in April 1980, the handheld console sold over 30 million units over the next 11 years, laying the groundwork for other handhelds such as GameBoy and Nintendo's further penetration into the games sector (Donovan 2010; Ryan 2013). But Yamauchi was not satisfied. To achieve his goal he now wanted to replicate the success Atari enjoyed with its VCS/2600. Again, Nintendo used the "withered technology" approach for its new home console. The Famicom—launched in 1984—was ordered to be a year ahead of the competition but also affordable (Donovan 2010). This goal was achieved using more mature technology— similar processors and components to the aging Atari—but engineering innovations in graphics and RAM that had not been possible just a few years earlier. Famicom was a massive success in Japan, but it was merely a step toward developing a new business model for Nintendo's global domination of video games.

Nintendo had achieved massive commercial success and cultural impact with 1981s *Donkey Kong*, an arcade smash soon ported to Game and Watch. Created by novice designer Shigeru Miyamoto, in collaboration with Gunpei Yokoi, *Donkey Kong* was the first Nintendo game to break North America, due to its innovative characterization and gameplay. Yamauchi had ordered the Famicom to emulate the Atari by being cartridge based, so he decided the console would ship with *Donkey Kong* plus two more Miyamoto games. And it was these games that were key to the new business model. Yamauchi believed the console was "just a tool to sell software"; Nintendo would make its *real* money from the higher margins afforded by selling games (Donovan 2010, p.158). This approach delivered instant success but soon there was a problem: Famicom had become so popular that Nintendo could not make games fast enough. Yamauchi took quick and drastic action by opening up the console to other publishers and developers, revolutionizing the entire industry in the process. In return for allowing licensees to make games for Famicom, Nintendo demanded upfront payment for manufacturing cartridges, a cut of the profits and the right to veto any game it did not like. Some licensees initially balked at these terms, but the booming market for Famicom games forced them to change their minds. This was a good situation for Nintendo, as the new licensing model ensured it always made a profit because licensees paid manufacturing costs whether a game sold or not. Nintendo was well on the road to dominating the Japanese games market.

Yamauchi and Nintendo had already achieved success by pivoting business models for new products and contexts. But when Famicom was first touted in the US—redesigned as the Advanced Video System (AVS)—it was an instant flop. Yamauchi, still focused on his single purpose of global domination, told son-in-law and president of Nintendo of America Minoru Arakawa to find a solution. With bad timing, the AVS had been revealed in 1984, just as the US home console market collapsed. Business experts now argued video games had been simply a fad, so retailers failed to order Nintendo's new console. But Arakawa disagreed with the experts. He believed people had not lost their desire to play games—the arcades were booming and so was the PC market—they had just got bored of the substandard games that had become the norm on the Atari. Based on this assumption, he decided to iterate Nintendo's business model still further for the US market. First, Arakawa would have the Famicom/AVS redesigned into a high-quality stand-alone entertainment system. Then he drew upon Nintendo's toy-making competencies and added a light gun and robot, helping retailers think of the new Nintendo Entertainment System (NES) more as a toy than a video game console. But still, orders remained scarce.

Crucially, Arakawa then decided to embrace the licensing model from Japan, turning the platform into a closed system by adding a security chip. This would enable Nintendo to control the quality of every game played on the NES. From now on, everything would revolve around the principle of quality and Nintendo controlling that quality throughout the value chain (Donovan 2010). Buoyed by this pivot, Arakawa and his small team also adopted the innovative approach of hustling the US market one big city at a time, starting with the toughest nut to crack: New York City. The US operation had adapted its purpose. Now instead of "global domination" or "conquering the US," the mission was simply to make the NES a success in one smaller market. Nintendo of America believed it had the right solution to playing games at home but still had to convince retailers and customers. The team did this by describing only an "entertainment system" when selling the product, not mentioning video games. It conducted all the merchandising, restocking and customer demonstrations. And it began a major regional advertising campaign in the New York area. Most importantly, Arakawa offered all retailers a money back guarantee on consoles that did not sell. This was a huge risk but Arakawa remained convinced his core assumption—that people still wanted to play high-quality video games—was right.

It was. After three months of exhausting work by the team, New York retailers sold over 50,000 units that Christmas (Kent 2001). Even better, most did not return the consoles after the holidays but continued to stock them. Arakawa and his team then moved on to Los Angeles, Chicago and San Francisco, with increasing success. As more high-quality games were released for the NES by Nintendo and its licensed publishers, demand increased exponentially and the console quickly conquered the US market. The story was similar in Europe. Nintendo would eventually become the principal player in the global games market for the rest of the 1980s and well into the next decade, gaining a 90% share of the US home video game market by 1990 (Kellon 2014). Its new business model—based on quality and licensing—would professionalize and reconfigure the global games industry, becoming the dominant model for all console development (Donovan 2010, p.177). But Yamauchi's goal had not been realized by "leaving luck to heaven"—the supposed English translation of Nintendo—but by the exact opposite: a single-minded purpose, clear principles and a willingness to adapt business models when the environmental context changed.

The Restaurant of Dreams

Anyone with even a passing interest in gastronomy will be aware of the restaurant explosion of the past few years. It has notably occurred in nations not traditionally known for gastronomic prowess: the Nordic countries, Australia and New Zealand, the UK and the US. In the US particularly, this golden age of restaurants has seen an explosion in "Hot New Food Towns" and "chef-driven, ambitious, fine-casual dining spaces that straddle the gap between neighborhood fixtures and destinations," according to American food writer Kevin Alexander (2016). But after a year of traveling the US talking to chefs and restaurant owners, Alexander now believes the US restaurant bubble is set to burst.

Focusing on the now-closed AQ restaurant in San Francisco, Alexander outlines problems affecting restaurants across the nation. When AQ opened, it was an immediate critical success, garnering awards and becoming a finalist for the Best New Restaurant in America. The restaurant initially increased revenue year on year but in its second year of operation, profits started to decrease. By 2016, the projected annual revenue was $1.6 million, down

$1 million from the year before. Instead of 240 covers served every night, the restaurant was now serving 100 (Alexander 2016). As the year progressed, the owners began to realize the game was up. AQ was no longer sustainable. With a heavy heart, they closed the doors.

Alexander identifies increasing labor and health care costs as a major factor in the impending crash. But he also blames market saturation, adherence to trends, business models based on faulty assumptions, rigid concepts and extortionate startup costs. All these are present in the demise of AQ. When the restaurant opened in late 2011, there were 3,600 restaurants in San Francisco; by 2016 there were 7,600 (Alexander 2016). That is *rapid* market saturation. AQ's on-trend hyper-seasonal approach also featured a menu that changed daily and decor that changed to match the mood of each new season. And while seasonality is laudable, as part of a business model it can be problematic. Traditionally, produce bought locally in season is cheaper than out-of-season food with longer supply chains. However, when seasonality becomes a trend and every chef wants the freshest local produce, the price shoots up. It's basic supply and demand. Also, when everything is cooked from scratch using fresh produce, wastage is an issue. Alexander quotes a New Orleans chef describing the current trend for restaurants making absolutely everything—bread, charcuterie, pickles, etc.—as "self-flagellating chef martyrdom at its best" (2016). The chef describes the substantial labor and raw materials required, adding that these items can usually be sourced cheaper and better from local specialists (think The Eagle and its Italian sausages from the local deli). Add 13 months and $1 million for startup into this mix and the cost implications of such an approach become substantial. And when you're paying to redecorate your $1 million restaurant every three months, it's no wonder things spiral out of control.

Now we're fans of good restaurants and scratch-made food with fresh local ingredients, but there are obvious flaws in this kind of business model. First, using so much time and money at startup before you have any evidence people want what you're offering is dangerous. It is the *Field of Dreams* approach: if you build it, they will come. Here assumptions about who your customer is and what they want only get tested after spending tremendous amounts of cash. The owners of AQ even admit that they had absolutely "no idea what to expect" on opening (Alexander 2016). It turned out people did want what AQ offered—but only for a moment before they abandoned it for the latest on-trend establishment. Being on-trend in your operating environment can be dangerous. If a successful business model has to present a better alternative to the way things are—plus tell a more compelling story—this is difficult when everybody is doing the same thing and telling the same tale. And trends are by nature ephemeral. The hyper-seasonal menu that changed daily and involved scratch-making everything was also a costly obsession. Alexander (2016) quotes AQ's owners as saying "If there was something new at the market, even just for a couple of weeks, chef was going to use it in a dish." This is cooking as selfish-making that ignores issues of either demand or organizational sustainability. The assumptions being made—and the economic logic underpinning this making-centered business model—are questionable at best. Worse, when these assumptions began to be invalidated, it appears no attempts to adapt the business model were made. Things just carried on until it was too late.

Alexander's article resonates for a few reasons. First, it describes the exact opposite of the business model that brought sustainable success to The Eagle, providing a template for Belben and others to adapt and scale with other businesses. Second, there are striking commonalities between what is happening to mid-level independent restaurants such as AQ and what is occurring in the independent games sector. There is no longer any doubt that the recent explosion of indie studios has led to a saturated marketplace where companies are struggling to scale or even sustain themselves. As discussed previously, this is a bubble where indie studios and games have become both genre and trend. And like the hyper-seasonal trend—also now a genre—when everyone is doing the same thing, it is more challenging to stand out and be discovered. Further, when a trend becomes mainstream, operators following that trend have to pander to mainstream customer expectations. And this usually leads to a fast, destructive race to the bottom. But if you're ploughing your individual furrow—perhaps inadvertently—or deliberately spearheading your own trend, this can be avoided. What you offer might not be for everyone, but as long as it resonates with enough people, who cares? Better to be defined by your principles and what you believe in than by a "proven" business model or established trend come genre. Another chef quoted by Alexander believes "the restaurant world is so saturated nowadays ... it requires so much extra work to keep yourself relevant" (2016). If you substitute "indie game making" for "restaurant," that statement remains equally valid.

The Maker Makes

The *Field of Dreams* approach is depressingly persistent throughout the game sector, where selfish and wasteful making is often encouraged through endless building of prototypes and "vertical slices" with little purpose. This can be exacerbated by the incessant game jams that have become so popular. These are fun and useful for developing competencies in making but should not be confused with a sustainable business model. The odd one-hit wonder exception celebrated in the game media proves the rule. If you endlessly build stuff purely for the sake of it, the people will not come. That only happens when you have a compelling story you can hustle and tell. The NES would have remained gathering dust in a warehouse if Minoru Arakawa and his team had not got out of the building and hustled—one city after another—to sell it. The Eagle would have failed if Michael Belben had not tirelessly hustled local office workers and respected food critics. Jazz masters like John Coltrane and Miles Davis loved to jam, but they didn't confuse it with making and selling an album. They knew they needed people who could hustle, who had the knowledge and chutzpah to package, promote and sell their wonderful but often challenging music to the public. Endless jam sessions did not change the culture and make these artists household names, *Birth of the Cool* and *A Love Supreme* did.

The wishful thinking approach also persists in many of the "incubation" or "hub" initiatives that are currently proliferating. Here people are given a limited funding runway, then encouraged to use it in the service of mindless making instead of testing their assumptions. By the time anyone mentions business models, customers, or selling things, it's too late. The young companies—yes, they are often also forced to waste resources "making" companies too—then disappear without trace. It should be no surprise this approach is espoused in many incubators or hubs because many of these utilize the same model themselves. Huge budgets are wasted on shiny buildings that demand extensive build-outs, rather than developing and running heuristic programs that encourage innovative and sustainable enterprise. That is because many of these initiatives are not honest in intent. Several are simply self-aggrandizement projects for people with big egos. Again, there is much to learn from The Eagle here. With a clear purpose, honest principles and a low-touch business model that repurposes existing spaces and demands minimal expenditure on refurbishment, there would be more money to fund transformative programs for promising entrepreneurs and startups. Maybe then, meaningful long-term change might occur instead of communities getting lumbered with half-empty, costly yet cut-price facsimiles of the Google campus, useful for glossy PR photographs but completely useless at encouraging sustainable enterprise.

This Year's Model

Whatever you're doing, it is clear you need some form of business model to guide action. You need a compelling story to tell about your business, product, or service. You need purpose and principles to drive your business model and constant testing and monitoring of assumptions to check it still works. If your assumptions are holding, then your model is currently sustainable, perhaps requiring the odd tweak to keep it resilient. But if your assumptions are invalidated, it is time to change. Remember what the Japanese concept of *wabi-sabi* says: "Nothing lasts, nothing is finished, nothing is perfect." The trick is never to leave things to chance or until it's too late, when the resources are almost gone and your destination is nothing but a blur receding on the horizon.

FIGURE 4.1   Side A of the original flyer for The Eagle. (Reprinted with permission from Michael Belben. © The Eagle 1991.)

FIGURE 4.2 Side B of the original flyer for The Eagle. (Reprinted with permission from Michael Belben. © The Eagle 1991.)

FIGURE 4.3   Nintendo *Donkey Kong* Game and Watch. (Courtesy of Roger Dahl, https://commons.wikimedia.org/wiki/File%3ANintendo_Donkey_Kong_Game_and_Watch.png.)

Let Me Be Your Fantasy

"We tell ourselves stories in order to live."

Joan Didion
The White Album (1979)

Not only do we tell ourselves stories in order to live, we tell them to feel alive. And when we are not telling stories, we want them told to us. Reason and logic are the bedrocks of scientific method and constructed argument, but they are not much fun without a compelling narrative. We want to be entertained. We want to find meaning. We want to find something intelligible in the incomprehensible. It is how we know we are alive. And sometimes, it is a way to escape our lives. Andy Warhol believed everyone must have a fantasy. And he was right. Why else would we spend so much time talking about "living the dream," American or otherwise? Stories and fantasies are powerful. And once you realize this, learning to construct and tell them becomes essential. But always remember: never let the facts get in the way of a great tale.

Riders on the Storm

"And your very flesh shall be a great poem."

Walt Whitman
Leaves of Grass (1855)

Since the beginning of Judaism, the Abrahamic religions have told stories of God. Religion gave purpose and meaning to whole cultures and societies. But by the late 18th century, another worldview was becoming dominant in Western Europe: the triumphant, rationalist, humanist Enlightenment (Hobsbawm 1962). The storm of the industrial revolution was accelerating everything. Science was rationalizing the natural world through categorization and positivist ideas of objective "truth" were peaking. Long-held religious "certainties"—now unprovable by science—began to be eroded. And as tales of God and the afterlife began to lose their grip, a small group of radicals searched for new secular stories to tell, new meanings to find, new ways of looking at and living in the world. They were the Romantics.

Romanticism might begin with Jean-Jacques Rousseau and young German poets such as Goethe, but it was in Britain where it fully bloomed. The initial wave included William Blake and Robert Burns, followed by the Lake Poets—Coleridge, Wordsworth and

Southey—then the more dramatic second wave of Byron, Percy and Mary Shelley, Keats and the Brontës. Romanticism also crossed the Atlantic, becoming an American proposition in the works of Irving, Cooper, Melville, Hawthorne and Whitman. The Romantics had been affected by the advances of rationalism and science, believing these could never satisfy the metaphysical dimensions of human existence. They feared mechanization, unthinking industrialization and the rationalization of everything—including nature—were enslaving people through imposed rules such as the enclosure of the fields or the tyranny of the mechanized clock (Ackroyd 2011a).

Defining Romanticism is hard, but its innovations and legacies still surround us. Marshall Berman (1984) argued that the creative breakthroughs of Romanticism nourished—and continue to nourish—a legion of revolutions, constituting a force at the heart of modernity that drives people to fight oppression. Certainly, the Romantics believed in the uniqueness of the individual, in the decency of common people and their right to liberty, free from oppression by monarchs and tyrants—essentially the founding principles of modern liberal democracies. In the face of dominant rationalism, they also valued individual feelings and emotions and specifically the potential of the individual imagination to transform the world through creative expression. It was Romanticism that articulated the first modern understanding of creativity. It believed in creative genius and its darker fellow traveler, melancholy. The Romantics extolled the virtues of imaginative tales of beauty, emotion, fantasy, mythology and gothic romance, because they believed that the creative imagination enabled people to transcend their circumstances (Forward n.d.). Romanticism also celebrated the beauty and sublimity of nature in all its awesome splendor, giving birth to both our learned enjoyment of the natural world and subsequent environmental movements (Ackroyd 2011b). Fundamentally, the Romantics were exploring how to understand, live and find meaning in an increasingly secular and rational world. And to find that meaning, they put trust in the power of a good story. Some even became the story.

Welcome to the Pleasuredome

"It may be bawdy ... but is it not life?"

Lord Byron
Don Juan (1824)

We live in a world of celebrity and secular icons. Our cultures elevate music and film stars, sports players, chefs, even the odd game designer, to the status of demigods. But the inventor of this modern notion of celebrity was none of these things. He was a poet. Famously described as "mad, bad and dangerous to know," Lord Byron was relentless in his pursuit of self-knowledge and self-gratification (Ackroyd 2011c). He was a leading light of the Romantic movement who believed "the great object of life was sensation—to feel that we exist" (cited in Marchand 1974, p.109). Byron refused to be forced into any rigid mold, preferring instead to craft his own. He was infamous for his recklessness with money, complete lack of moderation in love and sexual relationships across gender divides. After his travels through Europe, Byron wrote his first major work of poetry. Published in 1812, *Childe Harold's Pilgrimage* told tales of a noble but disaffected, smart yet cynical wanderer, who traveled distant lands in search of experiences after an earlier life of pleasure seeking and erotic excess. Byron was clearly recognizable in his debauched protagonist but decided to publish anyway (MacCarthy 2003). This decision would make him an overnight sensation, celebrated throughout Regency London and beyond. But according to Peter Ackroyd, it was his next decision "that would help define our modern world ... he chose to embrace celebrity, to live his life in public. This was his way of giving meaning to his own existence" (2011c). In a new secular world without God and religion, Byron would find that meaning in the worship of fans.

Childe Harold's Pilgrimage captured the imagination of its readers and Byron began to receive sacks of fan mail, most containing amorous proposals for trysts and assignations. To relieve debts, Byron had married Annabelle Millbanke, but he had also continued to conduct numerous affairs. Most notoriously there were rumors of an incestuous relationship with his half-sister, Augusta. Instead of dispelling these and moderating his behavior, Byron added fuel to the fire by accepting many of the salacious proposals he received. As his fame grew, scandalous scenes occurred at his Piccadilly house and in the local parks. Rumors of Byron's voracious infidelities became rife. Finally, in early 1816, his wife's legal representatives requested a separation. Practically unheard of at the time, this made things even worse. At first, Byron used the ensuing scandal to enhance his public image, reveling even deeper in being a "bad boy." But eventually, the maverick romantic image he had constructed began to work against him, particularly with the Establishment. Tales of debauchery, incest and homosexuality persisted. Whether these were true or not was now beside the point. In collusion with the press, Byron had constructed an image the rumors fitted only too well. It was time for a sharp exit.

Leaving England in April 1816—after signing the official separation document—Byron would never return. Instead, he would again wander Europe, perpetuating his personal romantic myth. He spent time with his friend Percy Bysshe Shelley—another Romantic adept at self-mythologizing—and Shelley's future wife, Mary. For a time they lived in a house by Lake Geneva. Here Mary would write *Frankenstein* and John William Polidori would invent the modern vampire literary genre, both inspired by conversations with Byron (Frayling 1992). After a while, Byron continued on his quest, traveling to Italy where he would write his masterpiece, *Don Juan*. This was a serialized tale of another cynical but smart, rebellious yet romantic hero. These repeated conventions came to define the classic "Byronic hero" today found everywhere from literature to video games. *Don Juan* celebrated liberty, reimagined the legend of the prolific lover, decried the earlier generation of Romantics as conservative sellouts and launched satirical attacks on the Establishment (Foreward n.d; Drummond n.d.). It was punk before punk was invented. Loved by some, hated by others, it was deeply provocative. Byron then moved on to Greece. Determined to liberate the Greek people from their subjugation under the Ottoman Empire, he sold his estate in Scotland to help fund the Greek insurgency and traveled to the island of Missolonghi to await battle. But the poet's quest for liberty failed to end in romantic glory. While waiting for battle to commence in April 1824, Byron developed an infection and died.

Despite his somewhat mediocre end, Byron remains the archetypal romantic hero. In Greece he is still revered as such. And there is little doubt he and the Romantics laid the groundwork for many aspects of our modern societies. Byron believed freedom and sensational experience were the keys to creative imagination. And Romanticism considered this imagination the key to a meaningful life. Those with such imaginations were presented as geniuses, driven by flashes of creative inspiration, accompanied by periods of melancholy. This became the foundation for our most enduring (if deeply flawed) understanding of creativity: the individual creative genius. Byron was also obsessive about his public image, carefully casting himself as the rebellious yet romantic hero valiantly challenging the status quo with his creative genius. He courted controversy while simultaneously attempting to control information and images that did not fit the fantasy (Drummond n.d.; Ackroyd 2011c). Byron was an expert in public relations, a spin doctor over 150 years before the term was invented (Safire 1986). Before Beatlemania there was Byronmania. And like The Beatles, Byron's phenomenal fame was not just the byproduct of artistic work, it was also the result of a carefully crafted and storied public image.

Every 18th century girl—and no doubt a few boys—dreamed of Lord Byron. He became their fantasy, his very flesh a great poem.

Fairy Tales and Centerfolds

"I think people are more apt to believe photographs, especially if it's something fantastic. They're willing to be more gullible. Sometimes they want fantasy."

Cindy Sherman
(quoted in Sussler 1985)

Cindy Sherman is fantasy and reality. The difficulty comes in distinguishing one from the other. Sherman is celebrated for "ferociously ironic photographs starring herself in different roles" that play with notions of identity and storytelling (Hughes 1997, p.615). But though millions have seen her in this work, few would recognize the "real" Cindy Sherman. That is because there are hundreds of Cindy Shermans: the vulnerable small-town girl in the big city, the virgin on the verge of womanhood, the exploited porn star, the damsel in distress, the Renaissance muse, or simply the "everyday" American woman. Sherman is all these, yet none of them.

Sherman's breakthrough work, 1978s *Untitled Film Stills*, comprises 69 photographs posing as stills from a variety of B movies, European art house films, or film noirs. Sherman "stars" in each, masquerading in different costumes and placing herself in implied situations, often stereotypical for female characters in film. The pictures are highly ambiguous, with "Sherman" always looking away from the camera. That each image is untitled adds to the ambiguity by refusing to impose or fix meaning with anchoring text. The photographs are disorientating yet strangely alluring. Each invites the viewer to map a story onto an isolated image. Joan Didion believes "we all live by the imposition of a narrative line upon disparate images" (1979, p.11), that we impose stories as an exercise in sense making, particularly when we are disorientated. Sherman describes how "some of the women in the outdoor shots could be alone, or being watched or followed ... or just come from a confrontation or a tryst" (Galassi 2003). It is this disorientating ambiguity that invites us to engineer a narrative fantasy to make sense of the unsettling images. And Sherman is complicit in this fantasy. For not only is she the subject of the photographs but the artist, the instigator, the provocateur. By dressing up and masquerading, Sherman is exploring her own imagination and providing a trigger for that of others. She is a willing co-conspirator in the fantasies of strangers.

Throughout her career, orthodoxy has foregrounded the feminist aspects of Sherman's work. But she argues feminism is not necessarily what drives her. When interviewed about *Untitled Films Stills*, she said the work was about "the way I was shooting, the mimicry of the style of black and white grade-Z motion pictures that produced the self-consciousness of these characters, not my knowledge of feminist theory" (quoted in Sussler 1980). More recently she has emphasized the centrality of dressing up, playful masquerade and performance in her work. She recalled how, from a young age, she would "spend a couple of hours turning myself into somebody else with makeup or clothes" whenever she felt moody or depressed, describing this as a form of catharsis (quoted in Smith 2004). An exhibition catalogue described her "obsession ... with dressing up, shopping, applying makeup and changing characters ... a girl who wore makeup when she was sick in bed and made cutout paper-doll clothes of everything in her closet to plan her outfits" (Smith 2004). And it is this chameleon-like behavior that gives real insight into Cindy Sherman's work. Simon Schama (2012) argues that "no living artist ... has more exactly nailed the masquerade we perform when we go about our business, public and private, social and erotic. No one has caught the futile compulsion to self-brand, to lock down an identity, with quite Sherman's psychological acuteness." For not only is Sherman's work a conspiratorial fantasy constructed between her and the viewer, it is an exploration of the fantasies each of us lives every hour of every day. It is a playful acknowledgement of that greatest fictional construct and performance: our individual self.

The Heart Is Deceitful above All Things

"It was fiction. It said that on the cover."

Laura Albert
(quoted in Langer 2013)

In 1999, Chris purchased a book called *Sarah* in a London bookstore. It was a tale of "lot lizards," sleazy pimps and truckers in West Virginia. The book explored themes of identity, gender, abandonment, abuse and poverty. It might sound difficult and depressing but the novel had magical realist qualities and humorous touches; it was an interesting read. *Sarah* soon became something of a sensation, praised in literary circles, loved by celebrities and inspiring a host of songwriters. As a result, author JT LeRoy began to be feted as a fresh, authentic voice in American literature, a new William Burroughs or Flannery O'Connor (Feuerzeig 2016; Rose 2016). But authentic was a poor choice of word to describe JT.

The JT LeRoy story is now the stuff of legend. As the author's fame exploded, revelations about his past emerged. His work was increasingly depicted as thinly veiled autobiography. More books and contributions to literary journals, magazines and newspapers only served to further reinforce LeRoy's supposed authenticity. In the early stages of success JT (or Jeremiah Terminator) was reclusive and mysterious. Public readings were conducted by fans on the premise that he was pathologically shy. Communications with him took place exclusively by phone, email, or fax. This was readily accepted because LeRoy had every reason to avoid the limelight. After all, his life had been an ordeal of being "pimped out as a cross-dressed prostitute by his mother at truck stops throughout the South" (Beachy 2005). The lack of public appearances even worked in LeRoy's favor. His reclusiveness fueled the myth and made fans ever more curious and devoted. Among these fans was a long list of celebrities, from Courtney Love to Gus Van Sant and Lou Reed. And, of course, Bono.

With such a level of attention, anonymity was no longer an option. As success went global, JT started appearing in public, always wearing sunglasses, hats, wigs and shapeless clothes. More emerged about his background. JT had multiple personality disorders. He was an HIV-positive junkie. He had developed a taste for literature from poetry-reading johns in hillbilly truck stops, communicated using a fax machine from modem-equipped restrooms, suffered abuse as a child at the hands of close family members. Sometimes JT felt like a he, sometimes a she. JT was the embodiment of innocence laid low by the evils of a heartless capitalist system. Now the author was trying to save himself through his art; he needed all the help he could get. Whatever the realities were, one thing was certain: JT LeRoy was the ultimate fantasy for the liberal-minded.

And that is just what he turned out to be: a fantasy, alter ego, avatar. The real author was Laura Albert, a mother in her early thirties. In her troubled teens, Laura started to phone crisis lines masquerading as a range of characters, including Jeremiah Terminator. Albert discovered listeners were more sympathetic when she impersonated a boy. In fact, after multiple calls, psychologist Terrence Owens encouraged Terminator to write down his experiences as a form of therapy. This was the beginning of Laura Albert's literary fantasy. Like JT, Albert had endured sexual abuse. But the rest was fiction. She had never been to West Virginia—or even a truck stop—but for the next decade she would tell tales of JT's teenage prostitution and abuse in these liminal spaces where the American Dream becomes nightmare. Albert would play JT in phone calls, faxes and emails, then assemble an expanding troupe of characters to star in a multilayered and increasingly absurd performance. Her sister-in-law, Savannah Knoop, would play JT LeRoy in public. Her husband, Geoffrey Knoop, acted as aspiring musician friend Astor. Albert herself played JT's British assistant and roommate, Speedie—in the least-believable gaw-blimey Cockney accent since Dick van Dyck. She also played wannabe rock star Emily Frasier, who wrote lyrics for JT's band. For a few years, nobody really questioned this impossible cast of misfits. But as the fiction became more fantastical and complex, it started to contradict itself and spiral out of control. Albert increasingly wanted to escape the world she had created—perhaps even get some recognition for her work—and began to tell confidants the truth. Or her version of it. Journalists also became suspicious. Finally, articles in the *New Yorker* and *New York Times* revealed that JT LeRoy and the whole absurd parade had been an elaborate hoax. The literary world and a gaggle of celebrities had been duped. The fantasy was over.

Once the hoax was busted, Laura Albert was castigated by the literary world as a liar. She was someone who had deliberately constructed a fantasy world to "trick" people and become famous. She found herself subject to a lawsuit and abandoned by the celebrity "friends" who had swarmed around JT. She withdrew for a time. It is still difficult to tell how deliberate the hoax was. Albert describes her penchant for creating characters as something she has always done to cope with a range of insecurities. She says the fantasy was as accidental as it was deliberate; once she started creating characters and spinning stories, she could not stop. However, she remains unapologetic. She describes JT as an avatar and believes "we should all be able to assume different voices. That's the idea of art, to be able to go to new worlds" (quoted in Langer 2013). Albert also points out that she never said the stories in the books were true: "It was fiction. It said that on the cover" (Feuerzeig 2016; Langer 2013). And as if to emphasize this fiction, she continually describes the moment the hoax was uncovered as "the big reveal."

Ultimately, "the truth" about JT LeRoy is unknowable and mostly irrelevant. But the whole episode illuminates how much people want—and often need—to believe in fantasies. And how much they are willing to participate in their construction. Celebrities in the art and literary worlds are so afraid of "losing their edge" that when something new and compelling comes along, they just have to be part of it. If the backstory is edgy, fits with their self-image and sense of moral authority, even better. As Albert says, "A lot of people signed up for the parade. The parade came to town and they loved it and it helped them. And when the reveal came, they could get attention for being injured" (quoted in Langer 2013). Those in the public eye were the most aggrieved at being "duped" or "tricked." Leroy's ordinary readers seemed ambivalent. They had wanted to be entertained by a fiction and the accompanying performance had fulfilled—maybe even surpassed—their desires. That LeRoy was also a fiction was entertaining in itself. But the credulous celebrities and experts had been complicit in the fantasy. As self-appointed cultural gatekeepers, they legitimized the JT LeRoy lie to enhance their own fantastical images. They had wanted to believe.

The Magic Cellar

The 2015 documentary *Sour Grapes* tells the story of oenophile Rudy Kurniawan. During the 2000s, Rudy performed perhaps the greatest wine fraud in history. He used his connoisseur knowledge to create fake bottles of expensive rare and vintage wines—particularly Burgundies—by blending relatively cheap bottles of Californian and French wines, then mimicking the labels, bottles and aging process through a DIY setup in his California home. In the process, Rudy conned millions of dollars from individual wine collectors and respected auction houses for years. In 2009, billionaire Bill Koch filed a lawsuit after discovering Rudy had swindled him out of $4 million for fake wine. The FBI got involved and in 2012 Kurniawan was arrested. He is currently serving 10 years in a correctional facility.

Rudy Kurniawan was a successful con artist not because he was a master forger. He wasn't. Sure, his sophisticated palate helped him approximate the taste of the wines he was forging, but he was also pretty slapdash. Most of the labels he made had spelling mistakes or incorrect details. Often he released more bottles of a rare wine than were ever made. And many of his approximations were simply not that good. But again, Kurniawan was successful because people wanted to believe in him. He had crafted an elaborate image and backstory that harnessed his victims' deepest fantasies. He was independently wealthy, dressed in expensive clothes, drove fast cars, had an art collection featuring the obligatory Damien Hirst and in the process created the myth that he was the go-to expert in the specialist domain of fine wine. He was what the majority of the people he conned either wanted to be or fantasized they were: rich, cultured experts.

Rudy understood that wealth plus cultural pretensions equaled opportunity. If he could tell a good enough story well enough for long enough, he could make a lot of money. What he did not quite realize—at least initially—was how simple it would be to become the "Great Gatsby of Generation X" (Atlas and Rothwell 2016). He could not have known how easily the experts, auction houses and wine collectors would be fooled. Nor how unwilling to admit their blunders they would be once suspicions were raised. If you watch the documentary and read about the case, it is clear that even now victims will not admit they were deceived. In the film, some maintain that although Rudy tricked hundreds of people, the wine that he sold them was the *real* deal. This is because they have too much skin in the game. People who consider themselves experts, who spent hundreds of thousands of dollars on wine that is still in their cellar, are unlikely to admit it is worthless. Or that their expertise is not much better. Revealingly, the person who finally busted the scam, Bill Koch, is so wealthy that the $4 million he lost did not particularly matter. For Koch, it was the principle of the thing.

Kurniawan fashioned "a collaboration between forger and dupe" (Atlas and Rothwell 2016). He told a great story, sucking people into the fantasy he was creating by mirroring their own. He hoodwinked gatekeepers—various wine experts and auctioneers—because they allowed themselves to be fooled. All this rare, expensive wine on the market was too good for business. And when gatekeepers are thinking too much about money, they become liable to compromise. Rudy was clearly a conman with very questionable morals—but he was also a magic seller.

Epilogue

Of course, we're not advocating conning people. We celebrate hustlers, not hucksters. But we do admire people who can craft images, narratives and situations that connect with other people—stories that make people forget reality and believe, if only for a little while. George Orwell (1944) once praised Charles Dickens for "telling small lies in order to emphasize what he regards as a big truth." Other writers in uncertain times have realized this, too. In the social and cultural maelstrom of the 1960s, a bunch of maverick journalists speculated that to connect, to emotionally resonate with their generation, just reporting "the facts" in a reasoned and supposedly objective way no longer cut the mustard. This cluster included Tom Wolfe, Norman Mailer, Truman Capote, Jimmy Breslin, Hunter S Thompson and Joan Didion—some of the greatest writers of the 20th century—and their approach became known as New Journalism. Author Marc Weingarten identifies the major tenet of New Journalism as the blurring of facts in order to arrive at some greater emotional or philosophical truth. Weingarten calls it "journalism that reads like fiction and rings with the truth of reported fact. It is the art of fact" (2006, loc.193). New Journalism caused an uproar with traditional journalists and editors, who thought its artistic license and subjective stance dishonest and heretical. But it connected immediately with a younger and more countercultural audience. And it is this ability to connect that is now so crucial in our postrational world.

Outliers like Trump or Brexit occur because their advocates tell better stories than the rationalized narratives of the liberal establishment. A phalanx of experts marshalled "the facts" against both but failed miserably. We have lost count how many times we heard experts laden with statistics predicting the adverse effects Brexit would have on the UK. These may turn out to be true but the statistical facts crumpled in the face of subjective fantasies. Conservative MP Michael Gove was only half right when he said "people ... have had enough of experts" (Sky News 2016). The experts were part of the problem, sure, but it was the data and statistics that pissed many people off. They were told there was no arguing with the data—the new deity of the early 21st century—so they chose to ignore it instead. People decided they would rather believe romantic myths than listen to rational arguments based on number-crunching. It turns out the Romantics were right: science and rationalism have never been enough. Whatever you're trying to do—whether it is selling games, running for office, or resisting authoritarianism—you had better tell the best story. It's not optional. It's not a luxury. Stories win elections and referenda. Stories connect. Stories resonate. Stories always trump statistics—because we need them in order to live.

Patronize Me, Please

"I think people have been obsessed with the wrong question, which is, 'How do we make people pay for music?' What if we started asking, 'How do we let people pay for music?'"

Amanda Palmer
The Art of Asking (2013)

Corporate Events

The most significant consequence of the internet revolution is the democratization of production and distribution. In the industrial era, power was derived from control over the means of production and the scarcity of distribution, in other words: supply. The internet era fundamentally changes how and where economic value is generated. As a result, power now resides in demand (Thompson 2017).

Artist Cory Arcangel calls it the "fourteen-year-old Finnish-kid syndrome," the modern phenomenon where any teenager with an iPhone can make something attention-grabbing (quoted by Chen 2017). It would be complacent to think game making is not well on its way to similar democratization, as tools such as *GameMaker*, *Twine*, *Source*, *Construct* and *Scratch* already demonstrate.

As we explored in previous chapters, the demise of industrial rationalization and the revival of the artisan is a positive step. The nostalgic fetishization of craft as a noun, however, is most definitely not. In a demand-driven economy, the artist still starves. It is the creative entrepreneur—the silo-smashing maker, marketer and merchant—who eats well.

Rather than taking your cue from the wolves of Wall Street or the techno-libertarians of Silicon Valley, Bruce Nussbaum suggests you take a closer look at the artisans of Bushwick and Rivington Street and their "indie capitalism" (2011). Swapping in the economics of efficiency and control for the economics of creativity and chance, Nussbaum argues these indie capitalists—we prefer "creative entrepreneurs"—are perfectly positioned to capitalize on the highly networked heterogeneity of the internet era (2013).

For Nussbaum, a defining characteristic of the indie capitalist is their reframing of capitalism as a social movement rather than a free market phenomenon. In such a space, social networks become the "basic building blocks of the economy," blurring the distinction between "creators, curators, founders and consumers" and cultivating an environment that is far more communal and experiential than it is clinically transactional (2013). Kickstarter, Nussbaum believes, perfectly illustrates his thesis. Not only is Kickstarter a transformative model for crowd funding but also for crowd building; it is a way to attract and organize an audience of like-minded people as well as a mechanism to capitalize on an existing audience. Such dialogic spaces make creators, capitalists and patrons of us all (Nussbaum 2013).

Democracy in Action

There is little argument that "the democratization of innovation" is a vapid slogan. As we discussed in the previous chapter, not only has innovation become conflated with invention, but it has become domesticated by corporations and hijacked by bottom-feeding creative consultants, gurus and experts. And what has democracy done for us lately, anyway? Zero-hours contracts, the erosion of egalitarianism and social welfare, myopic technocracy and populist insularity. Wonderful! Within such a context, it is easy to be cynical and dismiss the likes of Nussbaum, but it is important not to lose sight of the fact that innovation *has* been democratized and the opportunities this affords game makers *are* very real.

In mass-focused, manufacturer-centric innovation—a legacy of the industrial era—users rely on corporations to act as their "often very imperfect" agents, with homogenous results designed to meet the needs of and capture profits from, a mass market (von Hippel 2006, loc.35). But in the internet era—when user needs are more explicitly nuanced and individuals have the agency as well as the means of production and distribution—it is often more effective to just do it yourself. User-centric punk innovation extends beyond clinical commerce: communities of practice and patronage cluster around innovations, using open-source organization and cooperation to increase the speed and effectiveness of design, development and distribution. In many ways, user-centric innovation is the antithesis of the *Field of Dreams* strategy, catalyzing a Boydian-like OODA loop of continual feedback, iteration and curious mutation.

Sublime Interventions

Spelunky is the personification of user-centric innovation. A procedurally generated mashup of platformer and roguelike, *Spelunky* was designed and developed by Derek Yu and released in 2008 as freeware via niche online forum The Independent Gaming

Source (TIGSource), where its merits divided the community but delighted *Braid* creator Jonathan Blow. Championed to Microsoft by the ever-altruistic Blow, the game was remade and released on Microsoft Xbox Live Arcade (XBLA) in 2012. Interestingly, Yu elected not to simply rebuild *Spelunky Classic* but instead remix the original to create "fan fiction," Yu's rationale being that creating an original game is a very different creative act than reimagining an existing one. He preferred to be liberated by a mindset that "offers the same kind of bliss as lying on the grass and pointing out what the clouds remind you of" (2016, loc.1182). The XBLA version enjoyed (more than) reasonable critical acclaim and commercial success, but it would take an unsolicited user-initiated innovation for *Spelunky* to fully express itself.

Four months after *Spelunky*'s XBLA release, Yu received a serendipitous email from *JS Joust* designer Doug Wilson (2012), describing a whole new way to experience *Spelunky*:

> About a month ago, Nifflas and I started a daily tradition—a ritual, if you will. Every night, each of us gets one—and only one—*Spelunky* run. The other sits and watches, cheering along and providing advice. On rare days we'll indulge in a few practice runs, but it's only the "official" run that really matters—at least to us!
>
> This ritual has been deeply enjoyable for several reasons. First, the tradition gives us something to look forward to every evening. Second, the "stakes" of the game feel so much more real when you only get one shot. One error and you're done for the day. Nerve-wracking, but invigorating! Third and perhaps most importantly, I find that it's far more rewarding to play the game with somebody spectating—a witness with whom to share your triumphs and tribulations. After all, Spelunky is all about the stories you the player end up producing. As my hero Hannah Arendt puts it: "The presence of others who see what we see and hear what we hear assures us of the reality of the world and ourselves."
>
> Jokingly, before each run, we make a little prayer to Derek Yu, the game's creator. (For example: "Derek Yu, please grant us plentiful bombs and protect us from dark levels. Amen.") The prayer has itself become a key part of our daily ritual—to the point where we feel like we've almost created a Spelunky religion/cult. Like, why do bad things happen to good Spelunky players? And does Derek Yu even exist? Spelunky theology is tricky!

Wilson and "Nifflas" (game maker Nicklas Nygren) had turned *Spelunky* into an experience beyond the game's maker-defined boundaries. Excited by the framing and convinced by Wilson's "boundless enthusiasm" for this new way to play, Yu developed a Daily Challenge mode for the impending Steam version of *Spelunky* that riffed on Wilson's DIY innovation. Of course, Wilson's ritual only works if you have two or more people in the same physical space, so Yu once again turned to the community. Capturing the zeitgeist of *Let's Play* videos and Twitch and YouTube streaming, Yu turned the Daily Challenge from physically constrained local spectator sport to worldwide-networked broadcast experience. By seeding prerelease copies with prominent streamers to build buzz, *Spelunky* would sell 61,408 copies in its first month on Steam— more than double its XBLA performance—and more than half a million copies in its first two years of release (Yu 2016, loc.1781). *PC Gamer*'s Game of the Year in 2013 and ranked third on *Eurogamer*'s "Games of the Generation" list, *Spelunky* has sold over 1 million copies across all platforms and, more importantly, "every day, players are still drinking their daily cup of *Spelunky* coffee by playing the Daily Challenge" (Yu 2016, loc.1783).

Small Batch and Neat

In the summer of 2010, childhood friends Tom Gerhardt and Dan Provost began collaborating on a passion project—a tripod mount for the iPhone 4—on evening and weekends. After a couple of months sketching concepts, modeling designs and 3D printing prototypes, Gerhardt and Provost had an iteration worth making. They called it the *Glif* and it was an "elegant and simple" design they were both proud of (Gerhardt and Provost 2012, loc.74).

In the industrial era, this is where the story would have ended. Physically manufacturing the Glif would involve the process of injection molding, requiring considerable upfront investment. In the internet era, however, Gerhardt and Provost simply pitched their product on Kickstarter. Based on nothing more than a hunch, the unknown duo launched their Glif Kickstarter campaign in October 2010 with a modest funding goal of $10,000. Without spending a dime on advertising, they met their goal in just 12 hours and by the end of the 30-day campaign they had raised $137,417.

Gerhardt and Provost did not set out to create a legitimate business enterprise, nor did they dream of getting rich quick with a side income. They just wanted to embrace their love of iPhone photography and make a product that would scratch their own itch. And with completely unrelated day jobs—Gerhardt a software engineer and Provost an interaction designer—the duo had zero experience or expertise in industrial design, manufacturing, or retail when they pitched the Glif. All they had was a compelling pitch to catch the attention of like-minded people.

The campaign video for Glif was only 127 seconds long, yet it made a lasting impression on almost every iPhone aficionado who saw it. While the Glif was not for everyone—it was made for a particular phone (iPhone 4 only), a narrow use case (it was "just" a tripod mount to let you take better photos) and would only work under a specific set of conditions (naked: no case or screen protector allowed)—it was for someone. Too often, creators forget that patrons are people too, with their individual worldviews, biases and peccadilloes. But Gerhardt and Provost did not. They embraced individuality, making the Glif as opinionated, deceptively simple, beautifully designed and luxurious as the Apple product it served. That is why it resonated.

Kickstarter success is most often predicated on telling a resonant story: what desire is this fulfilling, who is it for, who is it not for, why should they care, how will it be brought to life? Gerhardt and Provost (2012) understand that as a patron you're "not buying a thing, you're buying a thing made by this person." This is a subtle but important distinction between curating storied, interactive journeys and quietly placing your product on someone else's overcrowded digital shelf. As Gerhardt and Provost (2012, loc.180) insightfully surmise:

> People want to know where things come from and who is behind the design. Products do not exist in a vacuum; they are designed and created by humans, which we sometimes forget.

Conscious of the often-ignored fact that good design and great products do not sell themselves, the duo were proactive in their marketing outreach. They focused on winning the hearts and minds of Apple influencers—such as *Daring Fireball*'s John Gruber—rather than taking the more traditional route of paid public relations or mainstream press lobbying. Active documentarians and writers, the duo used the campaign and the subsequent journey from prototype to commercial product to show their patrons "how the sausage is made," consequently building a deliberately human, thoughtful relationship with their backers. Arguing "you're not a faceless corporation, so why act like one?" Gerhardt and Provost were honest, direct and passionate (2012, loc.820). They did not try to gloss over their lack of experience or expertise in certain areas, nor did they temper their geeky enthusiasm for making the Glif for fear of appearing unprofessional. The duo liken crowdfunding to "having 5,000 bosses" (Gerhardt and Provost 2012, loc.335). Fortunately, they choose their superiors wisely.

A few months after the successful Glif campaign, Gerhardt and Provost quit their day jobs to go full time. To this day, they remain the only employees of Studio Neat and are completely focused on making things they care deeply about and are invigorated to work on. Gerhardt and Provost describe their agile venture as "small batch," in tribute to craft bourbon distilleries and their obsessive pursuit of handcrafted quality over mass-market proliferation and profit.

Since its initial success, Studio Neat has continued to curate its own microcosm of passionate patrons by simultaneously scratching its own itches and tapping into latent niche markets in desperate need of a little beautifully designed, handcrafted luxury. So far, Studio Neat adventures include cool tools for hobbyist cocktail connoisseurs, Apple TV remote stands hand-milled in Texas from a single piece of walnut and possibly the best wide-grip iPad stylus in the world. Genuinely uninterested in scaling to the mainstream, attracting venture capital, or abandoning its patrons in search of mass-market customers, Studio Neat is driven by the pursuit of one simple guiding principle: solve interesting problems and delight like-minded people. In doing so, it will continue to blur the lines between maker, marketer and merchant.

Punk Patronage

"BrewDog is an alternative small company, part owned by the people who love the beers we made. They are our shareholders, our best customers, our friends and the heart and soul of our business."

James Watt
Co-founder, BrewDog (2015)

Stretched to their banking credit limit but in need of an injection of capital to sustain their growth, our old friends at BrewDog decided to apply their punk approach to crowdfunding.

Equity for Punks was an innovative, alternative approach to business finance where BrewDog sold equity stakes in the company online to fans rather than professional investors. "Fast, furious and ruthlessly effective," Equity for Punks was "game changing" for the Scottish brewery and its co-founders, Martin Dickie and James Watt, helping them to fund their intensive expansion plans without having to dilute their clarity of purpose or control over its execution (Watt 2015, p.73).

As a concept, Equity for Punks was dismissed out of hand by the first seven legal companies BrewDog consulted. In their "expert" opinion, what BrewDog wanted to do was impossible. Undeterred, the company pressed ahead, gambling BrewDog's entire future on making it work. Inspired by rejection, BrewDog launched Equity for Punks with "all guns blazing," hiring a 1940s tank, plastering it with BrewDog logos and parking it outside the Bank of England and London Stock Exchange. James Watt (2015, p.76) wanted to send a message:

> Equity for Punks was not about tinkering with the established order. We wanted to strap on the dynamite. This was more Guy Fawkes than Rockefeller.

Since 2009, BrewDog has launched four Equity for Punks crowdfunding campaigns, creating over 46,000 patrons and raising in excess of £15 million in the process. Yet for Watt the real beauty of Equity for Punks is not the financial investment but the emotional one. As a scheme, Equity for Punks deeply strengthens the bond between the brewery and the people who enjoy its beers. In contrast to professional investment, crowdfunding means BrewDog investors are its best customers, most passionate ambassadors and co-conspirators in the brewery's growth and success (Watt 2015, p.73):

> We revel in the fact that people as passionate about craft beer as we are now own a slice of our business. No greedy hustlers, no fat cats (or dogs), no investment banks, no venture capitalists, no overbearing parent. Just loads of people who passionately love great beer.

Nowhere is their ideal of playful punk patronage better articulated than in *DIY Dog*, an open-source recipe book of every BrewDog beer ever created (BrewDog 2016):

> With DIY Dog we wanted to do something that has never been done before as well as paying tribute to our homebrewing roots. We wanted to take all of our recipes, every single last one and

give them all away for free, to the amazing global home brewing community.

We have always loved the sharing of knowledge, expertise and passion in the craft beer community and we wanted to take that spirit of collaboration to the next level.

So here it is. The keys to our kingdom. Every single BrewDog recipe, ever. So copy them, tear them to pieces, bastardise them, adapt them and most of all enjoy them.

They are well-traveled but with plenty of miles still left on the clock. Just remember to share your brews and your results. Sharing is caring.

Oh and if you're from one of the global beer mega corporations and you're reading this, your computer will spontaneously combust, James Bond style, any second now.

So leave the building immediately and seriously consider your life choices.

DIY Dog gives away all of the BrewDog magic formulas for free. In theory, anyone can now do it themselves and make a BrewDog beer. If making alone is responsible for the success of the brand, then BrewDog has not only radically democratized brewing but accelerated their own demise. But it is not the sole metric of success. Making is just making, a small—admittedly, crucial—component of a greater experience. And it is the greater experience that is responsible for the thousands of punks that patronize BrewDog.

Strange Currencies

Money is not the only measure of value. This is a lesson *The Stanley Parable* co-creator William Pugh learned by self-funding Crows Crows Crows—his experimental game making studio—instead of signing with a publisher or taking outside investment.

Rather than spend multiple years developing a long-form game that "would likely be mediocre" and "crushed by the expectations of *The Stanley Parable*," Pugh (2017) took the decision to release a flurry of short-form playful experiences for free. By trading short-term profit for long-term patronage, Pugh and his team were able to build a 50,000-strong email list within a single year. Through these releases, Crows Crows Crows has not only developed the production repertoire and rhythm to support future production of long-form content, but it has also built a passionate following that is ready and willing to lend its patronage when that time finally comes.

In the process, Crows Crows Crows has also created a unique, playful tone of voice to complement its prolific tone of action, as evidenced by the "UNPROFESSIONAL RANT ZONE" Pugh inserted into a Gamasutra guest editorial (2017):

OKAY WELCOME TO THE UNPROFESSIONAL RANT ZONE YOU FUCKING BORING GAMASUTRA READING FUCKER!! HERE I WILL EXPLAIN TO YOU IN MY REAL UNPROFESSIONAL VOICE WHAT THE SITUATION WITH EMAILS IS:

FUCK OFF WITH YOUR BULLSHIT MARKETING BULLSHIT EMAIL LIST THAT YOU HALF-HEARTEDLY ASK PEOPLE TO SIGN UP TO ON YOUR WORDPRESS SITE THEN POST BULLSHIT THAT PEOPLE WILL READ SOMEWHERE ELSE ANYWAY—DON'T YOU FUCKING DARE EMAIL YOUR FANS SOME BORING DRY WHITE BREAD PRESS COPY THAT SENDS THEM TO SLEEP!! I AM LOOKING AT YOU LITERALLY EVERYBODY WHO'S EVER SENT ME AN EMAIL!!

EMAILS FROM COMPANIES ARE LIKE "HAVE YOU FOUND JESUS CHRIST" LEAFLETS YOU GET HANDED IN THE STREET. NOBODY GIVES A FUUUCK—NOBODY GIVES A FUCK YOU FUCKING STUPID BUSINESS IDIOTS WHY AM I TELLING YOU THIS YOU DUMB FUCKING IDIOTS FUCK YOU. FUCK YOU. YOU NEED TO BE EXUDING YOUR STYLE & IDENTITY THROUGH YOUR EMAIL SHAPED PORES AND YOU NEED TO FUCK YOUR EMAIL LIST IN A CONFIDENT AND VIGOROUS AND CREATIVE MANNER THAT INVOLVES EVERYTHING THEY WANT INCLUDING:

- ORIGINAL FUCKING CONTENT MADE BY THE CORE CREATIVE TEAM THAT UTILISES AND SUBVERTS THE FUCKING ANCIENT MEDIUM IT IS PRESENTED IN
- SOME FUCKING COOL SHIT LIKE THE TEMPLE OF NO— PLEASE DEDICATE ACTUAL RESOURCES TO MAKE THINGS PEOPLE WILL ACTUALLY ENJOY NOBODY GIVES A FUCK ABOUT THE NEW BARRY THE BIRD CHARACTER REVEAL UNLESS YOU'RE BLIZZARD
- DO NOT FUCKING LET YOUR STUCK-ON-LIFE-SUPPORT- PR-MARKETING-MANAGER FROM THE 8TH CIRCLE OF CONVERSION TOUCH ANY OF YOUR COPY—IT IS TO BE HANDLED BY -> -> -> THE CREATIVE TEAM <- <- <-

YOUR COMMUNICATION DICTATES THE PERCEIVED REALITY OF YOUR COMPANY SO PLEASE NEVER EVER SEND ME SOMETHING THAT HASN'T HAD ACTUAL PRODUCTION TIME SCHEDULED FOR IT'S CREATION!! AND I WANT SHIT FROM

THE CORE CREATIVE TEAM PLLEEEEAAAASSSSEEEEE!!!!!! PLEASE FOR THE LOVE OF HOLY FUCKING CHRIST YOU IDIOTS SIGN UP TO THE CROWSCROWSCROWS.COM EMAIL LIST IF YOU WANT REALLY GOOD FREE GAMES THIS IS JUST PROMOTION FOR MY STUDIO THIS IS JUST PROMOTION FOR MY STUDIO THIS IS JUST PROMOTION FOR MY STUDI– [sic]

Pugh is part of a new wave of tricksters unafraid to turn the act of game making into a community-driven performance act. Through "performative game development," Vlambeer also turned *Nuclear Throne* into a self-sustainable venture while it was still in the early stages of production (Sheffield 2014). By live streaming development directly to patrons twice weekly, *Nuclear Throne* was "informed by the community, while also informing the community about game development," simultaneously blurring the lines and strengthening the bond between creator and patron to create a more impassioned, invested and educated community of backers (Sheffield 2014).

Modern Love

Writing about the "Creative Apocalypse That Wasn't," Steven Johnson (2015) highlights the irony of artists who once complained about the "rapacious pursuit of consumer dollars" by their industry paymasters now complaining the same industries are not profitable enough for them to exist within. Seeing this complaint as short-sighted, Johnson argues that the death of longstanding centralized institutions—"record labels or studios or publishing conglomerates"—would not represent a doomsday event, the genuine dystopian scenario would be the "the death of music or movies" themselves (2015). It is the ongoing prosperity of creatives and artisans that is truly important for culture and society; the industries they have been forced to operate within don't really matter. Any cuddly reinvention of industrialized institutions is, in reality, a ruthless act of self-preservation masquerading as egalitarianism. There is no better time to cut the umbilical cord and build your own communities of practice, patronage and playful experiences.

Punks and provocateurs: seize the moment, smash the monoculture, do it yourself!

#90
JACK HAMMER

RUTHLESS INDIA PALE ALE. HOPPY. BITTER. HOPPY.

ABV	IBU	OG
7.2%	250	1065

THIS BEER IS

Hopped beyond the point at which IBUs are measurable, only the most hardened palate will get beyond Jack Hammer's intensely resinous pithy bitterness and to the grapefruit, orange zest and dry biscuity malt beyond. You could brew this with less hops, but really, why would you bother?

BASICS

VOLUME	20L	5gal
BOIL VOLUME	25L	6.6gal
ABV		7.2%
TARGET FG		1010
TARGET OG		1065
EBC		15
SRM		7.5
PH		4.4
ATTENUATION LEVEL		84.6%

METHOD / TIMINGS

MASH TEMP

65°C	149°F	75mins

FERMENTATION

21°C	70°F

INGREDIENTS

 MALT

Extra Pale	5.81kg	12.8lb

HOPS

	(g)	Add	Attribute
Centennial	25	Start	Bitter
Columbus Extract	30	Start	Bitter
Centennial	18.75	Middle	Flavour
Columbus	18.75	Middle	Flavour
Centennial	50	End	Flavour
Columbus	25	End	Flavour
Amarillo	100	Dry Hop	Aroma
Citra	100	Dry Hop	Aroma
Simcoe	100	Dry Hop	Aroma

 YEAST

Wyeast 1272 - American Ale II™

FOOD PAIRING

Phall Curry

Pork burrito with a habanero and mango chilli salsa.

Ginger and grapefruit poundcake

PACKAGING

BREWER'S TIP

Be aware that this is probably the hoppiest beer you will ever make. Make sure you use fresh hops, for a massive fresh grapefruit hit. Have everything else in your store cupboard, and buy your hops last, as close to brew day as possible!

FIGURE 4.4 You can copy BrewDog's recipe for making *Jack Hammer* but can you re-capture the definitive drinking experience? (Reprinted with permission from BrewDog, Copyright © 2016 BrewDog. All Rights Reserved.)

Devolver Digital: A Case Study in Amplification

Devolver Digital is a publisher for game makers who don't need one. An antidote to the monolithic, monocultural game publisher, Devolver has pioneered a new kind of maker–publisher dynamic based on personal relationships, creative freedom and fair contracts.

Small, nimble and self-funded, Devolver takes risks with the artists it works with, the deals it offers and the niche titles it publishes. Its reward is a hard-won reputation as a mainstream purveyor of "magnificently handcrafted games"; our reward is a new wave of exciting, sustainable, independent game makers.

Twenty-Four-Hour Party Playthings

"If video games are in their 'indie period,' where is our Factory Records?"

Jamin Warren
Kill Screen (2012)

Factory Records needs little reintroduction. The iconic Manchester record label was set up in 1978 by that "freewheeling, free-thinking bundle of contradictions," Tony Wilson (Morley 2007). Using a curious cocktail of "regional pride, entrepreneurial elan and seductive brand of quasi-situationist hedonism," Wilson brought Joy Division, New Order, Happy Mondays and the Haçienda to the world (King 2012).

For Factory—and its contemporaries of the 1980s—the mission extended beyond breaking provocative acts and distributing great records. Independent record labels were the self-appointed antithesis of the mainstream music industry and the postindustrial gloom of Thatcher's Britain; they embodied a set of ideals, cultural theories and aesthetic sensibilities. The Smiths signed to an independent instead of a major label because, according to guitarist Johnny Marr, "The very act of being on Rough Trade at the time was a statement in itself" (quoted by King 2012).

In a world oversaturated by indie games, indie game makers and now, indie publishers, Warren's question regarding the whereabouts of our Factory Records seems more pertinent than ever. Perhaps, Devolver Digital—"the closest thing to an indie record label our industry has" (Roberts 2015)—provides an answer?

Highly Devolved

Devolver Digital was founded in 2009 by Mike Wilson, Harry A Miller IV, Rick Stults, Nigel Lowrie and Graeme Struthers after the global financial crisis forced the sale of their previous venture, Gamecock Media Group. In some ways, Devolver Digital is the continuation of the good work that began with Gamecock. A Miramax-type studio, Gamecock helped independent game makers publish their work by doing "all the stuff a developer needs a publisher to do, but none of the stuff that they don't need a publisher to do" (Wilson 2007). In other ways, Devolver is more of a contextual iteration. Where Gamecock had external investors—the catalyst for its ultimate demise—Devolver Digital is wholly independent and was initially a side project funded by day jobs. Where Gamecock wanted to scale and take the major labels on at their own game, Devolver prefers to stay small and leave the major publishers to eat themselves. Where Gamecock was built to solve a problem for independents in the boxed product retail era, Devolver foresaw the shift to smaller games, infinite niches and digital distribution and it positioned itself accordingly (Jagneaux 2016).

Since the release of its first title—*Serious Sam HD: The First Encounter*—Devolver Digital has published over 50 more. And it has worked with game makers as diverse and distributed as Vlambeer (Netherlands), Croteam (Croatia), Roll7 (UK), Le Cartel Studio (France), Ojiro Fumoto (Japan), Free Lives (South Africa), Coffee Powdered Machine (Argentina), Jay Tholen (US), Terri Vellmann (Brazil) and No Code (Scotland). With a ludography zig-zagging between the sublime and the ridiculous, it is hard to define Devolver. There are ludicrous first-person shooters (*Serious Sam HD*), retro arcade games (*Luftrausers*), pigeon dating simulators (*Hatoful Boyfriend*), philosophical puzzle games (*The Talos Principle*), surreal point-and-click tragi-comedies (*Dropsy*) and psychological-horror text adventure homages to *Stranger Things* (*Stories Untold*). The only common theme is that each release is a magnificently handcrafted provocation that somehow, feels distinctly "Devolver."

There may be a feel of what is Devolver, but there is no prescriptive checklist criteria or style guide. Devolver Digital seeks out mavericks and misfits capable of setting themselves apart from the modern "indie" homogeny through attitude, aesthetic and/or experience. According to Nigel Lowrie, the games Devolver is attracted to do not have to be revolutionary or perfect, they just have to "strike us in some indescribable way" (quoted by Roberts 2015).

At their peak, the independent record labels of the 1980s were a vital, vibrant "source of popular experimentation and improvisation that connected with a wide audience" (King 2012). The Devolver Digital mission is similar: help interesting independents create exciting experiences and expose them to a wider, willing audience.

You Don't Need a Publisher

Nigel Lowrie (2016) argues that "nobody needs a game publisher" because "self-publishing is better than a bad agreement." If game makers do seek a publisher, it should only be because they believe their target publishing partner can perform the dirty work involved in producing and publishing a successful game better than they could themselves. In contrast to the majority of publishers—even self-styled "indie publishers"—Devolver has a devastatingly simple strategy: scout interesting game makers and help them make and sell their work. They do not promise the world, nor do they enforce oppressive contracts or demand creative control in return for their support. Devolver (Wilson quoted by Messner 2016) cultivates personal relationships with the game makers it works with, relationships built around fair contracts, creative freedom and honesty:

> The traditional method of dealing with difficult talent is to buy them. The publishers then own their intellectual property and can continue to crank out sequels with less uppity game developers. That's the point of owning the developer, you never have to listen to them.

In contrast to this traditional command-and-control publisher relationship, the role Devolver plays is simply one of enabler. It affords game makers space, time and resources to "have an impact in their lives and help them bring their project to life" and involves itself in that process only as much as the artist chooses (Struthers quoted by Jagneaux 2016). This model works because Devolver invests in teams and their potential rather than seductive paper ideas or fully formed products. The scope of Devolver's involvement varies from project to project, but one thing it always brings is creative freedom laced with brutal honesty. The close personal relationships Devolver cultivate affords the opportunity to "argue like friends" with teams, challenging them on important things like time and money and telling them things they sometimes don't want to hear but need to. But, says Lowrie (quoted by McKeand 2016), at all times the team reserves the right to tell Devolver to "fuck off."

Without Devolver Digital, *Enter the Gungeon*—the 2016 hit retro dungeon crawler—would likely have run out of money and its maker, Dodge Roll Games, would have been "forced to release the game too early," admits Dave Crooks from the Washington, DC, developer (quoted by Jagneaux 2016). Crooks praises Devolver for not only pushing them to release a better game but also curating a better promotional campaign and exposing the game to a far wider audience through trailers and demos in Best Buys and GameStops around the US.

> *"When it comes to how we position ourselves and how we do things, we do whatever's best for the developer and getting their games out there, because ultimately they're the ones who want to find success and hopefully they will want to work with us again. They've trusted us with their livelihood and their art, so we have to be good stewards of that."*
>
> **Nigel Lowrie**
> *(quoted by McKeand 2016)*

Artists and Repertoire

Another thing that sets Devolver apart from other game publishers—and reinforces its independent label credentials—is a commitment to artists and repertoire (A&R). The A&R division of a record label are responsible for scouting talent, bringing them to the label and overseeing their development as recording artists. While major record labels have significantly scaled back on A&R—shifting toward a more conservative signing policy in a desperate bid to conserve the music business they understand and profit from—independents continue to use good A&R to their unfair advantage.

It is an unfair advantage for Devolver Digital, too. No other game publisher comes close to matching its commitment to uncovering talent and potential. Devolver may receive 10 new pitches every week but Lowrie still regularly trawls "everything from *TIGSource* to *IndieDB* and *Steam Greenlight*," as well as spending time walking the floors of festivals, to uncover hidden gems (Jagneaux 2016).

Titan Souls started as a small prototype made for Ludum Dare—the long-running, online 48-hour game jam event. Devolver Digital stumbled upon it, played it, liked its potential, sought out its creators—UK independent studio Acid Nerve—and offered to help the Mancunian duo turn it into a full game. Fifteen months later, Acid Nerve released its commercial debut simultaneously on Playstation 4, Playstation Vita, PC and Mac. Signed for its potential and funded through development without any dilution of creative control, it is difficult to see how *Titan Souls* would have realized its vision without the patronage and parenting of Devolver. This emphasis on personal relationships runs throughout the history of Devolver Digital. Its first release, *Serious Sam 3*, came about due to a longstanding relationship with the game's makers, Croteam. A long-term relationship with Vlambeer and the publishing of *Luftrausers* happened when Devolver approached the Dutch duo to "remix" *Serious Sam*. In turn, it was Vlambeer who tipped Devolver off that Jonathan "Cactus" Söderström—a Swedish avant-garde game maker—had decided that, after years of self-publishing free experimental games, he wanted to do something commercial (McKeand 2016).

Playful and Provocative

Devolver did not know what kind of game Söderström planned when it signed him up. According to founding partner Graeme Struthers, it only "knew who Cactus [Söderström] was" and "If the guy wanted to make a chess game we would have said yes" (quoted by Purchase 2012). What Dennaton Games—a collaboration between Söderström and artist Dennis Wedin—had in the works was not chess but "exceptional top down f***-em-up" (Purchase 2012)—*Hotline Miami*.

> *"I had no idea what kind of game was going to drop into our lap at that point. When I got my build, I was just so happy. The music and the colour palette—it all just really came together for me in one magic burst of pixel joy. I didn't connect with feeling queasy or worried by the violence, let alone thinking about the underlying story. I was just having a blast."*
>
> **Graeme Struthers**
> *Devolver Digital (quoted by Edge Magazine* 2013)

After experimenting with music, drawing and short film in his teens, Söderström settled upon game making as his creative outlet. Armed with a copy of *GameMaker*, he began releasing games under the pseudonym Cactus. Since 2004, he has published over 40 video games, mostly small in size and avant-garde in nature.

In 2011, Söderström teamed up with Dennis Wedin to make the psychedelic *Keyboard Drumset Fucking Werewolf*. Encouraged by the collaboration, Söderström and Wedin began developing *Life/ Death/Island* but abandoned it when the scope outgrew their finances. After years of giving his games away for free, Söderström needed to put a game out that would make some money. Trawling Söderström's considerable archive, Wedin came across an abandoned prototype called *Super Carnage*, a simple, top-down shoot 'em up. Created when Söderström was just 18, it was a "teen-age boy's game: sick and violent and little more than that" (Edge Magazine 2013). However, viewed through mature eyes and aspi-rations, its potential was apparent. Before starting development, Söderström and Wedin watched a bunch of movies, including the Miami drug wars documentary *Cocaine Cowboys* and Nicolas Winding Refn's visceral neo-noir movie *Drive*. Both helped shape the thesis at the heart of *Hotline Miami* and its subsequent success: "What if *Super Carnage* wasn't merely a game in which you killed people, but a game that posed questions about what it meant to kill people in a game?" (*Edge* Magazine 2013).

In his review of *Hotline Miami*—"The First Postmodern Videogame?"—Joseph Bernstein (n.d.) called out the "conservative sphere of refer-ence" deployed by independent game makers. Bernstein observed the tendency for independent games to be "creative iterations of games their creators played growing up, often spectacularly cre-ative ones, but still, iterations" (n.d.). It is here, knowingly, where *Hotline Miami*—an "unimpeachable" aesthetic document, as viewed by Bernstein—distances itself from the average independent game. Scratch beneath the superficial influence of *Smash TV* and the origi-nal *Grand Theft Auto* and you can see the deeper cultural connections to the likes of *Cocaine Cowboys*. Söderström himself admits that he was "pretty tired of crappy games that don't really want to do any-thing special, just make more of the same and don't try new things." Instead, he wanted to "express something interesting that you want to share with other people" (quoted by Procter n.d.).

Hotline Miami is an expression of Söderström's concern with the way games portray violence as a "clean act," and how this absolves the player of any responsibility (quoted by Webster 2012). To chal-lenge this portrayal and abdication of responsibility, Söderström adopts a Peckinpah-like approach to making violence feel disturb-ing and discomforting to the audience:

> *"We wanted to show violence in real terms. Dying is not fun and games. Movies make it look so detached. With 'The Wild Bunch,' people get involved whether they like it or not. They do not have the mild reactions to it."*
>
> **Sam Peckinpah**
> *(quoted in Ebert 1969)*

As *Edge* (2013) rightly argued, *Hotline Miami* is a "deliriously vio-lent … nihilistic murder simulator" that at the same time poses a powerful and searching question to the player: "do you like hurt-ing people? And if you don't, why are you still playing?"

Hit the Road

Hotline Miami did not need a publisher but it undoubtedly benefitted from the partnership with Devolver Digital. Six months before its October 2012 release, *Hotline Miami* went on tour, visiting independent-minded game expos and festivals. At the inaugural Rezzed in Brighton, *Hotline Miami* won "Game Of The Show" from both *Eurogamer* and *Rock, Paper, Shotgun*, with the latter calling it "a work of bloody art [that] stood out a mile even at a show already full of wonders" (Meer 2012).

From that point forward, the momentum kept gathering as the game delighted crowds at both the Eurogamer Expo and Gamescom. Relatively unknown outside of the Devolver inner circle before Rezzed, the exposure built a following among press and players, creating a demand that culminated in a gushing launch day review in *Eurogamer* and 130,000 copies in the first seven weeks of release (Purchase 2012).

The sales figures would have been even higher but for the downloading of bootleg copies through torrenting. Instead of trying to fight the piracy, Dennaton embraced it, releasing a patch to fix some bugs present in the bootleg version. Whether a customer or a pirate, it was important that everyone got to play the best version of *Hotline Miami* (Purchase 2012). This stance mirrors Devolver's attitude toward streamers and YouTubers. In a world where megacorp monoliths—even the saintly Nintendo—serve desist notices and demand a share of revenue, Devolver encourages anyone and everyone to use footage of their games with no rules or restrictions. If the question is "can I stream and monetize Devolver Digital games?" the answer is always "yes" (Kuchera 2015). For Devolver, streamers and YouTubers are a critical function of modern publicity—so much so that Lowrie (2016) counsels independent game makers that should their potential publisher's PR strategy does not include streamers and YouTubers, they should "walk out of the door, lock that door and set the building on fire because they don't know what they are doing."

Reigns

Industry experts will tell you that the mobile market is an "indie-hostile" space where "paid apps are truly dead"; even if you have a hit, unless it's a free-to-play cash cow, you cannot gross enough money to turn a profit (Fahey 2016; Haro 2016). Devolver Digital disagrees.

Handcrafted by Nerial and published by Devolver, *Reigns* is a strategic card game that sold over a million copies in its first quarter of release. The majority of these sales were made on mobile app stores at the premium price of $2.99 (Reigns 2016a, 2016b). Written and developed on a tiny budget by François Alliot—in collaboration with Mieko Murakami (art), Disasterspace (audio direction), Matéo Lugo (music) and Eric Van Amerongen (sound design)—*Reigns* is a playful, playable, political satire inspired by the absurdity of Brexit—the 2016 referendum where British citizens voted to exit the European Union on indefinite terms at an undefined future date. Alliot (2016) set out to mock the way societies confront the complexities of the modern world by reducing them to political binaries in the vein of *Tinder*:

> It's troubling to think that a deep and complex decision involving the future of a whole continent was defined by the same mechanic as a casual dating service: a binary choice made disappointingly simple, crushing every nuance that a complex subject demands. Swipe either right or left. Accept the huge geopolitical consequences.

The core strength of *Reigns* is that the entire experience—every aspect of production—was defined by this provocative perspective. Every aesthetic contribution—its tone, audio-visual style, smart writing, subtle depth of gameplay, tactility and how it makes the player think and feel—are all in service of its satirical message. Alliot admits that Nerial did not set out to make the perfect game but to amplify an experience; the joke that modern political complexity had been reduced to a series of yes/no, in/out, right/left, good/bad binary questions.

Alliot did not want a publisher for *Reigns*; he just wanted to work with Devolver Digital. A unique game needed a unique partner, Alliot (2016) thought, someone "akin to one of those cool indie record labels" who could help the game reach the audience it deserved:

> The essence of the label is hard to define: You don't know what sort of crazy game they're going to release next, but you know it will have something special. All their games share some sort of edge or sharpness associated with a promise of depth behind the pitch. It's not a formula producing copycat games; there's really not much in common between, for instance, *Hotline Miami* and *Hatoful Boyfriend*. Still ... both of them are definitely Devolver. They share that spirit, that wit. They love to scratch the very homogenous word of "gaming," and preferably not gently.

For a "dynasty-management-slash-narrative-game-à-la-Tinder" targeting a simultaneous multiplatform release, it was critical to have a partner who knew how to get things shipped onto various platforms and operated beyond lazy marketing demographics.

For Alliot (2016), that partner had to be Devolver because no one else had a proven track record of persuading players to take a chance on an esoteric game and demonstrating that the "carefully erected frontiers between devices and gamers are not that real." Without Devolver's help, *Reigns* would likely have been just another mobile misfire languishing in the digital landfill.

Magnificently Handcrafted Games

Devolver Digital continues to prove it is possible to consistently connect interesting, niche games to a broader audience and make a profit doing so. At the same time, it disproves the anachronistic, top-down model of traditional publishers and demonstrates that personal purposeful partnerships—independent-thinking labels, not corporatized publishers—represent the future. Ask Nigel Lowrie (2016) and he will tell you that independent game makers "don't need a fucking publisher" but that the right partner can make a real difference.

In his obituary for Factory Records founder Tony Willson, Paul Morley (2007) said:

> *"Without Wilson there may well have been in some form Joy Division and Factory and New Order and the Hacienda and Happy Mondays. There may well have been Peter Saville's dream designs and Martin Hannett's timeless production and a Manchester that managed to move on from its sad post-industrial decline. But none of it would have been so far-fetched, so dramatic and so fantastic."*

Devolver Digital may not be our Factory Records but without it sustainably esoteric independent game making would not be so vibrant, so provocative, or so fantastic.

Practical Provocations

- Which independent record label best matches your ideals, cultural theories and aesthetic sensibilities? Who is their equivalent for game making?
- What if your primary reference point was a documentary?
- What if you remixed an old prototype as cultural commentary?

FIGURE 4.5 The Devolver Digital logo starring Fork Parker, their fictional chief financial officer. (Reprinted with permission from Devolver Digital, ©Devolver Digital 2017. All rights reserved.)

FIGURE 4.6   A screenshot from *Reigns*. Made by Nerial, published by Devolver Digital. (Reprinted with permission from Devolver Digital, ©Devolver Digital 2017. All rights reserved.)

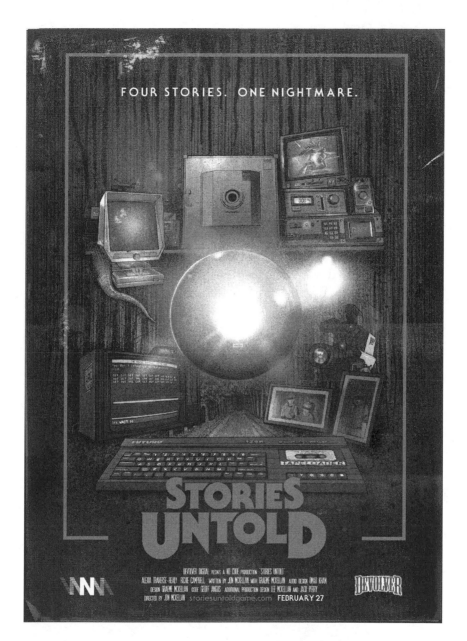

FIGURE 4.7 Cover art for *Stories Untold* from Glasgow's No Code. (Reprinted with permission from Devolver Digital, ©Devolver Digital 2017. All rights reserved.)

Conclusions

An Ending (Ascent)

"As soon as the 'd word'—as in definitive—passes your lips, the other 'd word' is true. You're dead."

Simon Schama
The Rest Is History (2000)

Defiantly Maybe

Throughout the writing of this book, a card sat tantalizingly in the "to do" list of our Trello board. It said simply: "Conclusion." That card represented a destination, a place where our thinking would converge into something concrete, into those neat takeaways that help us readers avoid thinking too much. But when we came to write those conclusions, we realized there were no neat answers, no fixed truths, no definitives. There were only more questions and triggers for action.

(Just Like) Starting Over

"You can be your own enemy
Or you can choose to be free ..."

Marshall Jefferson presents Truth
Open Our Eyes (1988)

So this is an ending—not the end. What follows is our manifesto. It might seem strange that the manifesto resides at the end of the book, but we didn't want to crack the code before you received the signal. And we wanted to finish with some food for thought. Plus, we're all about the unorthodox, as you know. Our manifesto intersects with core themes within this book, but instead of explicitly fixing them in definitive conclusions, it articulates stimuli and starting points. We believe in the manifesto now but can't promise we'll think the same in six or twelve months; what appears here has already evolved noticeably from the original written more than two years ago. But we're good with that. Adaptive evolution always trumps rigid stagnation. And by placing the manifesto at the end, we hope to keeps things more open-ended, offering space for new interpretations, fresh ideas, provocative triggers for speculation and creative action. Yours, we hope.

If you've got thoughts to share or stories to tell, let us know. We're always up for discussing ideals and ideas or revising our thinking. That's because creating playful experiences people want is complex. Contemporary game making—like anything in this world—is not a rigid either/or proposition. Anyone who thinks it is should stop now. There are no fixed rules, no certainties, no magic bullets. People who tell you different are merely hucksters. Game making is both effective and wasteful, rewarding and frustrating, comforting and risky, creative and mundane, simple and difficult, ugly and beautiful. It's a fluid adventure of living in flux, in the cracks and spaces, somewhere between the gutter and the stars. Embrace these uncertainties and contradictions. It's not always easy, but it can be done—as those mentioned in the preceding pages demonstrate. But doing so demands a heuristic mindset, unorthodox thinking and a deep-seated desire to do it yourself. In other words: true independence. And if we have managed to convince you only of this within these pages, then perhaps this is not an ending at all but simply a new beginning.

The *Punk Playthings* Manifesto

Uncertainty and change surround us. Game makers exist in a state of flux—with all that was solid melted into air. We must embrace the unknown and adapt. Seeking refuge in old certainties leaves us blind and immutable, groping for answers and retreating into orthodoxy.

Orthodoxy manifests in numerous ways: prescriptive processes deny adaptability, knowledge silos result in bunker mentalities, defined industry pathways negate artistic expression, identity ghettos restrict opportunity. All propel our medium and its artifacts into a creative cul-de-sac that negates meaning, resonance and sustainability.

Games are simultaneously eating and starving themselves. We need more diversity and sustenance in our diet. Know your context and become a curious explorer, ruthless remixer and imaginative conspirator. Be open, expressive and insightful. Be maverick, fluid and playful. Be truly independent of mind.

Here's how:

- **Remember, everything is connected.** Context is vital. Nothing exists in a vacuum

- **Smash the monoculture.** Eat culture, all you want, mostly not games. Expand your cultural capital, then remix and represent it

- **Always adapt.** Nothing is certain, nothing lasts forever. Fluidity beats rigidity. Only dead processes can be packaged

- **Celebrate ideals over ideas.** Find your purpose. Creativity and innovation will follow

- **Value people over process.** Mavericks over rules. Individuals over the mass

- **Form a band, not a company.** You must speculate not incorporate. Go easy, step light, stay free

- **Don't follow the yellow brick road.** There's more to life than established pathways. Take the road less traveled and arrive somewhere new

- **Refute gaming exceptionalism.** Games are no better or worse than any other medium. There are exceptional games, but there's nothing exceptional about games

- **Don't give up your day job.** Put on a show, find fans, procure patronage. Don't get caught in the lifestyle business trap

- **Sell out.** Money isn't the root of all evil; the worship of it is. Money can liberate creativity and experimentation. Get some, do good things

- **Do it yourself.** Always. Real punks are creative entrepreneurs.

References

Introduction

Anderson, C. (2012) *Quarrel vs. The Game Industry: Who's Right?* [Internet] *Gamasutra*, January 25, 2012. Available from: http://www.gamasutra.com/blogs/ColinAnderson/20120125/90784/Quarrel_vs_The_Games_Industry_Whos_Right.php [Accessed March 30, 2017].

Carmel, R. (2011) *Opinion: Is XBLA Past its Prime?* [Internet]. *Gamasutra*, October 3, 2011. Available from: https://www.gamasutra.com/view/news/37653/Opinion_Is_XBLA_Past_Its_Prime.php [Accessed March 30, 2017].

Morrissey, S.P. and Marr, J. (1983) *Jeane*. The Smiths et al. with Sandie Shaw. Recorded February 1984 [Vinyl]. RTT 130. London: Rough Trade.

Playboy. (1969) Playboy Interview: Marshall McLuhan: A Candid Conversation with the High Priest of Popcult and Metaphysician of Media. In: Mcluhan, E. and Zingrone, F., eds. (1997). *Essential McLuhan*. London: Routledge. pp. 233–270.

Public Image Limited. (1986) *Rise*. Public Image Limited et al. [Vinyl]. VS 841/12. London: Virgin Records Ltd.

Sawyer, K. (2006) *Explaining Creativity: The Science of Human Innovation*. Oxford: Oxford University Press.

Seabrook, J. (2006) *Game Master* [Internet]. *The New Yorker*, November 6, 2006. Available from: https://www.newyorker.com/ magazine/2006/11/06/game-master [Accessed December 15, 2016].

The Beloved. (1990) *Hello*. The Beloved et al. [Vinyl]. YZ 426T. London: WEA Records Ltd.

Turner, F. (2008) *From Cyberculture to Counterculture: Stewart Brand, the Whole Earth Network, and the Rise of Digital Utopianism*. Chicago, IL: The University of Chicago Press.

Wolf, G. (1996) *Steve Jobs: The Next Insanely Great Thing* [Internet]. *Wired*, February 1, 1996. Available from: https://www.wired.com/1996/02/ jobs-2/ [Accessed March 31, 2017].

Chapter 1: The Road Less Traveled

No Gods, No Masters

Chadwick, W. (1990) *Women, Art and Society*. London: Thames and Hudson.

Encyclopedia Britannica (2016). *Georgia O'Keeffe* [Internet]. Available from: https://www.britannica.com/biography/Georgia-OKeeffe [Accessed December 15, 2016].

House of Cards – Chapter 34. (2015) [Internet]. *House of Cards*, Season 3 Episode 8. TV Program: Netflix UK [Accessed February 14, 2017].

Imagine ... Georgia O'Keeffe: By Myself. (2016) [TV Programme]. BBC, BBC1, July 26, 2016 22:45.

Kent, S.L. (2000) *The Ultimate History of Video Games: From Pong to Pokemon and Beyond*. New York: Three Rivers Press.

Messinger, L. (2004) *Georgia O'Keeffe (1887–1986)* [Internet]. Available from: https://www.metmuseum.org/toah/hd/geok/hd_geok.htm [Accessed December 15, 2016]

NPR. (2017) *How I Built This: Atari & Chuck E. Cheese's: Nolan Bushnell*. [Podcast]. NPR, February 27, 2017. Available from: http://www.npr. org/podcasts/510313/how-i-built-this [Accessed March 18, 2017]

Ogilvy, D. (2013) *Confessions of an Advertising Man*. Harpenden: Southbank.

Seabrook, J. (2006) *Game Master* [Internet]. *The New Yorker*, November 6, 2006. Available from: https://www.newyorker.com/magazine/2006/ 11/06/game-master [Accessed December 15, 2016]

Tate. (2016) *Georgia O'Keeffe Exhibition at Tate Modern* [Internet]. Available from: http://www.tate.org.uk/whats-on/tate-modern/exhibition/georgia-okeeffe [Accessed December 14, 2016]

Tungate, M. (2007). *Ad Land: A Global History of Advertising*. London: Kogan Page.

Verlhac, P.H. and Dherbier, Y.B. eds. (2006). *Paul Newman: A Life in Pictures*. San Francisco, CA: Chronicle Books.

I Wanna Be Adored

Adejobi, A. (2016). *Independent vs Major Label: What Adele's £90m Sony Music Deal Means for XL Recordings* [Internet]. *International Business Times*, July 19, 2016. Available from: http://www.ibtimes.co.uk/independent-vs-major-label-what-adeles-90m-sony-music-record-deal-means-xl-recordings-1571439 [Accessed December 14, 2016]

BPI. (2016) *Certified Awards Finder* [Internet]. The British Phonographic Industry. Available from: https://www.bpi.co.uk/certified-awards.aspx [Accessed December 14, 2016].

Ellison, R. (1965) *Invisible Man*. London: Penguin.

Ellis-Petersen, H. (2016) *Adele Signs £90m Contract with Sony* [Internet]. *The Guardian*, May 23, 2016. Available from: https://www.theguardian.com/music/2016/may/23/adele-set-to-sign-90m-sony-deal [Accessed December 14, 2016].

Gamasutra Staff. (2013) *Indie Game Development on the Rise in a Big Way* [Internet]. *Gamasutra*, February 28, 2013. Available from: https://www.gamasutra.com/view/news/187540/Indie_game_development_on_the_rise_in_a_big_way.php [Accessed December 14, 2016].

Goldman, D. (2010). *Music's Lost Decade: Sales Cut in Half in 2000s* [Internet]. *CNN Money*, February 3, 2010. Available from: http://money.cnn.com/2010/02/02/news/companies/napster_music_industry/ [Accessed December 14, 2016].

Ingham, T. (2015) *Don't Dismiss Adele's Success as a Miracle. You're Better than that* [Internet]. *Music Business Worldwide*, November 27, 2015. Available from: https://www.musicbusinessworldwide.com/dont-dismiss-adeles-success-as-a-miracle/ [Accessed December 14, 2016]

Jonze, T. (2011a). *XL Recordings: The Record Label that's Tearing Up the Rule Book* [Internet]. *The Guardian*, February 16, 2011. Available from: https://www.theguardian.com/business/2011/feb/16/richard-russell-xl-recordings-dizzee-rascal-prodigy [Accessed December 14, 2016].

Jonze, T. (2011b) *How Adele Conquered the World* [Internet]. *The Guardian*, April 6, 2011. Available from: https://www.theguardian.com/music/2011/apr/06/adele-music-interview [Accessed July 27, 2017].

Juul, J. (2010) *A Casual Revolution: Reinventing Video Games and Their Players*. Cambridge, MA: The MIT Press.

Mateos-Garcia, J. and Bakhsh, H. (2014) *A Map of the UK Games Industry* [Internet]. London: Nesta/Ukie. Available from: http://www.nesta.org.uk/publications/map-uk-games-industry [Accessed December 14, 2016].

Music for Misfits: The Story of Indie. (2015) [TV Programme]. BBC, BBC4, October 9, 2015, 22:00.

Parker, L. (2011) *Rise of the Indie Developer* [Internet]. *GameSpot*, February 14, 2011. Available from: https://www.gamespot.com/articles/the-rise-of-the-indie-developer/1100-6298425/ [Accessed December 14, 2016].

PIAS. (2016) *Richard Russell: The Highlights from His Award Speech* [Internet]. *PIAS*, September 7, 2016. Available from: https://www.pias.com/blog/richard-russell-highlights-aim-awards-speech/ [Accessed December 14, 2016].

Rolling Stone. (2012) *Adele's "21" Earns XL Recordings $67 Million Profit* [Internet]. *Rolling Stone*, October 16, 2012. Available from: http://www.rollingstone.com/music/news/adeles-21-earns-xl-records-67-million-profit-20121016 [Accessed December 14, 2016]

Stewart, K. (2012). *Us and the Game Industry – How Indie Games Are the New Counterculture* [Internet]. *The Guardian*, March 12, 2012. Available from: https://www.theguardian.com/technology/gamesblog/2012/mar/12/us-and-the-game-industry-feature?CMP=share_btn_fb [Accessed March 21, 2017].

Sullivan, C. (2012) *Adele's Expected Brit Awards Underline Success of Indie Labels* [Internet]. *The Guardian*, February 20, 2012. Available from: https://www.theguardian.com/music/2012/feb/20/adele-brit-awards-indie-success [Accessed December 14, 2016]

Teather, D. (2007). *Still Kicking After All These Years* [Internet]. *The Guardian*, July 13, 2007. Available from: https://www.theguardian.com/business/2007/jul/13/musicnews.pop [Accessed December 14, 2016]

TIGA. (2016) *March of the Micro-Studios* [Internet]. *TIGA*, August 22, 2016. Available from: https://tiga.org/news/march-of-the-micro-studios [Accessed November 20, 2016].

Ukie. (2016) *UK Video Games Fact Sheet* [Internet]. *Ukie*, November 4, 2016. Available from: http://ukie.org.uk/research#Fact%20Sheet [Accessed November 20, 2016].

Witt, S. (2015). *What Happened When Music Got Free: The End of an Industry, The Turn of a Century, and Patient Zero of Piracy*. New York: Viking.

Weapons of Mass Destruction

BARB. (2017). *TV Since 1981* [Internet]. *The Broadcasters Audience Research Board*. Availble from: http://www.barb.co.uk/resources/tv-facts/tv-since-1981/1981/top10/ [Accessed July 27, 2017].

Brammer, J.P. (2016) *"The Latino Vote" Didn't Overwhelm Trump Because We're Not All the Same* [Internet]. *The Guardian*, November 9, 2016. Available from: https://www.theguardian.com/commentisfree/2016/nov/09/the-latino-vote-didnt-overwhelm-trump-because-were-not-all-the-same [Accessed January 5, 2017].

Buchanan, R. (1998) *Branzi's Dilemma: Design in Contemporary Culture*. In: Buchanan, R., et al., eds. *The Designed World: Images, Objects, Environments*. Oxford: Berg. pp. 13–28.

Cohn, D. and Caumont, A. (2016) *Demographic 10, Trends that Are Shaping the U.S. and the World* [Internet]. CNN, November 9, 2016. Available from: http://www.pewresearch.org/fact-tank/2016/03/31/10-demographic-trends-that-are-shaping-the-u-s-and-the-world/ [Accessed January 5, 2017].

Davies, R. (1966). *I'm Not Like Everybody Else*. The Kinks et al. Recorded May 1966, Pye Studio No.2, London. [Vinyl]. 7N 17125-B. London: Pye Records.

Dex, R. (2013) *Are You Taking the Piss? Hacienda Urinals Go on Sale for £15,000* [Internet]. *The Independent*, September 5, 2013. Available from: http://www.independent.co.uk/arts-entertainment/music/news/are-you-taking-the-piss-hacienda-urinals-go-on-sale-for-15000-8800535.html [Accessed July 27, 2017].

Gretton, R. (1992) *I Wanted A Place Where I Could Ogle Women*. Interviewed by Jon Savage, March 1992. In: Savage, J., ed., *The Hacienda Must Be Built*. Woodford Green: International Music Publications.

Hook, P. (1992) *Why Is the School Bully the School Bully?* Interviewed by Jon Savage, March 1992. In: Savage, J, ed., *The Hacienda Must Be Built*. Woodford Green: International Music Publications. p. 24.

Krogstad, J.M. (2016) *2016 Electorate Will Be the Most Diverse in U.S. History* [Internet]. Pew Research Centre, February 3, 2016. Available from: http://www.pewresearch.org/fact-tank/2016/02/03/2016-electorate-will-be-the-most-diverse-in-u-s-history/ [Accessed January 5, 2017].

Krogstad, J.M. and Flores, A. (2016) *Unlike Other Latinos, About Half of Cuban Voters in Florida backed Trump* [Internet]. Pew Research Centre, November 15, 2016. Available from: http://www.pewresearch.org/fact-tank/2016/11/15/unlike-other-latinos-about-half-of-cuban-voters-in-florida-backed-trump/ [Accessed January 5, 2017]

Krogstad, J.M. and Lopez, M.H. (2016) *Hillary Clinton Won Latino Vote But Fell Below 2012 Support for Obama* [Internet]. Pew Research Centre, November 29, 2016. Available from: http://www.pewresearch.org/fact-tank/2016/11/29/hillary-clinton-wins-latino-vote-but-falls-below-2012-support-for-obama/ [Accessed January 5, 2017].

Luhby, T. and Agiesta, J. (2016) *Exit Polls: Clinton Fails to Energize African-Americans, Latinos and the Young* [Internet]. CNN, November 9, 2016. Available from: http://edition.cnn.com/2016/11/08/politics/first-exit-polls-2016/ [Accessed January 5, 2017].

Morris, S. (1992) *That Was the Longest Walk of My Life*. Interviewed by Jon Savage, March 1992. In: Savage, J., ed., *The Hacienda Must Be Built*. Woodford Green: International Music Publications. p. 25.

Peter York's Hipster Handbook. (2016) [TV Programme]. BBC, BBC Four, November 10, 2016 00:00.

Pickering, M. (1992) *A Lot of the Best DJs and the Best Clubs ....* Interviewed by Jon Savage, March 1992. In: Savage, J., ed., *The Hacienda Must Be Built*. Woodford Green: International Music Publications. pp. 30–32.

Tyson, A. and Maniam, S. (2016) *Behind Trump's Victory: Divisions by Race, Gender and Education* [Internet]. Pew Research Centre, November 9, 2016. Available from: http://www.pewresearch.org/fact-tank/2016/11/09/behind-trumps-victory-divisions-by-race-gender-education/ [Accessed January 5, 2017].

Williams, R. (1963) *Culture and Society 1780–1950*. Harmondsworth: Penguin.

Wilson, A.H. (1992) *New Arms for Amputees, He Was a Lovely Man*. Interviewed by Jon Savage, March 1992. In: Savage, J., ed., *The Hacienda Must Be Built*. Woodford Green: International Music Publications. pp. 18–19.

Yesterday

Articles of Style. (2015) *The Art of Bespoke Denim* [Internet]. Available from: https://articlesofstyle.com/61683/the-art-of-bespoke-denim-feat-camillo-love/ [Accessed November 4, 2016].

Berman, M. (2010) *All That Is Solid Melts Into Air: The Experience of Modernity*. London: Verso.

Carpenter, E. (2011) *Social Making*. In: Charny, D. ed., *Power of Making: The Importance of Being Skilled*. London: V&A Publishing. pp. 48–56.

Craft Check. (2016) *FAQ/WTF/BBQ* [Internet]. Available from: http://www. craftcheckapp.com/ [Accessed December 7, 2016].

Frayling, C. (2011) *We Must All Turn to Crafts*. In: Charny, D. ed., *Power of Making: The Importance of Being Skilled*. London: V&A Publishing. pp. 28–38.

Frayling, C. (2013) *On Craftsmanship: Towards a New Bauhaus*. [Kindle Paperwhite]. London: Oberon.

Garrett, S. (1988) *Cut and Thrust: The Disco Mix Club. The Face*, April 1988. London: Nick Logan. p. 34.

Hospitality Ireland. (2016) *IFAI and HSE Investigating Mislabelling of Craft Beer in Pubs* [Internet]. Available from: http://www.hospitalityireland.com/ ifai-hse-investigating-mislabeling-craft-beer-pubs/32997 [Accessed November 4, 2016].

Lee, Y. (2013) *A Conversation with Roy Slaper* [Internet]. *Heddels*, September 17, 2016. Available from: https://www.heddels.com/2013/09/conversation-roy-slaper-roy-denim/ [Accessed November 8, 2016].

Lennon, J. and McCartney, P. (1966) *Yesterday*. The Beatles et al. Recorded June 1965, EMI Studios London. [Vinyl]. GEP 8948. London: Parlophone.

Murphy, M. (2016) *Heineken Claims Products Sold as Fake Craft Beer* [Internet]. *FFT.ie*, September 22, 2016. Available from: http://www. fft.ie/heineken-claims-products-sold-as-fake-craft-beer/13442 [Accessed November 5, 2016].

Pye, D. (1968) *The Nature and Art of Workmanship*. In: Adamson, G. ed., (2010). *The Craft Reader*. Oxford: Berg. pp. 341–354.

Roy Denim. (2016). *Story* [Internet]. Available from: http://www.roydenim. com/story [Accessed November 8, 2016].

Sellers, J. (2016) *Anthony Bourdain on Beer Snobs, Bad Food Trends and Roadhouse* [Internet]. *Thrillist*, October 27, 2016. Available from: https://www.thrillist.com/entertainment/nation/anthony-bourdain-interview-appetites-cookbook [Accessed March 21, 2017].

Wong, K., et al. (2014a) *Behind the Scenes: Monument Valley* [Internet]. Available from: https://www.youtube.com/watch?v=K2P-YKsHpNs [Accessed January 10, 2016].

Wiener, M.J. (1992) *English Culture and the Decline of the Industrial Spirit 1850–1980.* London: Penguin.

Williams, R. (1973) *The Country and the City.* London: Chatto and Windus.

Williams, M. (2013) *Get to Know the Goodness that is Levis Made and Crafted. [Internet]. A Continous Lean,* August 28, 2013. Available from: http://www.acontinuouslean.com/2013/08/28/get-to-know-the-goodness-that-is-levis-made-crafted/ [Accessed August 3, 2017].

Wong, K., et al. (2014b) *The Making of Monument Valley* [Internet]. Available from: https://www.youtube.com/watch?v=KT-JDV6KT4g [Accessed January 10, 2016].

Canon Fodder

Clarens, C. and Hirsch, F. (1997) *Crime Movies.* Boston, MA: De Capo Press.

Fitzmaurice, L. (2015) *Quentin Tarantino: The Complete Syllabus* [Internet]. *Vulture,* August 28, 2015. Available from: http://www.vulture.com/2015/08/quentin-tarantino-the-complete-syllabus.html [Accessed January 5, 2017].

Legend, T. (1968) *Time Will Pass You By.* Tobi Legend et al. [Vinyl]. Mala 591. New York: Mala Records.

Levi-Strauss, C. (1966) *The Savage Mind.* Chicago, IL: The University of Chicago Press.

Public Enemy. (1989) *Fight the Power.* Public Enemy et al. [Vinyl]. ZT 42878. Los Angeles, CA: Motown.

Rosenbaum, S. (2014) *Is Curation Overused? The Votes Are In* [Internet]. *Forbes,* March 28, 2014. Available from: https://www.forbes.com/forbes/welcome/?toURL=https://www.forbes.com/sites/stevenrosenbaum/2014/03/29/is-curation-over-used-the-votes-are-in/&refURL=&referrer=#373aabd9398c [Accessed January 5, 2017].

Stetsasonic. (1988) *Talkin' All That Jazz.* Stetsasonic et al. [Vinyl]. TB 918. New York: Tommy Boy Records.

Thornton, S. (1995) *Club Cultures: Music, Media and Subcultural Capital.* Cambridge: Polity Press.

Today with Bill Grundy. (1976) Interview with The Sex Pistols. [TV Program]. Thames Television, ITV, December 1, 1976 18:00.

Williams, A. (2015) *So What Do You Do: Ryan Schreiber, Founder and CEO of Pitchfork?* [Internet]. *MediaBistro,* October 15, 2015. Available from: https://www.mediabistro.com/interviews/so-what-do-you-do-ryan-schreiber-founder-and-ceo-of-pitchfork/ [Accessed January 5, 2017].

Willis, S. (1997) *High Contrast: Race and Gender in Contemporary Hollywood Films.* Durham, NC: Duke University Press.

thatgamecompany: A Case Study in Aesthetics

Alexander, L. (2012) *Changes at Thatgamecompany: Santiago Departs, New Game Underway* [Internet]. *Gamasutra*, March 29, 2012. Available from: https://www.gamasutra.com/view/news/163491/Changes_at_Thatgamecompany_Santiago_departs_new_game_underway.php [Accessed November 9, 2016].

Bramwell, T. (2009) *Flower* [Internet]. *Eurogamer*, February 9, 2009. Available from: http://www.eurogamer.net/articles/flower_4 [Accessed October 23, 2016].

Boyer, B. (2009) *MIGS: First Details on Thatgamecompany's Flower Debut* [Internet]. *Gamasutra*, November 29, 2009. Available from: https://www.gamasutra.com/php-bin/news_index.php?story=16414 [Accessed September 12, 2016].

"B_Squared". *Journey Apologies* [Online Forum Comment]. Available from: http://www.thatgamecompany.com/forum/viewtopic.php?t=1897 [Accessed October 27, 2016].

Caoili, E. (2012). *Journey developer no longer tied to Sony, thanks to new funding* [Internet]. *Gamasutra*, June 14, 2012. Available from: https://www.gamasutra.com/view/news/172404/Journey_developer_no_longer_tied_to_Sony_thanks_to_new_funding.php [Accessed November 14, 2016].

Carless, S. (2009). *GDC Europe: Thatgamecompany's Santiago On Flower's Emotional Search* [Internet]. *Gamasutra*, August 17, 2009. Available from: https://www.gamasutra.com/view/news/115822/GDC_Europe_Thatgamecompanys_Santiago_On_Flowers_Emotional_Search.php [Accessed November 22, 2016].

Chaplin, H. (2009) *Video Game Grad Programs Open Up the Industry.* [Internet]. *NPR*, March 23, 2009. Available from: http://www.npr.org/templates/story/story.php?storyId=102246406 [Accessed October 5, 2016].

Chen, J. (2006) *Flow in Games.* MFA thesis, University of Southern California, 2006. Available from: http://www.npr.org/templates/story/story.php?storyId=102246406 [Accessed October 14, 2016].

Chen, J. (2007) *Flow in Games (and Everything Else)* [Internet]. *Communications of the ACM*, 50(4), 31–34. Available from: http://www.jenovachen.com/flowingames/p31-chen.pdf [Accessed October 14, 2016].

Chen, J. (2009). *The Beautiful Game* [Internet]. Interviewed by Mary Jane Irwin. Gamesindustry.biz, February 19, 2009. Available from: http://www.gamesindustry.biz/articles/the-beautiful-game [Accessed October 21, 2016].

Chen, J. (2012a) *A Personal Journey: Jenova Chen's Goals for Games* [Internet]. Interviewed by Ed Smith. *Gamasutra*, May 18, 2012. Available from: https://www.gamasutra.com/view/feature/170547/a_personal_journey_jenova_chens_.php [Accessed October 5, 2016].

Chen, J. (2012b) *Game Designer Jenova Chen on The Art Behind His "Journey"* [Internet]. Interviewed by Kevin Ohannessian. *Fast Company*, March 12, 2012. Available from: https://www.fastcompany.com/1680062/game-designer-jenova-chen-on-the-art-behind-his-journey [Accessed November 1, 2016].

Chen, J. (2013) *An Interview with Jenova Chen: How Journey's Creator Went Bankrupt and Won Game of the Year* [Internet]. Interviewed by Dean Takahashi. *Venturebeat*, February 8, 2013. Available from: https://venturebeat.com/2013/02/08/an-interview-with-jenova-chen-how-journeys-creator-went-bankrupt-and-won-game-of-the-year/view-all/ [Accessed October 10, 2016].

Chen, J. (2015) *Jenova Chen: Journeyman* [Internet]. Interviewed by Simon Parkin. *Eurogamer*, July 21, 2015. Available from: http://www.eurogamer.net/articles/2012-04-02-jenova-chen-journeyman [Accessed October 4, 2016].

Clements, R. (2009) *Flower Review* [Internet]. Available from: http://www.ign.com/articles/2009/02/09/flower-review [Accessed October 22, 2016].

Csikszentmihalyi, M. (1990) *Flow: The Psychology of Ultimate Experience*. New York: Harper and Row.

Dyer, M. (2012) *How Thatgamecompany Struggled to Save Journey* [Internet]. *IGN*, August 14, 2012. Available from: http://www.ign.com/articles/2012/08/14/how-thatgamecompany-struggled-to-save-journey [Accessed November 14, 2016].

Fullerton, T., et al. (2006). *That Cloud Game: Dreaming (and Doing). Innovative Game Design* [Internet]. *Proceedings of the 2006 ACM SIGGRAPH Symposium on Videogames*. ACM. Available from: http://sandbox.siggraph.org/archives/papers/ThatCloudGame.pdf [Accessed November 20, 2016].

Govan, P. (2009) *Flower: The Interactive Poem/Videogame* [Internet]. *Wired*, February 26, 2009. Available from: https://www.wired.com/2009/02/flower-the-inte/ [Accessed October 22, 2016].

"Jo Pierce". (2012) *Journey Apologies* [Online Forum Comment]. Available from: http://www.thatgamecompany.com/forum/viewtopic.php?t=1897 [Accessed October 27, 2016].

Khaw, C. (2012) *What Went Wrong During the Making of Journey* [Internet]. *Gamasutra*, August 15, 2012. Available from: https://www.gamasutra.com/view/news/175966/What_went_wrong_during_the_making_of_Journey.php [Accessed November 10, 2016].

Liang, A. (2009) *Flower Review* [Internet]. Available from: http://www.1up.com/reviews/flower [Accessed October 9, 2016].

McCartney, G. (2012) *An Emotional Connection to the Games we Play* [Internet]. Available from: https://news.usc.edu/35337/making-an-emotional-connection-to-the-games-they-play/ [Accessed October 1, 2016].

"Monk". (2012) *Journey Apologies* [Online Forum Comment]. Available from: http://www.thatgamecompany.com/forum/viewtopic.php?t=1897 [Accessed October 27, 2016].

Museum of Modern Art (MoMA). *flOw* [Internet]. Gallery Label from Applied Design, March 2, 2013–January 31, 2014. Available from: https://www.moma.org/collection/works/164921 [Accessed October 20, 2016].

Parker, L. (2013) *A Journey to Make Video Games Into Art* [Internet]. *New Yorker*, August 2, 2013. Available from: https://www.newyorker.com/tech/elements/a-journey-to-make-video-games-into-art [Accessed November 1, 2016].

Parsons, Z. (2006) *Something Awful – The Littlest Developers* [Internet]. Available from: http://www.somethingawful.com/news/the-littlest-developers/ [Accessed November 14, 2016].

Postrel, V. (2003) *The Substance of Style: How the Rise of Aesthetic Value Is Remaking Commerce, Culture, and Consciousness*. New York: HarperCollins.

Santiago, K. (2009) *Interview: Kellee Santiago Talks thatgamecompany's Road Ahead* [Internet]. Interviewed by Brandon Sheffield. *Gamasutra*, July 1, 2009. Available from: https://www.gamasutra.com/view/news/24110/Interview_Kellee_Santiago_Talks_Thatgamecompanys_Road_Ahead.php [Accessed October 11, 2016].

Santiago, K. (2010a) *Fellows Friday with Kellee Santiago* [Internet]. Interviewed by Alana Herro. Available from: https://blog.ted.com/fellows-friday-with-kellee-santiago/ [Accessed September 27, 2016].

Santiago, K. (2010b) *thatgamecompany's Kellee Santiago* [Internet]. Interviewed by Phil Elliott. Gamesindustry.biz, July 2, 2010. Available from: http://www.gamesindustry.biz/articles/thatgamecompanys-kellee-santiago-interview [Accessed September 20, 2016].

Santiago, K. and Hunicke, R. (2010) *Interview: thatgamecompany's Santiago, Hunicke, On Designing for the Love* [Internet]. Interviewed by Patrick Dugan. *Gamasutra*, January 26, 2010. Available from: https://www.gamasutra.com/view/news/26910/Interview_ThatGameCompanys_Santiago_Hunicke_On_Designing_For_The_Love.php [Accessed November 22, 2016].

thatgamecompany. (2017a) *Journey* [Internet]. Available from: http://thatgamecompany.com/games/journey/ [Accessed October 10, 2016].

thatgamecompany. (2017b) *Something New from TGC* [Internet]. Available from: http://thatgamecompany.com/general/something-new-from-tgc/ [Accessed December 4, 2016].

Warren, J. (2013) *Is Journey Creator Jenova Chen the Videogame World's Terrence Malick* [Internet]. *Kill Screen*, February 12, 2013. Available from: https://killscreen.com/articles/journey-creator-jenova-chen-videogame-worlds-terrence-malick/ [Accessed November 19, 2016].

Wikipedia. (2016a) Thatgamecompany [Internet]. In: *Wikipedia: The Free Encyclopaedia*. Unknown eds. Available from: https://en.wikipedia.org/wiki/Thatgamecompany [Accessed October 20, 2016].

Wikipedia. (2016b) *Journey (2012 Video Game)* [Internet]. In: *Wikipedia: The Free Encyclopaedia*. Unknown eds. Available from: https://en.wikipedia.org/wiki/Journey_(2012_video_game) [Accessed October 20, 2016].

Chapter 2: Ideals Over Ideas

What Side Are You On?

Bauhaus: The Face of the 20th Century. (1994) [Film]. Directed by Frank Whitford. Germany: Art-Haus Musik.

BrewDog. (2010a) *Hop Propoganda 05* [Internet]. Available from: https://en.wikipedia.org/wiki/Journey_(2012_video_game) [Accessed August 22, 2017].

BrewDog. (2010b) *Hop Propoganda 02* [Internet]. Available from: https://www.brewdog.com/files/1425988310HopProp02.pdf [Accessed August 22, 2017].

BrewDog. (2015) *The BrewDog Charter.* In: *Equity for Punks AGM Update* [Internet]. Available from: https://www.brewdog.com/files/1425988310HopProp02.pdf [Accessed December 7, 2016].

Classic Rock. (2010) *Interview with Malcolm McLaren. Classic Rock*, June 2010, Issue 145. s.l.

Cobain, K. (1991) In *Bloom*. Nirvana et al. From the LP: *Nevermind*. Recorded April 1990–June 1991. [Vinyl]. DGC 424 425-1. New York: DGC Records.

Debord, G. (1967) *Society of the Spectacle.* Translated from French by Ken Knabb, 2004. London: Rebel Press.

Didion, J. (1979) *The White Album*. London: Penguin.

Gropius, W. (1919) *Bauhaus Manifesto and Program of the Weimar State Bauhaus* [Internet]. Available from: https://www.bauhaus100.de/en/past/works/education/manifest-und-programm-des-staatlichen-bauhauses/ [Accessed December 7, 2016].

McLaren, M. (2008) *This Much I Know* [Internet]. *The Guardian*, November 16. Available from: https://www.theguardian.com/lifeandstyle/2008/nov/16/malcolm-mclaren-punk-vivienne-westwood [Accessed March 30, 2017].

McLuhan, M. and Fiore, Q. (1967). *The Medium is the Massage: An Inventory of Effects.* New York: Bantam Books.

McLuhan, E. and Zingrone, F. eds. (1997) *Essential McLuhan*. London: Routledge.

Savage, J. (1991) *England's Dreaming: The Sex Pistols and Punk Rock*. London: Faber.

Schama, S. (2006) *Power of Art*. London: BBC Books.

Approximate Authenticity

Amis, M. (1989) *London Fields*. London: Jonathan Cape.

Basu, J. (2014) *Dishoom – An Iranian Cafe in London* [Internet]. *Asian News*, May 23, 2014. Available from: https://asianlite.com/lifestyle/dishoom-an-iranian-cafe-in-london/ [Accessed February 9, 2017].

Bauman, Z. (2007) *Liquid Times: Living in an Age of Uncertainty*. Cambridge: Polity Press.

Cobb, R. ed. (2014) *The Paradox of Authenticity in a Globalized World.* New York: Palgrave Macmillan.

Cook, R. (2001) *Robin Cook's Chicken Tikka Masala Speech* [Internet]. *The Guardian*, April 19, 2001. Available from: https://www.theguardian.com/world/2001/apr/19/race.britishidentity [Accessed February 9, 2017].

Cronberg, A.A. (n.d.) *Conversations on Slowness: Nigel Cabourn Interview.* [Internet]. *Vestoj*, n.d. Available from: http://vestoj.com/conversations-on-slowness/ [Accessed February 9, 2017].

De Tocqueville, A. (1856) *The Old Regime and the Revolution* [Internet]. Archive.org. Available from: https://archive.org/details/oldregimeandrev00toc-qgoog [Accessed March 27, 2017].

Edensor, T. (2006) *Automobility and National Identity: Representation, Geography and Driving Practice* [Internet]. *Theory, Culture & Society* 21(4–5), 101–120. Available from: http://journals.sagepub.com/doi/pdf/10.1177/0263276404046063 [Accessed February 9, 2017].

Featherstone, E. (2016) *Dishoom's Co-founder on Our Love Affair with Indian Food* [Internet]. *The Guardian*, June 17, 2016. Available from: https://www.theguardian.com/small-business-network/2016/jun/17/dishoom-cofounder-love-affair-indian-food [Accessed February 9, 2017].

Fielding, S.A. (2014). *Currying Favour: Authenticity, Cultural Capital and the Rise of Indian Food in the United Kingdom.* In: Cobb, R. ed., *The Paradox of Authenticity in a Globalized World*. New York: Palgrave Macmillan.

Giddens, A. (1991) *The Consequences of Modernity*. Cambridge: Polity Press.

Gieben, B.E. (2013) *Late Flowering Lust: Andrew Weatherall on the Asphodells* [Internet]. *The Skinny*, January 15, 2013. Available from: http://www.theskinny.co.uk/clubs/interviews/late-flowering-lust-andrew-weatherall-on-the-asphodells [Accessed February 9, 2017].

Hiscock, J. (2002) What Makes a Brand British? [Internet]. *Campaign*, June 6, 2002. Available from: http://www.campaignlive.co.uk/article/makes-brand-british-first-six-week-series-looking-british-brands-past-50-years-jennifer-hiscock-explores-brands-capitalise-perceptions-britishness/147546#LWCgUkw4yW6lpzJt.99 [Accessed February 9, 2017].

Khaleeli, H. (2012) *The Curry Crisis* [Internet]. *The Guardian*, January 8, 2012. Available from: https://www.theguardian.com/lifeandstyle/2012/jan/08/britains-curry-crisis-chefs-immigration [Accessed February 9, 2017].

Love, M. (2013) *The New Mini Hatch: Car Review* [Internet]. *The Guardian*, December 1, 2013. Available from: https://www.theguardian.com/technology/2013/dec/01/new-mini-hatch-car-review [Accessed February 9, 2017].

Peterson, R. (1999) *Creating Country Music: Fabricating Authenticity.* 2nd ed. Chicago, IL: University of Chicago Press.

Telegraph. (2015) *British Tourists Flock to India under New e-Visa System* [Internet]. *The Telegraph*, December 16, 2015. Available from: http://www.telegraph.co.uk/travel/destinations/asia/india/articles/British-tourists-flock-to-India-under-new-e-visa-system/ [Accessed March 14, 2017].

Walton, J. (1992) *Fish and Chips and the British Working Class: 1870–1940*. London: Leicester University Press.

Wilson, B. (2017) *Who Killed the Curry House?* [Internet]. *The Guardian*, January 12, 2017. Available from: https://www.theguardian.com/lifeandstyle/2017/jan/12/who-killed-the-british-curry-house [Accessed February 9, 2017].

Yelp, Inc. (2016) *The Yelp Top 100 UK Eateries* [Internet]. *Yelp*, February 10, 2016. Available from: https://www.yelpblog.com/2016/02/the-yelp-top-100-uk-eateries [Accessed February 9, 2017].

Bunker Busting

Ashley-Smith, J. (2000) *Science and Art: Separated by a Common Language?* [Internet]. Available from: http://www.vam.ac.uk/content/journals/conservation-journal/issue-36/science-and-art-separated-by-a-common-language/ [Accessed February 6, 2017].

Brand, S. (1995) *How Buildings Learn: What Happens after They're Built?* New York: Penguin.

Dash, A. (2016) *It's More Than Just "Teach Kids to Code"* [Internet]. *A Blog about Making Culture*, September 14. Available from: http://anildash.com/2016/09/its-more-than-just-teach-kids-to-code.html [Accessed February 6, 2017].

Drucker, P. F. (1989) *The New Realities*. New York: Routledge.

Ferguson, N. (2015) *Kissinger 1923–1968: The Idealist*. London: Penguin.

Garfinkel, S. (1987) *Building 20: The Procreative Eyesore* [Internet]. Available from: http://anildash.com/2016/09/its-more-than-just-teach-kids-to-code.html [Accessed February 2, 2017].

Gould, S. J. (2004) *The Fox, the Hedgehog and the Magister's Pox: Mending the Gap between Science and Humanities*. New York: Harmony Books.

Hockney, D. (2006) *Secret Knowledge: Rediscovering the Lost Techniques of the Old Masters*. 2nd ed. London: Thames and Hudson.

Jones, J. (2014) *DIY Vermeer Documentary Utterly Misses the Point About Old Masters* [Internet]. *The Guardian*, January 28. Available from: https://www.theguardian.com/artanddesign/jonathanjonesblog/2014/jan/28/tims-vermeer-fails [Accessed February 6, 2017].

McLuhan, E. and Zingrone, F. ed. (1997) *Essential McLuhan*. New York: Routledge.

Musashi, M. (2011) *The Book of Five Rings* [Kindle Paperwhite]. Translated from Japanese by T. Cleary. Boston, MA: Shambhala Publications.

O'Neill, F. and Palazzo-Corner, S. (2016) *Rembrandt's Self-portraits* [Internet]. *Journal of Optics*, 18(8). Available from: https://www. theguardian.com/artanddesign/jonathanjonesblog/2014/jan/28/ tims-vermeer-fails [Accessed February 6, 2017].

Richmond, S. (1984) *The Interaction of Art and Science* [Internet]. *Leonardo*, 17(2), 81–86. Available from: http://www.jstor.org/ stable/1574993?seq=1#page_scan_tab_contents [Accessed February 6, 2017].

Snow, C.P. (1961) *The Two Cultures and the Scientific Revolution*. London: Cambridge University Press.

Teitelbaum, M.S. (2014) *The Myth of the Science and Engineering Shortage* [Internet]. *The Atlantic*, March 19, 2014. Available from: https://www.theatlantic.com/education/archive/2014/03/the-myth-of-the-science-and-engineering-shortage/284359/ [Accessed February 6, 2017].

Turner, F. (2006) *From Counterculture to Cyberculture: Stewart Brand, the Whole Earth Network, and the Rise of Digital Utopianism*. Chicago, IL: University of Chicago Press.

Wilson, E.O. (1999) *Consillience: The Unity of Knowledge.* New York: Vintage Books.

Monument Valley: A Case Study in Craftwork

Bernstein, J. (2014) *The Unlikely Story Behind The Making Of "Monument Valley"* [Internet]. *Buzzfeed*, April 10, 2014. Available from: https:// www.buzzfeed.com/josephbernstein/the-unlikely-story-behind-the-making-of-monument-valley?utm_term=.ps4BPzo68#. bulvJbNrn [Accessed October 22, 2016].

Blake, J. (2015) *Monument Valley Gets "Insane" Boost from House of Cards* [Internet]. *BBC*, March 13, 2015. Available from: http://www.bbc. co.uk/newsbeat/article/31875551/monument-valley-gets-insane-boost-from-house-of-cards [Accessed October 25, 2016].

Bradley, D. (2017) *Monument Valley Talk: "The Kind of Game Apple Would Make If They Made Games"* [Internet]. *PocketGamer.biz*, April 24, 2017. Available from: http://www.pocketgamer.biz/news/65579/monument-valley-interview/ [Accessed May 1, 2017].

Catmull, E. (2008) *How Pixar Fosters Collective Creativity*. Boston, MA: Harvard Business School Publishing.

Dormehl, L. (2014) *Inside Monument Valley: How "Impossible" Sketches Became An Amazing Game* [Internet]. *Cult of Mac*, April 10, 2014. Available from: https://www.cultofmac.com/273790/inside-monument-valley/ [Accessed October 23, 2016].

Dredge, S. (2011) *Whale Trail iOS Game Tops 38k First-Weekend Sales in Pursuit of Angry Birds* [Internet]. *The Guardian*, October 24, 2011. Available from: https://www.theguardian.com/technology/appsblog/2011/ oct/24/whale-trail-iphone-ipad-ustwo [Accessed October 20, 2016].

Gray, D. (2013) *Extremely Welcome Attention* [Internet]. Available from: https://monumentvalleygame.squarespace.com/blog/2013/12/11/unexpected-awesomeness [Accessed October 21, 2016].

Gray, D. (2014) Interviewed by Myke Hurley. *Building Monument Valley, with Daniel Gray.* [Podcast]. *Inquisitive*, November 18, 2014. Available from: http://www.relay.fm/inquisitive/14 [Accessed October 20, 2015].

Gray, D. (2015) *Monument Valley in Numbers* [Internet]. Available from: https://monumentvalleygame.squarespace.com/blog/2015/1/15/monument-valley-in-numbers [Accessed October 21, 2015].

House of Cards – Chapter 31. (2015) [Internet]. *House of Cards*, Season 3 Episode 5. Available from: Netflix UK. [Accessed January 20, 2017].

Kollar, P. (2014) *Monument Valley: The Quest for a Game Everyone Can Finish* [Internet]. *Polygon*, March 18, 2014. Available from: https://www.polygon.com/2014/3/18/5522874/monument-valley-everyone-finish [Accessed April 4, 2017].

McFarland, N. (2015) Interviewed by 52 Insights. *Neil McFarland: A Monument to Gaming. 52 Insights* [Internet]. Available from: http://www.52-insights.com/neil-macfarland-a-monument-to-gaming/ [Accessed October 29, 2016].

Miller, M. (2012) Interviewed by Daniel McFerran. *Interview: Whale Trail Creator Us Two talks Mobile Game Development. Know Your Mobile*, February 9, 2012 [Internet]. Available from: http://www.knowyourmobile.com/games/16138/interview-whale-trail-creator-ustwo-talks-mobile-game-development [Accessed October 21, 2016].

Miller, M. (2013) Interviewed by Keith Andrews. *We Didn't Want to "Shoe-Horn" in F2P: Us Two's Mills on Opting for Ads in Blip Blup* [Internet]. *PocketGamer,* May 24, 2013. Available from http://www.pocketgamer.biz/interview/51104/we-didnt-want-to-shoe-horn-in-f2p-ustwos-mills-on-opting-for-ads-in-blip-blup/ [Accessed October 27, 2016].

Mistry, M. (2013) *Blip Blup: A Journey into Puzzle Games* [Internet]. Available from: https://ustwo.com/blog/blip-blup-a-journey-into-puzzle-games/ [Accessed October 19, 2016].

Schafer, T. (2014) *Monument Valley Is the Most Elegant Game I've Played...* [Twitter], April 11, 2014. Available from: https://twitter.com/timoflegend/status/454651464460156928 [Accessed October 23, 2016].

Sheffield, B. (2014) *When Quality Comes Before Making Money: Developing Monument Valley* [Internet]. *Gamasutra*, October 19, 2014. Available from: https://www.gamasutra.com/view/news/228094/When_quality_comes_before_making_money_Developing_Monument_Valley.php [Accessed November 22, 2016].

Wong, K. (2014a) *Monument Valley Out Now* [Internet]. Available from: https://ustwo.com/blog/monument-valley-out-now/ [Accessed October 21, 2016].

Wong, K. (2014b) *Why Does It Take So Long to Make New Levels* [Internet]. Available from: https://monumentvalleygame.squarespace.com/blog/2014/8/3/why-does-it-take-so-long-to-make-new-levels [Accessed October 21, 2016].

Wong, K. (2014c) *Monument Valley Is Apple's iPad Game of the Year* [Internet]. Available from: https://monumentvalleygame.squarespace.com/blog/2014/12/8/monument-valley-is-apples-ipad-game-of-the-year [Accessed October 21, 2016].

Wong, K. (2014d) *Seven Weeks of Monument Valley* [Internet]. Available from: https://monumentvalleygame.squarespace.com/blog/sevenweeks [Accessed October 21, 2016].

Wong, K. (2014e) *On Top of the World* [Internet]. Available from: https://monumentvalleygame.squarespace.com/blog/2014/4/7/on-top-of-the-world [Accessed October 21, 2016].

Wong, K. (2014f) *Monument Valley Prints Now Available* [Internet]. Available from: https://monumentvalleygame.squarespace.com/blog/printsavailable [Accessed October 21, 2016].

Wong, K. (2015) *Escher and Monument Valley* [Internet]. Available from: https://monumentvalleygame.squarespace.com/blog/2013/11/28/inspiration [Accessed October 21, 2016].

Chapter 3: Re-Make, Re-Model

Into the Unknown

Boyd, J.R. (1996) *The Essence of Winning and Losing* [Unpublished lecture notes] [Internet]. Available from: https://monumentvalleygame.squarespace.com/blog/2013/11/28/inspiration [Accessed March 28, 2016].

Catmull, E. (2014) *Creativity, Inc.: Overcoming the Unseen Forces That Stand in the Way of True Inspiration* [Kindle]. New York: Random House.

Fallows, J. (2016) *The Next Article You Should Read on the GOP Race: Military-Strategist Assessment of the Trump Wave*. The Atlantic, January 8, 2016. Available from: https://www.theatlantic.com/notes/2016/01/the-next-article-you-should-read-on-the-gop-race-military-strategist-assessment-of-the-trump-wave/423240/ [Accessed March 27, 2017].

Ford, D. (2010) *A Vision So Noble: John Boyd, the Ooda Loop, and America's War on Terror* [Kindle]. Daniel Ford.

Foster, N. (2008) *Norman Foster: My Green Agenda for Architecture* [Video file]. Available from: https://www.ted.com/talks/norman_foster_s_green_agenda [Accessed December 7, 2016].

Hammonds, K. (2002) *The Strategy of the Fighter Pilot* [Internet]. Fast Company, May 31, 2002. Available from: https://www.fastcompany.com/44983/strategy-fighter-pilot [Accessed December 7, 2016].

Kaplan, B. (2011) *Oren Jacob, Entrepreneur and Former Pixar CTO, Talks About Scaling Pixar, the Crisis Around Toy Story 2 and his First-Hand Encounters with Steve Jobs* [Internet]. Available from: https://www.twilio.com/blog/2011/11/oren-jacob-pixar-steve-jobs-twilio-conference.html [Accessed December 7, 2016].

Larivé, M.H.A. (2014) *Failure of Imagination – Rumsfeld's interpretation of American foreign policy.* [Internet]. Foreign Policy Association, April 27, 2014. Available from: http://foreignpolicyblogs.com/2014/04/17/failure-of-imagination-rumsfelds-interpretation-of-american-foreign-policy/ [Accessed March 28, 2017].

McChrystal, S. (2015) *Team of Teams: New Rules of Engagement for a Complex World* [Kindle]. London: Penguin.

McLaughlin, D. (2015) *Military Strategist Explains Why Donald Trump Leads – And How He Will Fail* [Internet]. December 16, 2015. Available from: http://thefederalist.com/2015/12/16/military-strategist-explains-why-donald-trump-leads-and-how-he-will-fail/ [Accessed March 27, 2017].

Nicholson, B. (2012) *Simogo and How Its Sausage Is Made* [Internet]. Available from: http://toucharcade.com/2012/02/29/simogo-and-how-its-sausage-is-made/ [Accessed December 7, 2016].

Parton, H. (2016) *Donald Trump Is an Evil Genius: How He Abandoned Political Strategy and Won Over the GOP's Bloodthirsty Base* [Internet]. *Salon*, February 25, 2016. Available from: https://www.salon.com/2016/02/25/donald_trump_is_an_evil_genius_how_he_abandoned_political_strategy_and_won_over_the_gops_bloodthirsty_base/ [Accessed November 30, 2016].

Rumsfeld, D. (2002) *DoD News Briefing – Secretary Rumsfeld and Gen. Myers* [Internet]. United States Department of Defence, February 12, 2002. Available from: http://archive.defense.gov/Transcripts/Transcript.aspx?TranscriptID=2636 [Accessed March 20, 2017].

Shafer, J. (2016) *The Fighter-Jock Doctrine that Explains Why Trump Is Winning* [Internet]. *Politico*, March 23, 2016. Available from: http://www.politico.com/magazine/story/2016/03/donald-trump-2016-fighter-jock-213761 [Accessed March 27, 2017].

Stokols, E. (2016) *Inside Jeb Bush's $150 Million Failure* [Internet]. *Politico*, February 20, 2016. Available from: http://www.politico.com/magazine/story/2016/02/jeb-bush-dropping-out-set-up-to-fail-213662 [Accessed November 30, 2016].

Tingen, P. (2001) *Miles Beyond: The Electric Explorations of Miles Davis, 1967–1991.* New York: Watson-Guptill.

Zorthian, J. *How Toy Story Changed Movie History* [Internet]. *Time*, November 19, 2015. Available from: http://time.com/4118006/20-years-toy-story-pixar/ [Accessed March 28, 2017].

After the Gold Rush

Anderson, C. (n.d.) *The Long Tail, in a Nutshell* [Internet]. Available from: http://www.longtail.com/about.html [Accessed November 29, 2016].

Ball, M. and Menon, P. (2014) *Future of Film, Part III: Saving Independent Filmmaking* [Internet]. Available from: https://redef.com/original/future-of-film-part-iii-saving-independent-filmmaking [Accessed November 29, 2009].

Barnes, B. (2014) *America's Next Wal-Mart: The Indie Film Industry* [Internet] *Salon*, February 22, 2014. Available from: https://www.salon.com/2014/02/22/americas_next_wal_mart_the_indie_film_industry/ [Accessed November 29, 2016].

Byrne, D., et al. (1988) (*Nothing But) Flowers*. Talking Heads et al. Recorded 1987. [Vinyl]. 12EM 53. London: EMI.

Chalabi, M. (2014) *What Do McDonald's Workers Really Make Per Hour?* [Internet]. *FiveThirtyFive*, May 22, 2014. Available from: https://fivethirtyeight.com/features/what-do-mcdonalds-workers-really-make-per-hour/ [Accessed March 8, 2017].

Chang, J. (2015). *Film Review: 'Tangerine'* [Internet]. *Variety*, January 15, 2015. Available from: http://variety.com/2015/film/news/sundance-film-review-tangerine-1201414093/ [Accessed March 8, 2017].

Cheshire, T. (2014) *Changing the Game: How Notch Made Minecraft a Ault Hit* [Internet]. *Wired*, September 15, 2014. Available from: http://www.wired.co.uk/article/changing-the-game [Accessed November 29, 2016].

Cook, D. (2016) *Autumn for Indie Game Markets* [Internet]. *Gamasutra*, October 16, 2016. Available from: https://www.gamasutra.com/blogs/DanielCook/20161121/285971/Autumn_of_Indie_Game_Markets.php [Accessed March 13, 2017].

Dredge, S. (2015) *How Much Do Musicians Really Make from Spotify, iTunes and YouTube?* [Internet]. *The Guardian*, April 3, 2015. Available from: https://www.theguardian.com/technology/2015/apr/03/how-much-musicians-make-spotify-itunes-youtube [Accessed November 28, 2016].

Economist. (2017) *It Is Easier than Ever to Fund an Indie Film, but Harder than Ever to Get People to See It* [Internet]. *Economist*, February 25, 2017. Available from: https://www.economist.com/news/business/21717422-median-box-office-return-low-budget-films-america-measly-45-cents [Accessed March 8, 2017].

Edery, D. (2009) *The Hits Get Bigger* [Internet]. Available from: http://www.edery.org/2009/08/the-hits-get-bigger/ [Accessed November 28, 2016].

Epstein, G. (2017) *Mass Entertainment in the Digital Age Is Still About Blockbusters, Not Endless Choice* [Internet]. *The Economist*, February 11, 2017. Available from: https://www.economist.com/news/special-report/21716467-technology-has-given-billions-people-access-vast-range-entertainment-gady [Accessed February 15, 2017].

Gamasutra. (2014) *Gamasutra Salary Survey 2014* [Internet]. Available from: https://www.economist.com/news/special-report/21716467-technology-has-given-billions-people-access-vast-range-entertainment-gady [Accessed November 28, 2016].

Jarvis, M. (2016) *Average Indie Game Steam Sales Halve Year-on-Year* [Internet]. *Develop Magazine*, April 28, 2016. Available from: http://www.develop-online.net/news/average-indie-game-steam-sales-halve-year-on-year/0219745 [Accesssed November 28, 2016].

Kelly, K. (2010) *The Shirky Principle* [Internet]. Available from: http://kk.org/thetechnium/the-shirky-prin/ [Accessed April 4, 2017].

Kelly, K. (2016) *1,000 True Fans* [Internet]. Available from: http://kk.org/thetechnium/1000-true-fans/ [Accessed December 10, 2016].

Koster, R. (2009) *Great Article on Indie Biz* [Internet]. Available from: http://www.raphkoster.com/2009/08/04/great-article-on-indie-biz/ [Accessed November 29, 2016].

Persson, M. (2010) *20000! Wow. :)* [Internet]. Available from: https://notch.tumblr.com/post/709098848/20000-wow [Accessed November 29, 2016].

Steam Spy. (2017) *Genre Search: Indie* [Internet]. Available from: http://steamspy.com/genre/Indie [Accessed March 8, 2017].

TIGA. (2016) *March of the Micro-Studios* [Internet]. *TIGA*, August 22, 2016. Available from: https://tiga.org/news/march-of-the-micro-studios [Accessed November 20, 2016].

Ukie. (2016) *UK Video Games Fact Sheet* [Internet]. *Ukie*, November 4, 2016. Available from: http://ukie.org.uk/research#Fact%20Sheet [Accessed November 20, 2016].

Wong, K. (2015) *Mobile Isn't the Games Industry You Recognize, and That's Great* [Internet]. *Polygon*, October 29, 2015. Available from: https://www.polygon.com/2015/10/29/9631436/mobile-ustwo-monument-valley-Bugbyte [Accessed March 13, 2017].

Wong, K. (2016). Interviewed by Christopher Dring. *"In Games, People Shy Away from Life and Death and Love and Sex"* [Internet]. *GamesIndustry.biz*, October 31, 2016. Available from: http://www.gamesindustry.biz/articles/2016-10-31-in-games-people-shy-away-from-life-and-death-and-love-and-sex [Accessed March 13, 2017].

Start a Band, Not a Business

Albini, S. (2014) *Steve Albini on the Surprisingly Sturdy State of the Music Industry – In Full* [Internet]. *The Guardian*, November 17, 2014. Available from: https://www.theguardian.com/music/2014/nov/17/steve-albinis-keynote-address-at-face-the-music-in-full [Accessed March 16, 2017].

Alvi, S. (2016a) Interviewed by Guy Raz. *How I Built This: Vice: Suroosh Alvi.* [Podcast] NPR, October 10, 2016. Available from: http://www.npr.org/podcasts/510313/how-i-built-this [Accessed February 20, 2016].

Baio, A. (2013) *The Indiepocalypse* [Internet]. January 31, 2015 Available from: http://waxy.org/2013/01/indiepocalypse/ [Accessed March 8, 2017].

David, S. (2015) *In the All-Night Café: A Memoir of Belle and Sebastian's Formative Year* [Kindle]. London: Little Brown.

Dunlevy, T. (2016) *Long Read: How a Little Magazine Called VICE Conquered the Media World* [Internet]. *Montreal Gazette*, February 29, 2016. Available from: http://montrealgazette.com/storyline/long-read-how-a-little-magazine-called-vice-conquered-the-media-world [Accessed February 21, 2017].

Friedman, M. (2015) *Steve Albini Shows That Punk Rock Ethics Are Good Business* [Internet]. July 7, 2015. Available from: https://www.psychologytoday. com/blog/brick-brick/201507/steve-albini-shows-punk-rock-ethics-are-good-business [Accessed March 16, 2017].

Hertzfeld, A. (n.d.) *Pirate Flag* [Internet]. Available from: https://www. folklore.org/StoryView.py?story=Pirate_Flag.txt [Accessed March 28, 2017].

McLaren, M. (2008) *This Much I Know* [Internet]. *The Guardian*, November 16, 2008. Available from: https://www.theguardian. com/lifeandstyle/2008/nov/16/malcolm-mclaren-punk-vivienne-westwood [Accessed March 16, 2017].

Parkin, S. (2014) *Why Indie Gaming's Obsession with Moneymaking Hurts Us All* [Internet]. *The New Statesman*, July 14, 2014. Available from: https:// www.newstatesman.com/culture/2014/07/why-indie-gaming-s-obsession-moneymaking-hurts-us-all [Accessed February 20, 2017].

Rose, L. (2016) *Vice's Shane Smith Asks, "You Think I Could Hoodwink Bob Iger, Jeff Bewkes and Rupert Murdoch?"* [Internet]. *Hollywood Reporter*, February 3, 2016. Available from: http://www.hollywoodreporter.com/features/ vices-shane-smith-asks-you-861226 [Accessed February 20, 2017].

Taylor, S. (2004) *The A to X of Alternative Music*. London: Continuum International.

Yakowicz, W. (2014) *Vice Media: From Voice of Montreal to Voice of the Millennial Generation* [Internet]. *Inc.*, November 24, 2014. Available from: https://www.inc.com/will-yakowicz/vice-media-finds-success-by-telling-different-story.html [Accessed February 21, 2017].

Stop Just Making Stuff

Blow, J. (2006) *Game Design Rant 2006: "There's Not Enough Innovation in Games!"* [Internet]. Available from: http://number-none.com/blow/ slides/rant_2006.html [Accessed March 28, 2017].

Bjergsø, M.B. (2014). *Better Beer for The World* [Video]. Available from: https://creativemornings.com/talks/education-better-beer-for-the-world/1 [Accessed December 11, 2016].

Caramanica, J. (2016) *Kanye West Is Fixing His Album in Public. You'll Want to Read the Edits* [Internet]. *New York Times*, February 19, 2016. Available from: https://www.nytimes.com/2016/02/21/arts/music/ kanye-west-life-of-pablo-tlop.html [Accessed December 13, 2016].

Chapple, C. (2016) *App Store Trends for November 2016: Average of 792 Games Submitted Every Day* [Internet]. *PocketGamer.biz*, December 5, 2016. Available from: http://www.pocketgamer.biz/news/64575/app-store-trends-for-november-2016/ [Accessed December 13, 2016].

Eleftheriou-Smith, L.M. *MTV VMAs 2016: Read Kanye West's Speech in Full* [Internet]. *The Independent*, August 29, 2016. Available from: http:// www.independent.co.uk/news/people/vmas-2016-mtv-kanye-west-speech-in-full-read-transcript-video-music-awards-a7214956.html [Accessed March 28, 2017].

Eno, B. (1996) *A Year with Swollen Appendices: Brian Eno's Diary*. London: Faber & Faber.

Eno, B. (2015) *Brian Eno's BBC Music John Peel Lecture 2015* [Podcast]. Available from: http://www.independent.co.uk/news/people/vmas-2016-mtv-kanye-west-speech-in-full-read-transcript-video-music-awards-a7214956.html [Accessed December 10, 2016].

Fincher, D. (2014) *"Movies Aren't Finished. They're Abandoned." – David Fincher on Why He Hates Watching His Films* [Internet]. Available from: https://www.filmindependent.org/blog/movies-arent-finished-theyre-abandoned-david-fincher-on-why-he-hates-watching-his-films/ [Accessed March 28, 2017].

Fox, D.J. (2016) *How the Lonely Island Changed the Internet, Comedy, and Especially Internet Comedy* [Internet]. *Vulture*, June 1, 2016. Available from: http://www.vulture.com/2016/05/lonely-island-changed-the-internet-comedy.html [Accessed December 13, 2016].

Greene, J. (2016) *The Life of Pablo* [Internet]. *Pitchfork*, February 15, 2016. Available from: https://pitchfork.com/reviews/albums/21542-the-life-of-pablo/ [Accessed December 13, 2016].

Hughes, R. (1988) *Requiem for a Featherweight* [Internet]. *New Republic*, November 21, 1988. Available from: https://newrepublic.com/article/105858/hughes-basquiat-new-york-new-wave   [Accessed December 10, 2016].

Jones, J. (2012) *Robert Hughes: The Greatest Art Critic of Our Time* [Internet]. *The Guardian*, August 7, 2012. Available from: https://www.theguardian.com/artanddesign/jonathanjonesblog/2012/aug/07/robert-hughes-greatest-art-critic [Accessed December 13, 2016].

Keyes, R. (2006) *The Quote Verifier: Who Said What, Where, and When*. New York: St. Martins Press.

McCracken, G. (2012) *Culturematic*. Boston, MA: Harvard Business Review Press.

McLaren, M. (2008) *This Much I Know* [Internet]. *The Guardian*, November 16, 2008. Available from: https://www.theguardian.com/lifeand-style/2008/nov/16/malcolm-mclaren-punk-vivienne-westwood [Accessed March 16, 2017].

Mikkeller. (2016) *Our Vision* [Internet]. Available from: http://mikkeller.dk/brewery/ [Accessed December 11, 2016].

O'Connell, S. (2016) *23% of Users Abandon an App After One Use* [Internet]. Available from: http://info.localytics.com/blog/23-of-users-abandon-an-app-after-one-use [Accessed December 13, 2016].

Solberg, D. (2016) *Kanye West Is Patching His Latest Album Like a Videogame* [Internet]. *Kill Screen*, March 21, 2016. Available from: https://killscreen.com/articles/kanye-west-is-patching-his-latest-album-like-a-videogame/ [Accessed December 13, 2016].

Topolsky, J. (2016) *Your Media Business Will Not Be Saved* [Internet]. Available from: https://medium.com/@joshuatopolsky/your-media-business-will-not-be-saved-1b0716b5010c#.pzlem4t7e [Accessed December 13, 2016].

Tzuo, T. (2016) *Kanye West's "The Life of Pablo" Is the First SaaS Album* [Internet]. *TechCrunch*, March 17, 2016. Available from: https://techcrunch.com/2016/03/17/kanye-wests-the-life-of-pablo-is-the-first-saas-album/ [Accessed December 13, 2016].

Weiner, J. (2014) *A Fight Is Brewing* [Internet]. *New York Times*, March 26, 2016. Available from: https://www.nytimes.com/2014/03/30/magazine/a-fight-is-brewing.html [Accessed December 11, 2016].

West, K. (2016) *Fixing Wolves 2day....* [Internet]. *Twitter*, March 15, 2016. Available from: https://twitter.com/kanyewest/status/709872072604913664 [Accessed December 13, 2016].

The Work of Play in the Age of Digital Reproduction

Barnett, J., et al. (2008) *Thinking with Portals: Creating Valve's New IP* [Internet]. *Gamasutra*, November 4, 2008. Available from: https://www.gamasutra.com/view/feature/132233/thinking_with_portals_creating_.php [Accessed February 12, 2017].

Benjamin, W. (2009) *One-Way Street and Other Writings* (Vol. 966). London: Penguin.

Bramwell, T. (2007) *Portal Review* [Internet]. *Eurogamer*, October 10, 2007. Available from: http://www.eurogamer.net/articles/portal-review [Accessed February 11, 2007].

Chang, D. (2016) *The Secret Code to Unleashing The World's Most Amazing Flavors* [Internet]. *Wired*, July 19, 2017. Available from: https://www.wired.com/2016/07/chef-david-chang-on-deliciousness/ [Accessed March 15, 2017].

Eames Office. (2013) *Powers of Ten and the Relative Size of Things in The Universe* [Internet]. October 9, 2013. Available from: http://www.eamesoffice.com/the-work/powers-of-ten/ [Accessed February 16, 2017].

Galenson, D. (2004). *A Portrait of the Artist as a Young or Old Innovator: Measuring the Careers of Modern Novelists* [Internet]. The National Bureau of Economic Research, January 2004. Available from: http://www.nber.org/papers/w16024 [Accessed February 13, 2017].

Galenson, D. (2010) *Understanding Creativity* [Internet]. The National Bureau of Economic Research, May 2010. Available from: http://www.nber.org/papers/w16024 [Accessed February 13, 2017].

Hill, D. (2012) *Dark Matter and Trojan Horses: A Strategic Design Vocabulary* [Kindle]. Moscow: Strelka.

Hofstadter, D.R. (2007) *I Am a Strange Loop*. New York: Basic Books.

McLuhan, M. (1969) *Playboy Magazine Interview. Playboy Magazine* March 26, 1969.

Pollan, M. (2009) *Food Rules: An Eater's Manual* [Kindle]. London: Penguin.

Ritzer, George. (n.d.) *What is McDonaldization?* [Internet]. Available from: http://www.mcdonaldization.com/whatisit.shtml [Accessed February 14, 2017].

Slow Food. (1989) *Slow Food Manifesto* [Internet]. Available from: http://www.mcdonaldization.com/whatisit.shtml [Accessed February 14, 2017].

Valve. (2012) *Valve: Handbook For New Employees* [Internet]. Available from: http://www.mcdonaldization.com/whatisit.shtml [Accessed March 29, 2017].

Threes: A Case Study in Itinerant Iteration

Byrne, D. (2012). *How Music Works* [Kindle]. London: Canongate Books.

Cameron, P. (2015). *Mending the Developer/Player Relationship with Threes Free-to-Play* [Internet]. *Gamasutra*, June 22, 2015. Available from: https://www.gamasutra.com/view/news/246612/Mending_the_developerplayer_relationship_with_Threes_freetoplay.php [Accessed October 31, 2016].

Chimero, F. (2011) *The Long, Hard, Stupid Way* [Internet]. Available from: http://www.frankchimero.com/writing/the-long-hard-stupid-way/ [Accessed November 22, 2016].

Cirulli, G. (2014) *2048, Success and Me* [Internet]. Available from: http://web.archive.org/web/20150102213534/http://gabrielecirulli.com/articles/2048-success-and-me [Accessed November 9, 2016].

Dormehl, L. (2014) *Monument Valley's Creator Picks His Top iOS Games* [Internet]. *Cult of Mac*, April 13, 2014. Available from: https://www.cultofmac.com/274255/monument-valleys-creator-picks-top-ios-games-exclusive/ [Accessed November 11, 2016].

Gruber, J. (2014) *Threes* [Internet]. Available from: https://daringfireball.net/linked/2014/02/10/threes [Accessed November 2, 2016].

Kerr, C. (2014) *Threes Creator Asher Vollmer on Growing Up, Going Indie, and the Dangers of Cloning* [Internet]. *Pocketgamer*, October 9, 2014. Available from: http://www.pocketgamer.biz/interview/60034/threes-creator-asher-vollmer-on-growing-up-going-indie-and-the-dangers-of-cloning/ [Accessed November 10, 2016].

Kuchera, B. (2014) *Why It Took a Year to Make, and Then Break Down, an Amazing Puzzle Game* [Internet]. *Polygon*, February 6, 2014. Available from: https://www.polygon.com/2014/2/6/5386200/why-it-took-a-year-to-make-and-then-break-down-an-amazing-puzzle-game [Accessed November 11, 2016].

Sorrell, M. (2014) *Threes! Review* [Internet]. *Eurogamer*, March 5, 2014. Available from: http://www.eurogamer.net/articles/2014-03-05-threes-review [Accessed November 10, 2016].

Vanhemert, K. (2014). *Design Is Why 2048 Sucks, and Threes Is a Masterpiece* [Internet]. *Wired*, May 7, 2014. Available from: https://www.wired.com/2014/05/threes-game-design/ [Accessed November 9, 2016].

Vollmer, A. (2015) *We Released a Free Version of @ThreesGame One Month Ago and Here's How It's Doing.* July 20, 2015 [Twitter]. Available from: https://twitter.com/AsherVo/status/623264369242013700 [Accessed October 20, 2016].

Vollmer, A. and Wohlwend, G. (2014) *The "Threemails"*. [Internet]. Available from: http://asherv.com/threes/threemails/ [Accessed November 11, 2016].

Volmer, A. and Wohlwend, G. (2015) *We Are the Folks That Made Threes, a Popular Mobile Puzzle Game Cloned by the Even More Popular 2048, AMA* [Internet]. Available from: https://www.reddit.com/r/IAmA/comments/3x9b2n/we_are_the_folks_that_made_threes_a_popular/ [Accessed November 9, 2016].

Webster, A. (2014) *By the Numbers: "Threes" Is Your New iPhone Addiction* [Internet]. *The Verge*, February 6, 2014. Available from: https://www.theverge.com/2014/2/6/5361708/threes-ipad-iphone-puzzle-game [Accessed November 11, 2016].

Webster, A. (2015) *One Year Later, Mobile Puzzle Game Threes Is Going Free* [Internet]. *The Verge*, June 11, 2015. Available from: https://www.theverge.com/2015/6/11/8722909/threes-free-to-play-launch-ios-android [Accessed November 2, 2016].

Wohlwend, G. (2014) *Show Business: Marketing for Those That Hate Marketing* [Internet]. Available from: https://aeiowu.tumblr.com/post/80292757667/show-business-marketing-for-those-that-hate [Accessed November 9, 2016].

Dear Esther: A Case Study in Challenging Assumptions

Briscoe, R. (2009) *Mods and the Motherland!* [Internet]. Available from: http://www.littlelostpoly.co.uk/mods-and-the-motherland/ [Accessed September 14, 2016].

Briscoe, R. (2012a) *A Retrospective/Post-Mortem on Dear Esther* [Internet]. Available from: http://www.littlelostpoly.co.uk/my-retrospectivepost-mortem-on-dear-esther/ [Accessed September 14, 2016].

Briscoe, R. (2012b) Interview with Martin Davies. *Back To The Source: Dear Esther Reborn* [Internet]. *Gamesindustry.biz*, March 1, 2012. Available from: http://www.gamesindustry.biz/articles/2012-03-02-back-to-the-source-dear-esther-reborn [Accessed September 26, 2016].

Briscoe, R. and Pinchbeck, D. (2012a) Interviewed by Lewie Procter. *Interview: Dan Pinchbeck & Rob Briscoe on Dear Esther* [Internet]. Available from: http://indiegames.com/2012/01/interview_dan_pinchbeck_rob_br.html [Accessed September 23, 2016].

Briscoe, R. and Pinchbeck, D. (2012b) Interviewed by John Polson. *Road to the IGF: Thechineseroom's Dear Esther* [Internet]. *Gamasutra*, February 20, 2012. Available from: https://www.gamasutra.com/view/news/40391/Road_to_the_IGF_Thechineserooms_Dear_Esther.php [Accessed September 21, 2016].

Curry, J. (2012) Interviewed by Emily Reese. *Jessica Curry and Dear Esther on Top Score* [Podcast]. *Top Score*, October 4, 2012. Podcast. Available from: https://www.classicalmpr.org/story/2012/10/03/jessica-curry-dear-esther-top-score [Accessed November 2, 2016].

Denby, L. *Touched By the Hand Of Mod: Dear Esther* [Internet]. May 15, 2009. Available from: https://www.rockpapershotgun.com/2009/05/15/touched-by-the-hand-of-mod-dear-esther/ [Accessed September 13, 2016].

Indie Fund. (2017) *About Indie Fund* [Internet]. Available from: https://indie-fund.com/about/ [Accessed April 3, 2017].

Pinchbeck, D. (2008a) *Dear Esther* [Internet]. July 7, 2008. Available from: https://developer.valvesoftware.com/wiki/Dear_Esther [Accessed September 15, 2016].

Pinchbeck, D. (2013) Interviewed by Rainer Sigl. *"Games Are Architectures for an Emotional Experience" – An Interview with Dan Pinchbeck* [Internet]. Available from: http://videogametourism.at/content/games-are-architectures-emotional-experience-interview-dan-pinchbeck [Accessed September 24, 2016].

Pinchbeck, D. (2014a) *Dear Esther- Two Years In... (Part One)* [Internet]. Available from: http://www.thechineseroom.co.uk/blog/blog/dear-esther-two-years-in-part-one [Accessed September 13, 2016].

Pinchbeck, D. (2014b) *Dear Esther- Two Years In... (Part Two)* [Internet]. Available from: http://www.thechineseroom.co.uk/blog/blog/dear-esther-two-years-in-part-two [Accessed September 13, 2016].

Pinchbeck, D. (2016) Interviewed by James Pickard. *Talking "Walking Sims": The Chinese Room's Dan Pinchbeck on the Pointlessness of the Debate* [Internet]. Available from: http://www.pcgamesn.com/dear-esther/dan-pinchbeck-interview-are-walking-sims-games [Accessed November 3, 2016].

Smal, P. (2016) *Jessica Curry: A Musical Journey Towards [Everybody's Gone to] "the Rapture"* [Internet]. *Gamasutra*, March 31, 2016. Available from: https://www.gamasutra.com/blogs/PieterSmal/20160331/269062/Jessica_Curry_A_musical_journey_towards_Everybodys_Gone_to_quotthe_Rapturequot.php [Accessed September 13, 2016].

Stuart, K. (2016) *How Walking Sims Became as Important as the First-Person Shooter* [Internet]. *The Guardian*, September 20, 2016. Available from: https://www.theguardian.com/technology/2016/sep/20/how-walking-sim-first-person-shooter-dear-esther [Accessed November 23, 2016].

Wikipedia. (2016) Dear Esther [Internet]. In: Wikipedia: The Free Encyclopaedia. Unknown eds. Available from: https://en.wikipedia.org/wiki/Dear_Esther [Accessed September 20, 2016].

Chapter 4: Success Doesn't Suck

Abstract

Temkin, M. (n.d) Aeiowu-a-Lot-of-Indies-Dont-Want-to-Market [Internet]. Available from: http://blog.maxistentialism.com/post/80593829689/aeiowu-a-lot-of-indies-dont-want-to-market [Accessed May 1, 2017].

It's Just a Business Model

Alexander, K. (2016) *There's a Massive Restaurant Industry Bubble, and It's About to Burst* [Internet]. *Thrillist*, December 30, 2016. Available from: https://www.thrillist.com/eat/nation/american-restaurant-industry-bubble-burst [Accessed March 1, 2017].

Belben, M. (2017) *Interview with Michael Belben*. Interviewed by Chris Lowthorpe. *The Eagle*, February 26, 2017. [In Person].

Donovan, T. (2010) *Replay: The History of Video Games*. Lewes: Yellow Ant.

Drucker, P. (1994) *The Theory of Business* [Internet]. *Harvard Business Review*, September–October 1994. Available from: https://hbr.org/1994/09/the-theory-of-the-business [Accessed March 1, 2017].

Green, E. (1991) *The Whammy Awards Go to the Italians*. *The Independent*, February 9, 1991.

Kellon, L. (2014) *Sega vs. Nintendo: Sonic, Mario and the 1990s Console Wars* [Internet]. *BBC News*, May 13, 2014. Available from: http://www.bbc.co.uk/news/technology-27373587 [Accessed March 1, 2017].

Kent, S.L. (2001) *The Ultimate History of Video Games*. New York: Three Rivers.

Magretta, J. (2002) *Why Business Models Matter* [Internet]. *Harvard Business Review*, May 2002. Available from: https://hbr.org/2002/05/why-business-models-matter [Accessed March 1, 2017].

Maurya, A. (2012) *Running Lean: Iterate from Plan A to a Plan That Works*. 2nd ed. Sebastopol, CA: O'Reilly.

Meades, J. (1991) *Popped In, Pigged Out*. *The Times*, August 3, 1991.

Mesure, S. (2016) *The Eagle: Britain's First Gastropub Celebrates Its 25th Birthday* [Internet]. *The Independent*, 2016. Available from: http://www.independent.co.uk/news/uk/home-news/the-eagle-britains-first-gastropub-celebrates-its-25th-birthday-a6804221.html [Accessed March 1, 2017].

Reagan, R. (1989) *Farewell Address to the Nation* [Internet]. Washington, DC: The White House. Available from: http://www.presidency.ucsb.edu/ws/?pid=29650 [Accessed March 27, 2017].

Ryan, J. (2013) *Super Mario: How Nintendo Conquered America*. London: Penguin.

Slade, M.E. (1998) *Beer and the Tie: Did Divestiture of Brewer-Owned Public Houses Lead to Higher Beer Prices?* [Internet]. *The Economic Journal*, 108, 565–602. Available from: http://onlinelibrary.wiley.com/doi/10.1111/1468-0297.00305/pdf [Accessed March 1, 2017].

Steinbeck, J. (1962) *Travels with Charly: In Search of America*. London: Penguin.

The Eagle. (2017) *The Eagle Alumni* [Internet]. Available from: http://www.theeaglefarringdon.co.uk/alumni [Accessed March 1, 2017].

Welsh, I. (2002) *Porno*. London: Jonathan Cape.

Let Me Be Your Fantasy

Ackroyd, P. (2011a) *The Romantics: Liberty*. BBC4. Available from: https://learningonscreen.ac.uk/ondemand/index.php/prog/005737E0 [Accessed February 15, 2017].

Ackroyd, P. (2011b) *The Romantics: Nature*. BBC4. Available from: https://learningonscreen.ac.uk/ondemand/index.php/prog/005737E0 [Accessed February 15, 2017].

Ackroyd, P. (2011c) *The Romantics: Eternity*. BBC4. Available from: https://learningonscreen.ac.uk/ondemand/index.php/prog/005737E0 [Accessed February 15, 2017].

Atlas, R. and Rothwell, J. (2016) *Sour Grapes* [Internet]. Directed by Reuben Atlas and Jerry Rothwell. USA. Met Film Production. VOD. Available from: http://www.sourgrapesfilm.com/screenings [Accessed March 1, 2017].

Beachy, S (2005). *Who Is the Real JT LeRoy? A Search for the True Identity of a Great Literary Hustler* [Internet]. New York. Available from: http://nymag.com/nymetro/news/people/features/14718/ [Accessed March 1, 2017].

Berman, M. (1984) *The Signs in the Street: A Response to Perry Anderson* [Internet]. *New Left Review*, March–April 1984. Available from: https://newleftreview.org/I/144/marshall-berman-the-signs-in-the-street-a-response-to-perry-anderson [Accessed March 1, 2017].

Byron, G.G. (1824) *Don Juan* [Internet]. Archive.org. Available from: https://archive.org/details/donjuan05byro [Accessed August 4, 2017].

Didion, J. (1979) *The White Album*. London: Penguin.

Drummond, C. (n.d.) *Lord Byron: 19th Century Bad Boy* [Internet]. Available from: https://www.bl.uk/romantics-and-victorians/articles/lord-byron-19thcentury-bad-boy [Accessed March 1, 2017].

Feuerzeig, J. (2016) *The J.T. LeRoy Story* [Internet]. Directed by Jeff Feuerzeig. Amazon Instant Video. VOD. Available from: https://www.amazon.co.uk/d/Amazon-Video/Author-JT-LeRoy-Story-Jeff-Feuerzeig/B01M0HU6BU [Accessed March 1, 2017].

Forward, S. (n.d.) *The Romantics* [Internet]. Available from: https://www.bl.uk/romantics-and-victorians/articles/the-romantics [Accessed March 1, 2017].

Frayling, C. (1992) *Vampyres: Lord Byron to Count Dracula*. London: Faber & Faber.

Galassi, P. (2003) *Cindy Sherman: The Complete Untitled Film Stills*. New York: The Museum of Modern Art.

Hobsbawm, E. (1962) *The Age of Revolution: 1789–1848*. London: Abacus.

Hughes. R. (1997) *American Visions: The Epic History of Art in America*. London: Harvill.

Langer, A. (2013) *Laura Albert* [Internet]. Interview, July 22, 2013. Available from: http://www.interviewmagazine.com/culture/laura-albert#_ [Accessed March 1, 2017].

MacCarthy, F. (2003) *Byron: Life and Legend*. London: Faber and Faber.

Marchand, L.A. ed. (1974) *Byron's Letters and Journals*. Cambridge, MA: Harvard University Press.

Orwell, G. (1944) *A Hundred Up: The Centenary of Martin Chuzzlewit*. The *Observer*, February 13, 1944.

Rose, S. (2016) *JT LeRoy Unmasked: The Extraordinary Story of a Modern Literary Hoax* [Internet]. *The Guardian*, July 20, 2016. Available from: https://www.theguardian.com/film/2016/jul/20/jt-leroy-story-modern-literary-hoax- [Accessed March 1, 2017].

Safire, W. (1986) *On Language: Calling Dr. Spin* [Internet]. *New York Times*, August 31, 1986. Available from: http://www.nytimes.com/1986/08/31/magazine/on-language-calling-dr-spin.html?Src=longreads [Accessed March 1, 2017].

Schama, S. (2012) *Cindy Sherman Talks to Simon Schama* [Internet]. *Financial Times*, February 3, 2012. Available from: https://www.ft.com/content/1cec0df6-4d4f-11e1-8741-00144feabdc0 [Accessed March 1, 2017].

Sky News. (2016) [Television Broadcast]. *Sky News*, June 3, 2016.

Smith, R. (2004) *Art Review: The Ever-Shifting Selves of Cindy Sherman, Girlish Vamp to Clown* [Internet]. *New York Times*, May 28, 2004. Available from: http://www.nytimes.com/2004/05/28/arts/art-review-the-ever-shifting-selves-of-cindy-sherman-girlish-vamp-to-clown.html?ref=cindysherman&_r=0 [Accessed March 1, 2017].

Sussler, B. (1985) *Cindy Sherman Interview with Betty Sussler* [Internet]. *BOMB Magazine*, No. 12, Spring 1985. Available from: http://bomb-magazine.org/article/638/cindy-sherman [Accessed March 1, 2017].

Weingarten, M. (2006) *The Gang That Wouldn't Write Straight: Wolfe, Thompson, Didion, and the New Journalism Revolution* [Kindle Paperwhite]. New York: Three Rivers Press.

Whitman, W. (1855) *Leaves of Grass* [Internet]. Archive.org. Available from: https://archive.org/details/LeavesOfGrass1855Edition [Accessed August 4, 2017].

Patronize Me, Please

BrewDog. (2016). *DIY Dog* [Internet]. Available from: https://www.brewdog.com/diydog [Accessed February 2,7 2017].

Chen, A. (2017) *Brad Troemel, The Troll of Internet Art* [Internet]. *New Yorker*, January 30, 2017. Available from: https://www.newyorker.com/magazine/2017/01/30/brad-troemel-the-troll-of-internet-art [Accessed February 26, 2017].

Gerhardt, T. and Provost, D. (2012) *It Will Be Exhilarating* [Kindle]. Austin, TX: Studio Neat.

Johnson, S. (2015) *The Creative Apocalypse That Wasn't* [Internet]. *New York Times*, August 19, 2015. Available from: https://www.nytimes.com/2015/08/23/magazine/the-creative-apocalypse-that-wasnt.html [Accessed February 20, 2017].

Nussbaum, B. (2011) *4 Reasons Why the Future of Capitalism Is Homegrown, Small Scale, and Independent* [Internet]. *Fast Company*, December 5, 2011. Available from: https://www.fastcodesign.com/1665567/4-reasons-why-the-future-of-capitalism-is-homegrown-small-scale-and-independent [Accessed February 28, 2017].

Nussbaum, B. (2013) *How "Indie" Capitalism Will Replace Our Stagnant Economic System* [Internet]. *Wired*, March 5, 2017. Available from: https://www.wired.com/2013/03/how-to-put-the-indie-in-capitalism/ [Accessed February 26, 2017].

Palmer, A. (2013) *Amanda Palmer: The Art of Asking* [Video]. TED 2013, February 2013. Available from: https://www.ted.com/talks/amanda_palmer_the_art_of_asking [Accessed March 20, 2014].

Pugh, W. (2017) *William Pugh's Journey from the Stanley Parable into Crows Crows Crows* [Internet]. *Gamasutra*, January 19, 2017. Available from: https://www.gamasutra.com/view/news/288395/William_Pughs_journey_from_The_Stanley_Parable_into_Crows_Crows_Crows.php [Accessed February 27, 2017].

Sheffield, B. (2014) *Vlambeer's Performative Game Development – The Way of the Future* [Internet]. *Gamasutra*, March 17, 2014. Available from: https://www.gamasutra.com/view/news/213339/Vlambeers_Performative_Game_Development_the_way_of_the_future.php [Accessed February 28, 2017].

Thompson, B. (2017) *Manifestos and Monopolies* [Internet]. *Stratechery*, February 21, 2017. Available from: https://stratechery.com/2017/manifestos-and-monopolies/ [Accessed February 26, 2017].

Von Hippel, E. (2006) *Democratizing Innovation* [Kindle]. Cambridge, MA: MIT Press.

Watt, J. (2015) *Business for Punks: Break All the Rules – The BrewDog Way* [Kindle]. London: Penguin.

Wilson, D. (2012) *Spelunky Glory, Videogame Rituals, and Nifflas' Miracle* [Internet]. Available from: https://gutefabrik.com/blog/?p=2016 [Accessed March 14, 2017].

Yu, D. (2016) *Spelunky (Boss Fight Books 11)* [Kindle]. Los Angeles, CA: Boss Fight Books.

Devolver Digital: A Case Study in Amplification

Alliot, F. (2016) *How We Mixed Tinder and Politics to Make a Premium Hit on Mobile* [Internet]. *Polygon*, September 15, 2016. Available from: https://gutefabrik.com/blog/?p=2016 [Accessed September 15, 2016].

Bernstein, J. (n.d.) *Hotline: Miami, The First Postmodern Videogame?* [Internet]. *Kill Screen*. Available from: https://killscreen.com/articles/kill-screen-review-hotline-miami-first-postmodern-videogame/ [Accessed July 7, 2016].

Edge Magazine. (2013) *The Making of Hotline Miami* [Internet]. Available from: http://willingtobe.com/the-making-of-hotline-miami [Accessed November 24, 2016].

Fahey, R. (2016) *Mobile Has Become an Indie-Hostile Market* [Internet]. *Gamesindustry.biz*, August 26, 2016. Available from: http://www.gamesindustry.biz/articles/2016-08-24-mobile-has-become-an-indie-hostile-market [Accessed September 5, 2016].

Haro, S. (2016) *The #1 app in US Paid Apps List Is on Position #235 in the Top Grossing List. Paid Apps Are Truly Dead* [Twitter]. August 11, 2016. Available from: https://twitter.com/sulka/status/763725926819651584?ref_src=twsrc%5Etfw [Accessed September 1, 2016].

Jagneaux, D. (2016) *How Devolver Digital Came to Rule the World of Indie Games* [Internet]. *Playboy*, July 5, 2016. Available from: http://www.playboy.com/articles/how-devolver-digital-came-to-rule-the-world-of-indie-games [Accessed October 7, 2016].

King, R. (2012) *How Indie Labels Changed the World* [Internet]. *The Guardian*, March 22, 2012. Available from: https://www.theguardian.com/music/2012/mar/22/indie-record-labels-changed-world [Accessed October 10, 2016].

Kuchera, B. (2015) *Devolver Digital Shows Nintendo How It's Done with YouTube Monetization Statement* [Internet]. *Polygon*, January 30, 2015. Available from: https://www.polygon.com/2015/1/30/7952605/devolver-digital-nintendo-youtube [Accessed August 20, 2016].

Lowrie, N. (2016) *You Don't Need a F-ing Publisher. Game Developers Conference (GDC)*, San Francisco, CA. March 15, 2016. Available from: http://www.gdcvault.com/play/1023495/You-Don-t-Need-a [Accessed October 8, 2016].

McKeand, K. (2016) *Meet Devolver Digital, Gaming's Own Death Row Records* [Internet]. *The Telegraph*, August 31, 2016. Available from: http://www.telegraph.co.uk/gaming/what-to-play/meet-devolver-digital-gamings-own-death-row-records/ [Accessed October 9, 2016].

Meer, A. (2012) *Rezzed: Our, and Your, Game of the Show* [Internet]. July 18, 2012. Available from: https://www.rockpapershotgun.com/2012/07/18/rezzed-our-and-your-game-of-the-show/ [Accessed August 13, 2016].

Messner, S. (2016) *How Devolver Digital Is Redefining Videogame Publishing* [Internet]. Available from: http://www.pcgamer.com/how-devolver-digital-is-redefining-videogame-publishing/ [Accessed October 8, 2016].

Morley, P. (2007) *Idealist, Chancer, Loyal Friend: Why I Will Miss Tony Wilson* [Internet]. *The Guardian*, August 12, 2007. Available from: https://www.theguardian.com/music/2007/aug/12/tonywilson [Accessed October 10, 2016].

Peckinpah, S. (1969) Interviewed by Roger Ebert. *Sam Peckinpah: "Dying Is Not Fun and Games* [Internet]. *Chicago Sun-Times*, June 29, 1969. Available from: http://www.rogerebert.com/interviews/sam-peckinpah-dying-is-not-fun-and-games [Accessed June 24, 2016].

Procter, L. (n.d.) *Cactus on Hotline Miami: "I'm Pretty Tired of Crappy Games That Don't Really Want to Do Anything Special* [Internet]. Available from: http://www.pcgamesn.com/indie/cactus-hotline-miami-im-pretty-tired-crappy-games-dont-really-want-do-anything-special [Accessed August 27, 2016].

Purchase, R. (2012) *The Hotline Miami Sales Story, and More* [Internet]. *Eurogamer*, December 11, 2012. Available from: http://www.euro-gamer.net/articles/2012-12-11-the-hotline-miami-sales-story-and-more [Accessed October 13, 2016].

Reigns. (2016a) *Thanks! A Majority* [Twitter]. September 14, 2016. Available from: https://twitter.com/reignsgame/status/776075024763674624 [Accessed April 3, 2017].

Reigns. (2016b) *Reigns Has Crossed 1 Million Copies Sold, Thank You Loyal Subjects* [Twitter]. December 23, 2016. Available from: https://twitter.com/reignsgame/status/812320859968983044 [Accessed April 3, 2017].

Roberts, D. (2015) *Digital Humanity: How Devolver Is the Sub Pop of gaming* [Internet]. Available from: http://www.gamesradar.com/digital-humanity-how-devolver-sub-pop-gaming/ [Accessed October 8, 2016].

Warren, J. (2012) *If Videogames Are in Their "Indie" Period, Where's Our Factory Records?* [Internet]. *Kill Screen*, March 29, 2012. Available from: https://killscreen.com/articles/if-videogames-are-their-indie-period-wheres-our-factory-records/ [Accessed October 7, 2016].

Webster, A. (2012) *Blood and Pixels on the Beach: The Story of "Hotline Miami"* [Internet]. *The Verge*, October 1, 2012. Available from: https://www.theverge.com/2012/10/1/3437500/hotline-miami-dennaton-interview [Accessed October 12, 2016].

Wilson, M. (2007) Interviewed by Brandon Sheffield. *From God to Cock: Mike Wilson on GameCock's Publishing Party* [Internet]. *Gamasutra*, August 29, 2007. Available from: https://www.gamasutra.com/view/feature/1666/from_god_to_cock_mike_wilson_on_.php [Accessed October 8, 2016].

An Ending (Ascent)

Jefferson, M. (1988) *Open Our Eyes (Celestial Mix)* [Vinyl]. New York: Big Beat.

Schama, S. (2000) *The Rest is History* [MP4 File]. *BBC2*, October 3, 2000. London: BBC.

Colophon

Font
Open Sans

Style Guide
This book follows *The Guardian and Observer* style guide.
Available from: https://www.theguardian.com/guardian-observer-style-guide-a

References
This book follows Harvard referencing style.

Technical
This book was written in Google Docs, tracked in Trello and discussed in Slack.

Index